DAYTRIP ILLINOIS

A Travel Guide to the Land of Lincoln

Written by
Patricia O'Rourke
and
Lee Godley

Layout Design by
Patricia O'Rourke

Cover Design
and
Book Illustrations by
Debora Humphrey

Maps Created by
Paul Wentzel

State Park Maps
Illinois State Parks Magazine
© 1999 American Park Network

Statewide Listing of
State Historic Sites
Illinois Historic Preservation Agency

Illlinois Facts

Nickname — The Prairie State
Motto — State Sovereignty, National Union
Slogan — Land of Lincoln
State Bird — Cardinal
State Tree — White Oak
State Flower — Native Violet
State Song — "Illinois"
State Insect — Monarch Butterfly
State Mammal — White Tailed Deer
State Fish — Blue Gill

Highest Point — Charles Mound, 1,235 feet
Lowest Point — Mississippi River, 279 feet
Mean Elevation — 600 Feet

DAY TRIP ILLINOIS
SECOND EDITION

Copyright © 2000 by Aphelion Publications, Inc. All rights reserved. Printed in the United States of America. No part of this publication may be reproduced, stored in a retrieval system, or transmitted, in any form or by any means, electronic, mechanical, photocopying, recording, or otherwise, without the prior written permission of the publisher. All information included in the book was accurate at the time of printing.

ISBN # 0-9651340-3-2

Aphelion Publications, Inc.
5 Herring Drive
Fulton, MO 65251
Voice 573 642-4437
Fax 573 642-6341

Printed by Ovid Bell Press

Galena Complex State His. Site
P.O. Box 333, Galena, IL 61036
Phone: 815/777-3310
(U.S. Grant Home, Old Market
House, Washburne House)

Jubilee College State His. Site
11817 Jubilee College Road
Brimfield, IL 61517
Phone: 309/243-9489

**Lincoln Log Cabin State
Historic Site**
P.O. Box 100
Lerna, IL 62440
Phone: 217/345-6489

**Lincoln's New Salem State
Historic Site**
Rt. 1, Box 244-A
Petersburg, IL 62675
Phone: 217/632-4000

**Lincoln Tomb State
Historic Site**
Oak Ridge Cemetery
Springfield, IL 62702
Phone: 217/782-2717

**Metamora Courthouse State
Historic Site**
113 East Partridge, Box 776
Metamora, IL 61548
Phone: 309/367-4470

**Old State Capitol/
Lincoln Herndon Law
Office State Historic Site**
1 Old State Capitol Plaza

Springfield, IL 62701
Phone: 217/785-7960

**Pierre Menard Home State
Historic Site**
4320 Kaskaskia Street
Ellis Grove, IL 62241
Phone: 618/859-3031

**Postville Courthouse/Mount
Pulaski Courthouse**
914 Fifth Street, P.O. Box 355
Lincoln, IL 62656
Phone: 217/732-8930

**Shawneetown Bank State
Historic Site**
Route 1
Old Shawneetown, IL 62984
Phone: 618/269-3303

**Vandalia Statehouse State
Historic Site**
315 West Gallatin
Vandalia, IL 62471
Phone: 618/283-1161

**Illinois Historic Preservation
Agency** 217/782-4836
1 Old State Capitol Plaza
Springfield, IL 62701-1507

• *Lincoln's New Salem is featured on the next page (viii).*

Lincoln's New Salem State Historic Site

Illinois Route 97 about two miles south of Petersburg

Lincoln's New Salem State Historic Site is a reconstruction of the village where Abraham Lincoln spent his early adulthood. The six years Lincoln spent in New Salem formed a turning point in his career. From the gangling youngster who came to the village in 1831 with no definite objectives, he became a man of purpose as he embarked upon a career of law and statesmanship.

Although he never owned a home here, Lincoln was engaged in a variety of activities while he was at New Salem. He clerked in a store, split rails, enlisted in the Black Hawk War, served as postmaster and deputy surveyor, failed in business, and was elected to the Illinois General Assembly in 1834 and 1836 after an unsuccessful try in 1832.

The six years that Lincoln spent in New Salem almost completely encompass the town's brief history. The community was thriving when Lincoln settled here in 1831, but growth stalled before his 1837 move to Springfield to practice law. The 1839 establishment of the county seat at Petersburg hastened New Salem's decline.

More than 20 reconstructed log buildings nestled in the midst of tree-lined hills make visitors feel as though they have walked into the 1830s. A new visitors center, two gift shops, and restaurants cater to the needs of visitors. Seasonal special events feature staff and volunteers in period costumes re-enacting historically accurate events and activities. The sites open daily free of charge, and is administred by the Illinois Historic Preservation Agency. —*David Blanchette*

Daytrip Illinois
Interstate 55

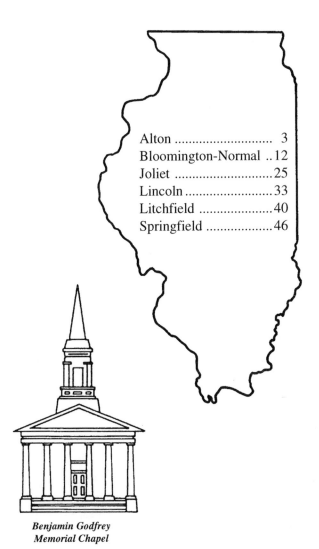

Benjamin Godfrey
Memorial Chapel

Alton
All Around Alton

Location

Alton is located west of Interstate 55 on IL 140.

History

Alton was originally settled by Jean Baptiste Cardinal in 1783. He stayed in the settlement until he was taken prisoner by the Indians. Meriwether Lewis and William Clark spent the winter of 1803-1804 here before making their historic expedition into the Northwest. The town of Alton, was founded by Col. Rufus Easton and named for one of his sons, was incorporated in 1833. River traffic on the Mississippi became very important to Alton.

The murder of Elijah Lovejoy, noted abolitionist, in 1837 illustrated the importance of the slavery issue. The last of the Lincoln-Douglas senatorial debates was held in front of Alton's city hall in 1858. The famous Lincoln-Shields duel of 1842 almost took place on a sandbar near the river. State Auditor James Shields challenged Lincoln to a duel after Mary Todd, Mr. Lincoln's fiancee, ridiculed the official in a newspaper column. The future president chose broad swords, and when the two men met by the river, the combatants agreed the article was not that derogatory.

Local industry sustained the town's growth long after the steamboats ceased operating.

Getting Started

Begin your visit by stopping at the Greater Alton/Twin Rivers Convention & Visitors Bureau, 200 Piasa Street or call in advance for more information 1-800-258-6645 • (618) 465-6676.

Attractions

Clark Bridge
Engineering Masterpiece

Linking Illinois and Missouri on Route 67 is the Clark Bridge which is a cable-stay bridge, one of the most unusual bridges in the United States. The bridge was named for William Clark who went with Meriwether Lewis in 1804 on a two-year 5,000 mile expedition up the Missouri River to reach the Pacific Northwest. The bridge is a gateway for thousands of visitors to "Discover the River Bend" region. Near Alton the Mississippi River changes direction for a short distance to run west to east. The bridge is earthquake resistant because its seismic design was based on wind testing and geological studies.

Confederate Monument
1 800 258-6645
Rozier Street
The monument is in remembrance of the 1,354 Confederate prisoners who died while imprisoned in the Alton Military Prison between February 1862-June 1865.

Confederate Prison
1 800 258-6645
Williams Street
In 1857 the Alton Penitentiary closed and moved to Joliet because of its horrendous conditions. The building was reopened in 1862 as a Confederate prison and part of the structure is still standing.

Eagle Watching
1 800 258-6645
From 200 to 400 American bald eagles winter in this area.
✪ Free admission

Lincoln Douglas Square
1 800 258-6645
Market Street
The last senatorial debate between Abraham Lincoln and Stephen A. Douglas was held here in 1858.

Lovejoy Monument
1 800 258-6645
Monument and Fifth Streets
The monument was constructed in honor of Elijah P. Lovejoy, the abolitionist editor, who was murdered because of his belief in and support of freedom of the press.
✪ Free admission

Photo by L. Allen Klope

Lincoln Douglas Square

Melvin Price Locks and Dam

Reservations required by calling (618) 462-1713

The construction of the locks was started in 1979 and completed in 1994. The project is at river mile 200.8 between the mouth of the Illinois River, 15 miles upstream, and the Missouri River, eight miles downstream. The valves of the dam are opened and closed hydraulically while the locking chamber is filled and emptied through the natural pull of gravity. Tours scheduled March 15 through November 15. Groups of 25 visitors or less Mondays, Wednesday, Fridays 10am, 1 and 3pm. Groups of 25 visitors or more Tuesdays and Thursdays 10am. 1 and 3pm. Saturday tours are at 1pm. Other groups by appointment. Visitors must be 13 or over.

✪ Free admission

Museum of History and Art

(618) 462-2763

Loomis Hall

You will find exhibits about the lives of Robert Wadlow and Elijah Lovejoy. Wadlow, known as the friendly giant, had the record as the tallest man in the world at 8 feet 11 inches tall according to the *Guinness Book of Records*. A monument in his honor is located at 2800 College Avenue across the street from the museum. The newspaper editor Lovejoy was known for arguing for freedom of the press, freedom of speech, and freedom from slavery. The history of Alton's involvement in the Civil War and Mississippi River steamboats is the main feature of the museum.

✪ Suggested donation $1

Piasa Bird

1 800 258-6645

The Piasa Bird is a Native American pictograph that was discovered high on a limestone bluff overlooking the Mississippi River in 1673 by Pere Marquette.

Sam Vadalabene Bike Trail

Route 100

1 800 258-6645

Enjoy some of the most scenic views of the Mississippi River along the 20-mile trail extending between Alton and Pere Marquette State Park and passing Elsah and Grafton. Bike rentals are available in Grafton.

✪ No charge to ride the trail

Lewis and Clark Historic Site

Off Illinois Highway 3, approximately two miles north of Interstate 270 is the monument commemorating the famous expedition to the Pacific coast. The site is located at the confluence of the Missouri and Mississippi Rivers, where Lewis and Clark trained and outfitted the exploring party. Their winter headquarters, called Camp DuBois, was used from December 12, 1803, to May 15, 1804, which is the longest time they spent in any one place. The party of forty-five men were known as the Corps of Discovery.

✪ Free admission

Satellite Attractions

✺ **Godfrey**

Benjamin Godfrey Memorial Chapel
(618) 466-3411 ext. 3001
Located a few miles north of Alton is an historic college founded 30 years after the Lewis and Clark Expedition of 1804-1806. It was originally founded as Monticello Female Seminary in 1835 by Benjamin Godfrey, and in 1970 the named was changed to Lewis and Clark Community College. The campus is home to the historic Benjamin Godfrey Memorial Chapel, built in 1854. The chapel is now on the National Register of Historic Places in Illinois and is one of the six most authentic copies of New England church architecture. It was moved in 1991 across the highway from its original location. The moving of the chapel brought over 2,000 spectators. The chapel may be rented for weddings, lectures, meetings and performing arts groups.

✪ Fees vary

✺ **Jersey County**

American Bald Eagle Roosting Area
Jersey County received its name due to the many early settlers who migrated there. It is the third largest roosting area for the American bald eagle. The eagles feed and patrol the river valley along the Great River Road and into Pere Marquette State Park. Spectacular panoramic bluffs rise up hundreds of feet. The area is one of the most scenic drives in Illinois and the nation. Discover small villages and communities such as Grafton and Elsah. January and February are the peak eagle viewing times.

✪ Free from November through February

✺ **Jerseyville**

Court House Square
Built in 1894 the courthouse is a beautiful example of architecture with a dome that towers 124.5 feet.

✺ **Elsah**

During the steamboat days "Jersey Landing," now known as Elsah, was an important river stop. The quaint village overlooks the Mississippi River and stands today as a reminder of the way small villages were during the 1800s. It is on the National Historic

Register as one of the best preserved 19th century villages.

❦ Grafton

Brussels Ferry
On the Great River Bend Road discover one of the few remaining free ferries in the country. The ferry runs year-round, 24 hours per day, weather permitting.

❦ Kampsville

Center for American Archeology
(618) 653-4316
The CAA is located in Calhoun County and is known as one of the world's richest archeological regions. The valley where the Illinois River joins the Mississippi has been significant in excavations and discoveries that help track nearly 10,000 years of human habitation on this continent. Interesting artifacts, exhibits and displays can be found in the Visitors Center. All ages come to work at active sites where they can have a hands-on introduction to the field of archeology. Enjoy browsing through the museum located at Kamps Store and now on the National Register of Historic Places, so named in 1994. ◗Visit by bridge or ferry.

Annual Events
Alton offers a variety of annual events. For a current calendar of events call 1-800-258-6645 or 1-618-465-6676.

January
- American Bald Eagle Tours
- Nature Tours — Various Dates
- Alton Little Theatre

February
- American Bald Eagle Tours
- Masters of the Sky

March
- Alton Museum of History & Art Exhibit
- Alton Symphony Orchestra
- Alton Little Theatre
- Underground Railroad Tours
- Greater Alton Concert Asso.

April
- Alton Spring Blossom Self-guided Driving Tour
- Greater Alton Concert Association, Inc.
- Alton Multiple Sclerosis Society Annual Walk
- Easter Egg Hunt
- Earth Day Education for Kids
- Grafton Riverside Flea Market
- Spring Bird Walk
- Alton Symphony Orchestra
- Calhoun County Spring Blossom Tour

May
- Y2K Encampment
- Calhoun Co. Historical Society Annual Quilt and Antique Car/Tractor Show
- Grafton Riverside Flea Market
- Center for American Archeology Field Schools
- Memorial Day

June
- Roxana Auto Show
- Concerts in the Park
- Sports Fest
- Grafton Riverside Flea Market

July
- Fireworks on the Mississippi
- Concerts in the Park
- Annual Tour De Donut
- Grafton Riverside Flea Market

August
- Drum and Brass Review
- Concerts in the Park
- Archeology Day
- Grafton Riverside Flea Market

September
- Lighted Boat Parade
- Bethalto Homecoming
- Barn Storming Tour, A Break Away Bicycle Tour
- Alton Exposition
- Grafton Riverside Flea Market
- Heritage Days

October
- Haunting of the Grand
- Pride, Inc. Annual Chili Cook Off
- Landmarks House Tour
- Alton Cultural Festival
- Echoes Off the River, Marching Bands Competition
- Kampsville Old Settler's Day
- Riverbend Jamboree, Country Music Shows
- Grafton Riverside Flea Market
- Halloween Parade
- Lincoln-Douglas Days
- Haunted History Tours

November
- Alton Road Runners Race
- Celebration of Christmas
- Lovejoy Commeration

December
- Community Christmas Tree Lighting, Downtown
- Ole Alton Arts and Crafts Fair
- Middletown Victorian Christmas
- Riverbend Jamboree Country Music
- German Christmas at the Koening House
- Last Chance Arts and Crafts Show

Shopping and Dining

In the heart of downtown Alton you will find a shopping district featuring more than 60 antique and specialty shops. Less than a 10 minute drive from downtown you will find the Alton Square Mall. It is a "Shop Til' you Drop Opportunity."

Dining is at its best in Alton from the all-American cheeseburger to the finest of dining. All types of cuisine are offered. Many of the restaurants in the area have provided brochures and menus to the Visitors Center so stop by for brochures, look through the files or ask a staff member for suggestions to help you make your selection.

We invite group tour directors to call the Group Sales Department of the Greater Alton/Twin Rivers Convention and Visitors Bureau to set up tours.

Conclusion

For further information contact:
Greater Alton/Twin Rivers
Convention & Visitors Bureau
200 Piasa Street
Alton, IL 62002
1-800-258-6645 • (618) 465-6676
website: www.visitalton.com

A team of tourism professionals at the Visitors Center will help you find new haunts. They offer patrons information about a view of the panoramic Great River Road, the picturesque corridor referred to as the Grand Canyon of the Midwest. The white cliffs in the region provide roosts for nearly 400 American Bald Eagles each winter. People from all over the world come to enjoy the splendor.

Tips

✔ While Eagle watching, come dressed with the layered look. It is cold.

✔ We are only 30 to 45 minutes from St. Louis International Airport.

✔ Golf course rates in the Alton area are available in a number of price ranges.

✔ Recreation and sports facilities are an inviting feature of the region.

✔ Athletic tournaments and competitions can be held at Lewis and Clark Community College in Godfrey.

66 Welcome to our region which is literally bordered by one of the mightiest rivers in the world — the Mississippi. Much of Alton's and the region's history is connected to the river.

The Greater Alton/Twin Rivers Convention and Visitors Bureau proudly serves a three-county area including Jersey, Calhoun and parts of Madison County. The Visitors Center, located in the heart of downtown Alton, is open seven days a week. To locate the Visitors Center, find the intersection of Piasa and Broadway Streets (the intersection of Rt. 67 and 100). If you are already in town, use the tall, white Con Agra Grain Elevator and the river as landmarks. We're practically just across the street.

Call or stop by the Visitors Center where you can obtain a wealth of information about the area. The Illinois Room at Hayner Public Library in Alton can also be a source of information.

Area historians have taken great efforts to record and preserve elements of the region's rich heritage. Historical programs and museums are available, but many have abbreviated hours. For optimum scheduling of your trip, call the Visitors Center or the museum in advance to confirm operating hours. In some circumstances and for groups, advance arrangements can be made to open the museum by appointment.

If you enjoy your trip so much that you would like to plan an extended stay or repeat visit with a group, contact the bureau's sales department for assistance planning your itinerary. Remember us too when planning family reunions, retreats, meetings, conventions, conferences and school field trips. We have a variety of overnight lodging options and interesting activities to complete a schedule for groups of all sizes.

We're pleased to share our region with you. Give us a call at 1-800-ALTON IL (800) 258-6645 and we will help you create a memorable visit *All Around Alton* **99**

—The Board and Staff
Greater Alton/Twin Rivers
Convention and Visitors Bureau

HISTORIC SITES

1. Alton Museum of History and Art, Loomis Hall (E5)
2. Confederate Cemetery (C4)
3. Confederate Prison (D5)
4. Lewis & Clark National Trail Site #1 (F8)
5. Lovejoy Monument (D5)
6. Alton Museum of History and Art, Koenig House (D5)
7. Pere Marquette Cross (A4)
8. Robert Wadlow Monument (E4)
9. Lewis & Clark Historic Marker (F6)
10. Wood River Massacre (F4)
11. Lincoln Douglas Square (D5)
12. Melvin Price Lock and Dam #26 (E6)
★ Greater Alton/Twin Rivers Convention & Visitor's Bureau

Map from Greater Alton/Twin Rivers Convention & Visitors Center

Bloomington-Normal
Twin Cities —We'd Love Your Company

Location

Bloomington-Normal is located in Central Illinois at the crossroads of Interstates 55, 75 and 39 as well as Routes 51 and 9. The twin cities are halfway between Chicago and St. Louis.

History

The seat of McLean County was originally known as Keg Grove in 1822 when the first settlers began to settle in the area. Later the name was changed to Blooming Grove. An early settler by the name of James Allin was instrumental in getting the newly created county of McLean to have as its seat his donated land adjacent to Blooming Grove. The town of Bloomington was the result of this decision.

In 1853 Illinois Wesleyan University was founded in the town, and in 1854 the rails of the Illinois Central, Chicago and Mississippi Railroads came to the town. In 1857 the Illinois State Normal University was created in North Bloomington.

The local publishing of Wakefield's *Almanac* in the late 1800s spread the town's name far and wide.

The Illinois State Republican Party was organized here in 1856. Abraham Lincoln's political career was greatly assisted by the Bloomington *Pantagraph*, a newspaper which was started in 1846. Two Bloomington natives, John M. Hamilton and Joseph Fifer, eventually became state governors. The city was also home to Adlai Stevenson,I, vice-president under Grover Cleveland.

➥ Getting Started

Stop by the Bloomington-Normal Convention and Visitors Bureau located on 210 South East Street for tour opportunities, brochures and updates on things to do while visiting in McLean County.

Attractions

✦ BLOOMINGTON

Beer Nuts Inc.
(309) 827-8580
103 N. Robinson
Beer Nuts, sold around the world, originated in the mid-1930s as

David Davis Mansion

"Virginia Redskins" peanuts. Bloomington is the only place in the world where they are manufactured. Visit the company store where free samples are available and watch a 15-minute video (by appointment only to groups of 15 or more).

David Davis Mansion
(309) 828-1084
1000 E. Monroe Street
The home of Supreme Court Justice David Davis, mentor to Abraham Lincoln and the man who convinced Lincoln to run for president, was a 19th century estate built in 1872. The Renaissance style house depicts the lifestyle of the wealthy and powerful of its day. The beautiful Victorian manor has eight fireplaces with Italian marble mantles, a large library accented with elegant English tile and French plate glass. Outside you will find formal gardens, the original carriage barn, stable and woodhouse. Sixty minute tours are from 9 a.m.-4 p.m., Thursday-Monday. Closed Thanksgiving, Christmas and New Years Day. For additional information call (217) 785-7929.

Franklin Park Historic District
Walnut, McLean, Chestnut and Prairie Streets in Bloomington feature many 19th century Victorian Homes that border the park. Adlai Stevenson's and "Private Jo" Fifer's homes are among the homes.
✪ Private residences

Illinois Coaches Association Golf Hall of Fame
(309) 823-4217 ,
502 Sale Barn Road
The IGA Golf Hall of Fame, located at the Prairie Vista Course, honors Illinois high school golf coaches and others on behalf of junior and high school golfers at the local, state and national levels of the game.

Illinois Wesleyan University
(309) 556-3031
Located on 60 acres the ivy covered buildings create a pleasant atmosphere for the 1,800 plus students. Illinois Wesleyan University was named the best small college in the Midwest by *U.S. News and World Reports* for 5 consecutive years.

Illinois Wesleyan University — Evelyn Chapel
(309) 556-3161
1301 N. Park Street
The Chapel has won international acclaim for both architecture and interior design. The chapel houses a Casavant-Freres organ that has more than 1,650 pipes. The organ is an integral part of the buildings design. Concerts are open to the public during the school year.
✪ Pre-arranged visits are welcome, with a tour guide provided.

Korean/Vietnam Memorial
Miller Park—At Morris Avenue and Wood Street stands a black granite memorial surrounded by red sidewalks with the names of Central Illinois residents who were killed or missing in action during the Korean and Vietnam battles.

McLean County's Children's Discovery Museum
(309) 829-6222
716 E. Empire
Known as Kid's Crossing the museum offers hands-on discovery centers in the arts, sciences and humanities. Open Tuesday and Thursday 10-5 p.m., Friday and Saturday 10-6 p.m. Closed except on school holidays.

Kathryn Beich, Inc. a Nestle Company
(309) 829-1031
2501 Beich Road
Come view the candy-making process of such classic candies as Katydids, Imps, Truffles, Gold Crumbles, Bit-O'Honey and 10 different flavors of Laffy Taffy. Tours are offered Monday-Friday at 9 a.m., 10 a.m., 11 a.m., 1 p.m.

Nestle•Beich

and 2 p.m. (depending on production schedules). Candy store open to purchase items after the tour.
✪ Reservations are required.

McLean County Soldiers & Sailors Civil War Monument
Miller Park, Morris Avenue
The monument dedicated in 1913 is inscribed with the names of all McLean County soldiers at that time.

Miller Park Zoo
(309) 823-4250
1020 S. Morris Avenue
A Bloomington-Normal landmark since 1891, Miller Park Zoo is one of only five zoos' in central Illinois and the only one to feature Sumatran tigers. You will discover an indoor tropical rain forest where you can spot 20 species of exotic birds, an outdoor exhibit where you will see Indian lions and snow leopards. Take time to visit the petting zoo, sea lions, and recently they have added red wolf and wallaby exhibits. Open everyday of the year except Christmas.
✪ Classroom facilities available for groups if scheduled in advance. Children under 3 admitted free with paid adult.

Old Courthouse Museum
(309) 827-0428
200 N. Main Street
The Old Courthouse Museum and Library is located in the former county courthouse, which was

built after the great fire of 1900 that destroyed four square blocks of downtown Bloomington. The courthouse is one of the finest examples of American Renaissance architecture, and the building's dome is an excellent reproduction of the dome of St. Peter's Basilica in Rome. The courthouse is listed in the National Register of Historic Places. Enjoy a self-guided tour through the history of McLean County learning about life on the prairie, its people, farming, work, politics and all that went into the growth of the area. There is a hands-on exhibit "Pioneer Neighborhood" where *please touch* is the rule.

✪ An orientation lecture or guided tour can be provided groups of 10 or more by appointment. Admission free on Tuesdays.

Prairie Aviation Museum
(309) 663-7632
Central Illinois Regional Airport at Bloomington-Normal
See the history behind the current aviation technology. The headquarters building houses a theater, aircraft models, an engine, an escape capsule, photos, uniforms and Ozark Airlines memorabilia. Revolving displays document many facets of our aviation heritage. Outside and hangar displays include a 1942 DC-3 (listed in the National Register of Historic Places), A-7A Corsair II, T-38, T-

33, 1958 Cessna 310B, Marine Corps Sea Cobra Helicopter, and several military ground vehicles. Tuesday 5pm-8pm April-November, Saturday 11am-4pm, Sunday Noon-4pm. Other times by appointment. Group tours available.
✪Donation suggested

Twin Cities Ballet of Bloomington
(309) 829 9333
510 E. Washington, Suite 320
Under the direction of Alexander Bennett, formerly of London's Royal Ballet and Ballet Rambert, the Twin Cities Ballet provides an exceptional dance curriculum.

✦ NORMAL

Aquaculture Research and Demonstration Facility
(309) 438-5654
W. Gregory Street
The prototype facilities, located on the ISU Farm, specialize in raising of fish as an agricultural product in an indoor, controlled environment. This facility is the only publicly-owned facility in the Midwest. With educational groups only, you can see a dairy operation and animals fed by computer.
✪ Tours by appointment

Eyestone One-Room School House
(309) 438-5414

Corner of College Avenue &
School Street
In this 1899 classroom, visitors
relive an era where antique wood-
en desktops and slateboards were
used to study the 19th century
curriculum.

Illinois State University Farm
(309) 438-7021
W. Gregory Street
When you tour this farm you will
see a dairy operation, beef cattle,
swine, sheep and the new aquaculture area where fish are grown.
The farm is open year round.
✪ One hour guided tours are
available.

ISU Planetarium
(309) 438-2496 (current showings)
(309) 438-8756 (private showings)
Corner of College Avenue and
School Street, Normal
The majesty of the "night" sky is
recreated in this 100-seat celestial
theater in-the-round by ISU's
Physics Department Planetarium.
Complex special effects are used
to demonstrate the wonders of
astronomy. Presentations are 60
minutes. Private showings are
available by appointment only,
Thursday-Friday 9am-4pm
✪Admission charge

Normal Theater
(309) 454-9720
209 North Street

Opened in 1937 it was the first
theater built specifically for sound
films. The theater has a strong art-
deco/modern design which at the
time was avant-garde for a small
Illinois town. It has been completely restored and is ready for
viewing.

Site of Major's Hall
Front and East Streets
A plaque commemorates a speech
Abraham Lincoln gave to a room
of delegates in the Hall on May 29,
1856. The address was to become
known as his *"lost speech"*. No
one took notes that day because the
audience was so enthralled with
the oration favoring the abolition
of slavery.

Stevenson Graves
(309) 827-6950
Grave sites of Bloomington's
honored natives, Adlai I, who was
vice-president of the United States
under Grover Cleveland and his
grandson, Adlai II, former Governor of Illinois, United States
Ambassador to the United Nations
and twice the Democratic can-
didate for the Presidency.

Recreational Facilities

Constitution Trail
The trail runs through both
Bloomington and Normal. It is a
multi-use trail made possible by a

Bloomington - Normal
Constitution Trail

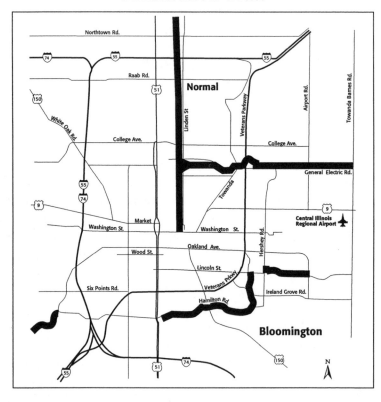

Northtown Rd.

Raab Rd.

Normal

Linden St

Veterans Parkway

Airport Rd.

Towanda Barnes Rd.

White Oak Rd.

College Ave.

College Ave.

General Electric Rd.

Towanda

Market

**Central Illinois
Regional Airport**

Washington St.

Washington St.

Hershey Rd.

Wood St.

Oakland Ave.

Lincoln St.

Six Points Rd.

Veterans Prkwy

Ireland Grove Rd.

Hamilton Rd.

Bloomington

N

Constitution Trail–a unique 9.2-mile linear park has become a hit with the community. Ideal for jogging, walking, cycling, and rollerblading, the north-south segment follows the abandoned Illinois Central Gulf railroad. The east-west segment intersects the north segment and continues east to Towanda-Barnes Road. The "Liberty Branch" is a new addition on Bloomington's southeast side.

Bloomington and Normal have jointly developed a master plan for trail development. Long-range plans call for extensions to connect neighborhoods with parks, greenspaces, schools, places of work, and historical sites in the Bloomington-Normal community.

Map courtesy of Bloomington Parks and Recreation Department

joint venture with the City of Bloomington and the Town of Normal. It is open from dawn until dusk. The Trail was officially dedicated September 17, 1987, and opened on May 6, 1989. The Trail follows the I.C.G. Railroad line from Normal City Hall to Washington Street in Bloomington. The east-west segment intersects the north segment at Normal Parks and Recreation Office, City Hall Annex and continues to Airport Road in Bloomington. The cities have jointly developed a master plan for trail development. The long-range plan calls for extensions to connect and encircle the city of Bloomington and extend from Normal City Hall to Lake Bloomington.

The trail is open to walkers, runners, in-line skaters, skateboarders, cyclists, wheelchair users, and other non-motorized forms of transportation. During winter months the trail is not cleared of snow, so is available to skiers, weather permitting.

Parks

The Recreation Departments of Bloomington-Normal maintain more than 30 parks in the Twin Cities. For information on the parks and seasonal recreation activities contact each city's Park and Recreation Department. Bloomington (309) 823-4260 • Normal (309) 454-9540.

Indoor Rock Climbing
Upper Limits
1-800-964-7814 or 829-TALL
Upper Limits is the tallest climbing facility in the world and one of the largest in the country. With more than 20,000 square feet of climbing surface, it has 44 separate lines of roped routes and eight overhangings and/or roof routes. Upper Limits offers a warm-up area, pro shop, equipment rental, instruction classes and seminars, group rates, locker rooms and an artificial waterfall in the winter months which is advantageous for ice climbing. Come see why Upper Limits has been featured and showcased by such popular media as Good Morning America, Sports Illustrated and ESPN

Bicycling
You will find many ideal places for bicycling. Contact the McLean County Wheelers Bicycle Club by calling (309) 454-1541 for a list of cycling events scheduled each year.

Satellite Attractions

⍦ Chenoa

Matthew T. Scott Home
(815) 945-4555
(25 miles north of Blm-Nrml, off I-55)
Home to Matthew T. Scott and his

wife Julia Green Scott, one of the founders of the Daughters of the American Revolution. Tour the Victorian home restored to its original condition.

❂ Guided tours by appointment only.

❧ Heyworth

Simpkin's War Museum
(309) 473-3989
20 minutes from Bloomington
Memorabilia from the Civil War through Vietnam is on display in the museum. In the personal collection of Gary Simpkins you will find over 900 American shoulder patches, over 300 pieces of military headgear, over 100 uniforms, more than 50 rifles and much more.

❂ Free admission by appointment throughout the year.

❧ LeRoy

LeRoy Museums
(309) 962-3331 • 962-9380
(15 miles east of Bloomington-Normal, off Interstate 74)
You will find three museums in LeRoy. The Rike House, built in 1853 by a local blacksmith, has been restored and includes the first piano in LeRoy. All museums are open during special events.

❂ By appointment only.

❧ Lexington

Patton Cabin
(309) 365-3091
(15 miles north of Blm-Nrml, off I-55)
John Patton, one of the area's first white settlers, built his cabin in 1829. Patton made peace with the local Indians after his first winter there, after which they helped him build his cabin.

❧ McLean County

The Apple Barn
(309) 963-5557
Route 4, (5 miles west of Blm-Nrml, County Rd. 1650 N.)
McLean's County's oldest commercial orchard. Apples, tasty treats and other surprises are available. Jacob Birckelbaw started the orchards in 1918. This is a great family outing. In the fall "Harvest Days" featuring wagon rides, craft demonstrations, food and fun is held the first full weekend in October. The following week-end is "Pumpkins Weekend" where families can go to the field by wagon to pick their own pumpkin. July-October 8-6, M-F; 8-5 Saturday 8-5; November 8-5, M-Saturday; open Sunday 9-5 mid-July-Thanksgiving.

Route 66 Museum and Hall of Fame
Dixie Truckers Home—McLean

(309) 874-2323
(15 miles south of Blm-Nrml, off I-55)
Come celebrate the legend and lore of historic Route 66 in the Hall of Fame Museum. The museum features displays and plaques of the fabled highway that winds through the prairies of Illinois on its way to the Pacific Ocean.

ᴥ Rural Hudson

Comlara Park Visitor Center
(309) 726-2022
(8 miles north of Blm-Nrml on I-39)
This Environmental Education Facility of the Illinois Department of Conservation has permanent wildlife displays, artifacts, a summer rotating exhibit program and other educational displays.
➲ Open year-round

ᴥ Shirley

Funk Prairie Home/Gem & Mineral Museum
(309) 827-6792
(13 miles southwest of Blm-Nrml, off I-55)
Drive to the restored 1864 residence of Lafayette Funk, he was an Illinois State Senator, co-founder and director of Chicago's Union Stockyard, known as the cattle-king of Illinois. The home is a fully restored Civil War Era mansion where one can hear an original, working Victrola or see the first-ever electric kitchen island. There is a dazzling display of many rare and beautiful gems.
➲ Tour reservations required (90 minute tour).

Funk Grove Pure Maple Sirup
(309) 874-3360
(13 miles southwest of Blm-Nrml, off I-55)
During the months of February and March guided tours are offered to show sirup-making by the "boiling down" process.
➲ Tours for groups up to 30 must be arranged in advance.

Art Events

Arts and entertainment groups along with offerings from the two universities give diverse opportunities to the community. Call the numbers listed with each facility for upcoming events.

- *American Passion Play*
  (309) 829-3903
  110 E. Mulberry, Bloomington
- *Community Players Theatre*
  (309) 663-2121
  201 Robinhood Lane, Bloomington
- *Heartland Theatre*
  (309) 452-8709
  1100 N. Beech Street, Normal
- *Illinois State University Galleries*
  (309) 438-5487
  110 Center for the Visual Arts,

Normal
- *Illinois Shakespeare Festival*
  (309) 438-2535
  Ewing Manor (Towanda Avenue at Emerson Street), Bloomington
- *ISU Music*
  (309) 438-3838
  Centennial East Building, Normal
- *ISD Redbird Area*
  (309) 438-2000
  W. College Avenue, Normal
- *ISD "Stars on Stage" Series*
  (309) 438-5444
  ISU Braden Aud., Normal
- *ISU Theatre*
  (309) 438-7314
  ISU Center for the Visual Arts, Normal
- *Illinois Symphony Orchestra*
  (800) 401-7222, Bloomington
- *IWU Merwin Art Gallery*
  (309) 556-3140
  302 E. Graham St., Blmg.
- *IWU School of Drama*
  (309) 556-3232
  McPherson Theatre, 304 E. Graham Street, Bloomington
- *IWU Shirk Center (Illinois Wesleyan University)*
  (309) 556-3203
  302 E. Emerson Street, Bloomington
- *IWU School of Music*
  (309) 556-3061
  Westbrook Auditorium, Presser Hall, Bloomington
- *McLean County Arts Center*

(309) 829-0011
601 N. East Street, Bloomington

Annual Events

The major events for the Bloomington/Normal area are listed below. The Calendar of Events is published four times a year with over 200 events taking place. Call (309) 829-1641 for new events and continual updates.

February
- International Fair
- Bloomington Barber Shoppers Show

February-May
- ISU's "Stars on Stage" Series

February-March
- Funks Grove Maple Sirup

March-May
- American Passion Play

April
- Gamma Phi Circus

May-October
- Third Sunday Market

May-September
- Music and Theatre Under the Stars

June
- Illinois Special Olympics Summer Games

June-August
- Illinois Shakespeare Festival

Mid-June
- Prairie Brass Review Drum & Bugle Corps Show
- Comlara-Fest Pioneer Days

July 4th
- Spirit of McLean County Sky-concerts

July
- Taste of Country Fair
- Sugar Creek Arts Festival
- McLean County Fair
- Civil War Re-Enactment

August
- Prairie Air Show
- Corn Festival
- LeRoy Fall Festival
- Cultural Fest

September
- Fall Carlisle Mid-West Collector Car Flea Market and Car Corral
- PACRACC (Pantagraph Area Cyclist Ride Around Corn Country), Labor Day Weekend
- Labor Day Parade, Labor Day Weekend

September-December
- ISU's "Stars on Stage" Series

October
- Fall Colors Family Day
- The Apple Barn Harvest Days Celebration
- Comlara Cycle-Cross

November-December
- Illinois University Madrigal Singers Dinner
- The Nutcracker by Twin Cities Ballet
- A Holiday Celebration at the David Davis Mansion

Shopping and Dining

You'll find shopping galore in the Bloomington-Normal area. You will find two malls, many antique and specialty shops, unique boutiques, and the larger retailers. All bring people from all across the central part of Illinois.

Dining at its finest with just the right atmosphere is any place you choose from elegant to just plain good 'ole country cookin'.

In Conclusion

For more information contact:
Bloomington-Normal Area Convention and Visitors Bureau
P.O. Box 1586
Bloomington, IL 61702-1586
(309) 829-1641
1-800-433-8226
website:
www.visitbloomingtonnormal.org

Tips

✔ June and September are usually the most comfortable months of the year.

✔ More than 2,000 hotel rooms from which to chose.

Bloomington-Normal Area
Convention and Visitors Bureau

66 Bloomington-Normal is second-to-none in location. It is located halfway between Chicago and St. Louis, with three major interstates connecting all parts of Illinois. Bloomington-Normal/McLean County, continues to maintain positive economic growth in the Central Illinois market. The diverse, stable and recession resistant economy has its strength in insurance, education, agribusiness and industry. This information is an enticing factor to many for attracting business to the area. What many do not realize is Bloomington-Normal is also a diverse and exciting travel destination.

Bloomington-Normal is home to two universities which offer a wide variety of events from sports to music, to theater plus a whole lot more. Other educational venues include the David Davis Mansion, Old Courthouse Museum, Children's Discovery Museum and Prairie Aviation Museum to name a few.

Bloomington-Normal also is known for its industrial tours. One can tour the Kathryn Beich Candy Factory that produces such favorites as Bit O'Honey and Laffy Taffy. Mitsubishi Motor Manufacturing of America is the only place in the United States to produce Mitsubishi cars. Beer Nuts, the only place in the world where Beer Nuts are produced, offers a video of the plant's process along with an outlet shop.

Bloomington-Normal is home to a wide variety of seasonal events. Two of the most popular ones are the American Passion Play and the Illinois Shakespeare Festival. Bloomington-Normal is home of the oldest continuously performed Passion Play with over 70 seasons. Bloomington-Normal's Passion Play dramatizes the entire ministry of Jesus Christ, not just the Passion Week like other plays. Another seasonal event is the Illinois Shakespeare Festival which features three Elizabethan classics which rotate nightly. A cultural highlight in Illinois, this festival under the stars and magic in the night, includes the Illinois State University Madrigal singers, love scenes, sword fights and more.

The above mentioned activities are just the tip of the iceberg for things to do in the area. A look through all of the promotional materials will show the infinite number of things to do in Bloomington-Normal.**99**

Manager-Motorcoach Group Tour Sales

Joliet
The Heart of the Heritage Corridor

Location

Joliet is located at the crossroads of America on Interstate 55 and Interstate 80 less than an hour from downtown Chicago.

History

In 1831, Charles Reed established the initial settlement in the region. The Black Hawk War caused Reed and the later arrivals to leave the area, but all returned in 1834, and a town was laid out in earnest.

The town's early name was Juliet, prompting a nearby settlement to call itself Romeo. When Will County was formed in 1836, Juliet became its seat of government.

When the first boats arrived in 1848 along the Illinois and Michigan Canal, Joliet grew to accommodate the river traffic. Local limestone deposits enabled the area to export its own materials for wealth. By the 1850s, limestone was shipped as far away as New York.

In 1852 a railroad, the Rock Island Line, came to town. Five additional rail lines curtailed profits for the canal business. But it was the steel industry's interests in local soft coal deposits that spurred real growth in Joliet. The manufacturing of spikes, track bolts, and other railroad materials created new factories for the town.

Getting Started

Begin your visit by stopping by the Heritage Corridor Convention and Visitors Bureau Office located at 81 N. Chicago Street in Joliet. You will receive the latest brochures and tourist information. They are located across the street from the Rialto Square Theatre, City Center.

Attractions

Empress Casino Joliet
Toll Free: 1-888-4EMPRESS
2300 Empress Drive
Over 1,000 slots and 50 table games. Three restaurants, a lounge, a ballroom and nightclub.

Harrah's Joliet Casino
1-800-HARRAHS
151 N. Joliet Street

Experience the hottest casino action in Chicagoland. Featuring 3 restaurants and a hotel.

Haunted Trails Family Amusement Park
(815) 722-7800
1423 N. Broadway (Rt. 53)
14 acres of year-round family amusement featuring hundreds of games, indoor and outdoor rides, go-karts, miniature golf, batting cages and restaurant. Group party packages available.

Joliet Iron Works Historical Site
(815) 727-8700
Collins Street just east of City Center. Naturalist led tours of the blast furnace ruins. Groups of 10 or more. Reservations required.
○ Free

Jacob Henry Mansion
(815) 722-2465
20 S. Eastern Avenue
Elegant National Historical Landmark offers unique Victorian settings for your particular dining occasions. Groups and or tours welcome.
○ Reservations required

Joliet Area Historical Society Museum
(815) 722-7003
17 E. Van Buren Street
Area history and special exhibits changing often.

Barber and Oberwortmann Horticultural Center
(815) 741-7278
227 N. Gouger Road
Features shows, exhibits, a resource center, programmed learning opportunities, gift shop and outdoor covered deck.

Bird Haven Greenhouse and Conservatory
(815) 741-7278
225 N. Gouger Road
Gougar Road, near Route 30
Displays a beautiful array of plants. Italian Renaissance-style Greenhouse offers year-round attractions with tropical house, cacti-room and show house.

Joliet-A-Midwestern Mosaic
(815) 727-2323
Joliet City Center Walking Tour
Self-guided mural and architecture walking tours.

Midewin National Tallgrass Prairie and Abraham Lincoln National Cemetery
(815) 423-6370
30071 S. State Route 53, Wilmington
19,000 acres of protected open space with native grasses and plants. Being developed are hiking, biking and environmental education opportunities.

Rialto Square Theatre

Pilcher Park Nature Center
(815) 741-7277
Gouger Road near Route 30
Includes display rooms, observation windows for bird watching, large aquariums, indoor turtle pond and hands-on-displays.

Rialto Square Theatre
(815) 726-7171 (815) 726-6600
102 N. Chicago Street
Historical vaudeville/movie theater listed on the National Register of Historical Places. Presenting a wide variety of popular, country, cultural and educational performances.

Route 66 Raceway
(815) 722-5500
3200 S. Chicago Street
The first "Stadium of Drag Racing" race track facilities which includes a half mile clay oval, a one mile off road course and a 35 acres driving school pad.

Slovenian Women's Heritage Museum
(815) 727-1926
431 N. Chicago Street
Established to preserve the rich ethnic Slovenian heritage and to honor immigrants who settled in the area.

Photo credit Diane Meredith

Joliet Union Station
(815) 727-2323
50 E. Jefferson Street
Crossroads to three national train lines. Listed on the Register of Historical Places.

Will/Joliet Bicentennial Park Historical Bluff Street Walk
(815) 740-2216
201 W. Jefferson Street
Boulders marked with bronze plaques mark important sites from the early days of Joliet and form a historic walk where early merchants and artisans established their homes and businesses

Satellite Attractions

🌿 Lockport

Gaylord Building
200 W. 8th Street
A beautifully restored landmark building along the banks of the I & M Canal.
• *I&M Canal Visitor Center* — (815) 838-4830. Exhibits on the state park system, I&M Canal

Riverwalk

and Gaylord Building.

- *Illinois State Museum*, Lockport Gallery — (815) 838-7400. Rotating exhibitions highlight the most distinctive fine, ethnographic and design arts in Illinois.
- Public Landing Restaurant — (815) 838-6500. Modern, regional American cuisine.

Will County Historical Society I&M Canal Museum
(815) 838-5080
803 N. State Street
Presents the history of the Illinois and Michigan Canal by costumed docents.

Annual Events

Call 1-800-926-CANAL for dates, times and a complete schedule of events and activities.

June
- NHRA Fram — Route 66 National Raceway Joliet
- Lockport Old Canal Days — Walk the trails or enjoy a horse-drawn tour wagon or carriage ride.
- City Center Car Show — Joliet weekend filled with demonstrations, displays, food and entertainment.
- Street Machine National — Route 66 Racing Joliet

July
- Dulcimer Festival — Annual musical event, jam session, top performers, workshops and more!
- Waterway Daze — Celebrate the economic and recreational vitality of the area waterways.

September
- I&M Canal Rendezvous — Columbia Woods, Willow Springs (708) 352-4110. Gathering of fur traders, trappers, settlers and entertainers along the banks of the Des Plaines River. Fun for all.
- Grundy County Corn Fest — Downtown Morris (815) 942-2676. Celebrate harvest time.

October
- Pumpkin Fest — Joliet (815) 724-4040 Bicentennial Park is turned into a Halloween pictacular

November
- Festival of Trees —Louis Joliet Mall, Joliet. (815) 727-6693. A dazzling display of Christmas trees along with local entertainment for children and adults.

December
- Poinsettia Show Bird Haven Greenhouse, Pilcher Park, Joliet (815) 741-7278. View spectacular poinsettias amongst the twinkling lights of the holiday.

Shopping and Dining

The merchants of Joliet invite you to browse through its many stores, specialty and antique shops.

You will not go away hungry from Joliet. There is a large variety of dining choices. Eating establishments vary from exquisite cuisine to casual dining. Many restaurants specialize in pizza and pasta dishes.

Conclusion

For further information contact:
Heritage Corridor Convention and Visitors Bureau
81 North Chicago Street
Joliet, IL 60431
1-800-926-2262
Fax: (815) 727-2324
website:
www.heritagecorridorcvb.com

❝ Get to the heart of life in the Illinois and Michigan Canal National Heritage Corridor. Your journey through time begins just 30 minutes southwest of Chicago. Experience the heart stopping moment before the roulette wheel finishes its rotation at one of our casinos. Revive yourself with a heart-pumping bike ride or hike along the I&M Canal towpath. Slow a racing heart in a nostalgic setting of a quaint town. Feel the welcome of outstretched arms when you step back in time at one of our museums and historical sites. Meet costumed docents from the past at festivals and big name entertainers of today at ballrooms and theatres. Connect with nature in any of the 11 State parks offering a backdrop of beauty that will simply take your breath away. Whatever the beat, find your heart's desire! **Willow Springs** — Get your heart pumping in the "Gateway to the Heritage Corridor". Where "take a hike" is more than a mere suggestion. Hiking and biking enthusiasts can discover the 11 paved miles of outdoor splendor on the I& M Canal Trail or take a break and enjoy a variety of nearby fishing spots and wooded groves.

Discover romance and history at the Willowbrook Ballroom. Founded in 1921 and rebuilt in the 1930's, the Willowbrook has hosted many dancers through the ages. Kick up your heels on the landmark ballroom's floor or celebrate privately in one of the banquet rooms. It's THE PLACE to be!

Joliet — Get your heart racing in the "Heart of the Heritage Corridor". From a spin of the roulette wheel to the ground shaking excitement of a drag race, Joliet is teaming with unbelievable action!

The first "Stadium of Drag Racing", Route 66 Raceway features 240-acres of excitement! With a drag strip, half-mile clay oval, one-mile off-road course and 35-acre driving school pad the Raceway has it all —and more to come. Showcasing in the spring 2001-NASCAR comes to the motorsport park.

Explore the heart of the city. The Joliet Iron Works Historical Site offers blast furnace ruins amid a beautiful backdrop of nature. Walk past murals and architecture that highlight three Joliet eras —Settlement and Growth; 1830-1850: Stone and Steel; 1860-1900: Prosperity; 1920-1935. Step back to vaudeville days in the historic Rialto Square Theatre. Entertainment today runs the gamet from popular and country music to cultural and educational performances.

Utica — Get to know your heart in the "Soul of the Heritage Corridor". Explore unique shops and sample a variety of cuisines as you connect to the simple life. Relax and enjoy the tranquility of Starved Rock State Park. Sample nature at its finest as you travel the many trails or paddle a canoe on a lazy river. Sit back, relax and enjoy!" ❞

—Christine Kirsch

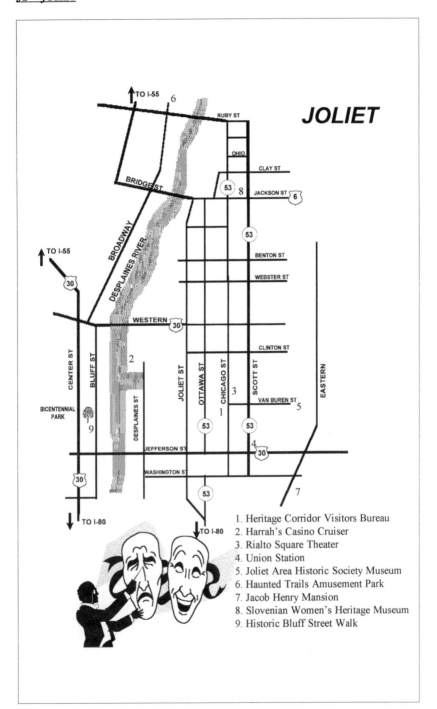

JOLIET

1. Heritage Corridor Visitors Bureau
2. Harrah's Casino Cruiser
3. Rialto Square Theater
4. Union Station
5. Joliet Area Historic Society Museum
6. Haunted Trails Amusement Park
7. Jacob Henry Mansion
8. Slovenian Women's Heritage Museum
9. Historic Bluff Street Walk

Lincoln
Land of Lincoln

Location

Lincoln is located in Logan County, the geographic center of the state on Interstate 55 with intersections of Route 10, 66, 121 and 155.

History

The city of Lincoln, Logan County, Illinois, is given special attention because it claims the distinction of being the first city in the United States to be named for Abraham Lincoln, with his full consent and knowledge.

It received the name in 1853, when three prominent men of Central Illinois acquired a new town site in Logan County. They employed Abraham Lincoln, attorney at law, to draw up the legal papers necessary to create the town and decided to name it for their lawyer who was a personal friend.

Christening Site of the town of Lincoln

The Alton and Sangamon Railroad Company made preparations early in 1853 to extend its lines from Springfield across Logan County to Bloomington. They located a station about halfway between these two places at a point which happened to be near Postville, Logan County. It soon became evident this site was centrally located and having railroad transportation would be an ideal place for the county seat.

Mr. Lincoln drew up the contracts for a public sale of town lots and was present when the sale was held on August 27, 1853. It was at that time that he christened the town.

The Christening Ceremony was very short. Lincoln selected a watermelon from a pile close by. He opened the melon with his pocket knife, he cut out the core, squeezed the water into a tin cup saying "Gentlemen: I am requested by the proprietors of this town site to christen it. I have selected the juice of a melon for the purpose of pouring it on the ground. Therefore, in your presence and hearing, I now christen this town site. It's name is "Lincoln."

Getting Started

Begin your visit by stopping by the Abraham Lincoln Tourism Bureau of Logan County at 303 S. Kickapoo. You can pick up brochures, maps, tour information and other general information. (217) 732-TOUR (8687).

Attractions

Heritage in Flight Museum
Located at the Logan County Airport in Lincoln, the building originally served as an army training facility and was brought to its present location from Camp Ellis. German prisoners of World War II were housed there. The museum is filled with memorabilia from all the military conflicts dating back to World War I.

Lincoln College
The college was founded and named for President Lincoln in 1865. The University Hall cornerstone was laid the same day. Today it is a National Historic Landmark. On the campus you will find a statue of Lincoln, the student. Lincoln College's McKinstry Library houses two museums. The Lincoln Museum contains the Abraham Lincoln collection valued over a quarter of a million dollars. Over 2,000 Lincoln volumes, manuscripts, art and related items of historic interest are housed there. The second museum is the Museum of Presidents, designed to honor the chief exe-

Merle Gage Statue at Lincoln College

cutives from Washington to the present day.

Logan County Courthouse

Located "On-the-Square"

The neo-classical structure, topped with a renaissance-style dome was completed in 1905. The building is a working courthouse that still houses county offices and records dating back to 1839. Points of interest include: a dome of 52 feet and a height of 60 feet from the base to the summit of the dome proper, a Seth Thomas clock with

four glass faces each nine feet in diameter; memorial tablets, carved in stone at each entrance depicting events from the founding county until the new courthouse was built; a Broadway entrance tablet that pays homage to Lincoln, who practiced law there; a rotunda that continues to the roof of the third floor covered with stained glass that illuminates with natural light during the day and artificial light after dark. There are other features too numerous to mention. You are welcome to come and browse at your leisure through the courthouse.

Postville Courthouse

(217) 732-8930

914 Fifth Street

The original courthouse was built in 1841 and was Logan County's first courthouse. The original structure was purchased by Henry Ford and moved to Dearborn, Michigan, where it stands as a Lincoln memorial at his Greenfield Village. The courthouse is now a state shrine. The State of Illinois built a replica building based on the original courthouse. The courthouse now houses a local museum collection on the first floor, while the second floor houses a courtroom and office furnished and arranged as they might have been in the 1840s when Abraham Lincoln visited the

Postville Courthouse.

✪ Suggested donations
Adults $2, Children $1.

Satellite Attractions

🍂 **Atlanta**

Atlanta Public Library

The octagon-shaped building was built in 1908 and one of the few in Illinois. The Library is on the National Register of Historic Places. It features classic details of the 1840s. It has high ceilings, doomed rotunda, high narrow windows, and has obtained its original solid oak woodwork and old fashioned fireplace. In 1973 the museum was established in the basement of the library. It houses museum pieces of local history, tools and artifacts of the original settlers.

🍂 **Elkart**

John Dean Gillett Memorial Chapel

Located on Elkart Hill is a chapel built by Mrs. Gillett in memory of her husband. The chapel is the only privately-owned, self-supporting church in the state. Mr. Gillett was known as the "Cattle King of the World" due to his breeding of Shorthorn cattle. He was a personal friend of Abraham Lincoln and Governor Richard Oglesby. Oglesby was elected

Governor in 1864, 1872, and 1884. John Dean Gillett and Richard Oglesby are both buried in Elkhart Cemetery.

🍂 **Mt. Pulaski**

Mt. Pulaski Courthouse
Downtown Pulaski

The courthouse is located in downtown Pulaski and has been placed on the National Register of Historic Places. The courthouse is a two-story brick building which served as Logan County Courthouse from 1847 to 1853. It is one of two remaining courthouses on Abraham Lincoln's eighth judicial circuit.

🍂 **Middletown**

Middletown Stage Coach Inn

The wooden structure Inn is over 150 years old. It stood on Middletown's public square and was on the stage coach Route 541 between Springfield and Peoria. It was purchased in 1874, and moved to the Thomas Davy, Sr.'s farm, where it was used as a home. It has been moved back to Middletown two blocks from the original sight.

Annual Events

Call (217) 732-8687 for dates, times and updates on events and activities. Free brochures available.

February

- Lincoln's Birthday open house, Mt. Pulaski State Historic Site. 100 candles will illuminate the building and period music can be heard from 6pm-7:30pm.
  ✪ Free admission
  (217) 792-3919

May

- Fiber Jubilee at Postville Courthouse —Demonstrations of natural dying, carding, spinning, weaving, quilting, and lace making with fibers such as wool, linen, cotton, angora, and mohair. Hours 10am-4pm
  ✪ Free admission

June

- Cedar Creek Shows — Antiques and Crafts Festival held at the Logan County Fairgrounds. Over 300 vendors (309) 263-0932.

July

- Elkhart Homecoming — Town-wide Garage Sales. Evening meals, hill rides and more.

July-August

- Logan County Fair—Fairgrounds, 4-H judging, open class horse racing, carnival, nightly entertainment, merchant displays, food, demolition derby, attendance prizes and more.
  ✪ Handicapped accessible
  (217) 732-3311

August

- Lincoln Art and Balloon Festival — Logan County Fairgrounds

Postville Courthouse State Historic Site

Art and Balloon Fest

and Latham Park. Over 45 hot air balloons, juried art show at Latham Park, food, carnival, car show, craft show, doll show entertainment.

✪ Free (217) 735-2385

• 1800's Craft Fair — Postville Courthouse, various artisans demonstrating skills from the 1800s such as blacksmithing, quilting, flax to linen, spinning, rope making, bobbin-lace making, wood carving, and broom making. Traditional music by various groups.

✪ Free (217) 732-8930

September

• Mt. Pulaski Fall Festival — Downtown Mt. Pulaski. Carni-val, food, parade, free entertainment, merchant booths, evening meals and more. (217) 792-5845 or 792-3904

• Atlanta Fall Festival — City Park, parade, carnival, food, free entertainment. Fire engine rides for youngsters and more.

• Cedar Creek Show

Shopping and Dining

Relax and enjoy shopping in Logan County. The merchants are ready to extend a warm welcome as you browse through their many shops. You will also find dining opportunities in abundance when visiting us.

Conclusion

For further information contact:
Abraham Lincoln Tourism Bureau
of Logan County
303 S. Kikapoo
Lincoln, IL 62656
732-TOUR (8687)

Tips

✔ Parks for your enjoyment include Atlanta City Park, Atlanta Ball Parks, Edward R. Madigan State Park, Kickapoo Creek Park, Latham Park, Memorial Park and Mt. Pulaski Ball Park.

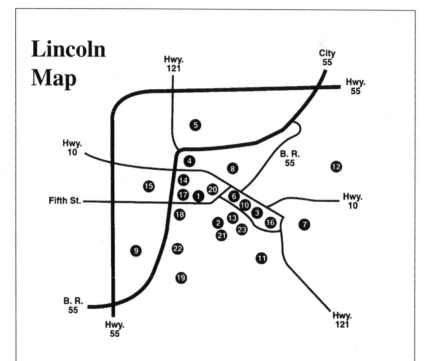

Lincoln Map

1. Abraham Lincoln Memorial Hospital
2. Great Lincoln Area Chamber of Commerce
3. City Hall & Fire Department
4. Exchange Park
5. Kickapoo Creek Park
6. Latham Park
7. Lincoln Christian College
8. Lincoln College
9. Lincoln Memorial Park
10. Lincoln Public Library
11. Lincoln Recreational Center
12. Logan County Airport

13. Logan County Courthouse
14. Logan County Fairgrounds
15. Logan County Health Department
16. Logan County Public Safety Complex
17. Postville Courthouse
18. Postville Park
19. Edward R. Madigan State Park
20. Ralph Gale Field
21. Scully Park
22. Union Cemetery
23. U.S. Post Office

Map from Abraham Lincoln Tourism Bureau of Logan County

Litchfield
Thriving With Industry and Community Spirit

Location

Litchfield is located at the intersection of I-55 and Illinois Route 16 (exit 52) approximately 38 miles from Springfield, IL and 52 miles from St. Louis, MO in Montgomery County.

History

The history of Litchfield is that of a typical central Illinois town. It began with the movement of men westward to new farmlands, the development of a railroad, and the formation of a land speculation group.

In 1849 several families settled their land on a site where the town would later be laid out. A surveyor in 1853 laid out the original plot of the town in a cornfield that belonged to the Litchfield Town Company. It was divided into 236 lots which became Huntsville, and later Litchfield. A charter was granted by the state legislature on February 16, 1859.

In 1866 the first coal shaft was sunk and in 1878 a second. During this time several oil wells were drilled and natural gas was found. In 1876, the Litchfield Car and Machine Company was formed and in 1881 Planet Mills opened with a capacity of 600 barrels of flour a day. By the spring of 1883 it jumped to 2,000 barrels a day, making it the largest mill in the country. In 1881 a third railroad was extended to Litchfield and in 1905 the Litchfield Grocer Company was incorporated. The Litchfield Creamery opened in 1917, later to become known as Milnot Company, and in 1971 began processing Chili Man Chili.

Henry F. Henrich Publications began publication of the world famous "Sunshine Magazine" in 1925 and by 1929 the Schutt Manufacturing Company began its operations.

➠ Getting Started

Begin your visit by stopping by the Litchfield Chamber of Commerce, 311 N. Madison Street. We will start you on your visit by providing brochures and to answer any of your questions about our county. (217) 324-2533

Attractions

Lake Lou Yaeger

Boaters and skiers are welcome to splash the waters while swimmers and sunbathers can enjoy the beach. Fisherman are welcome.

Old Route 66

Capture the past of Old Highway 66. You will find the only drive-in theatre in the state located on the old road.

Party in the Park

A gala 2-day festival of craft and food booths, carnival and entertainment. District chili cookoff.

Satellite Attractions

❦ Butler

Butler is a historic village located on Highway 127 formerly known as the Springfield Road. It was a very busy crossroads in the early 1800s. Butler has now become mostly residential but is home to the Montgomery County Fair. (217) 532-6697.

❦ Coffeen

For the avid fisherman you will find large mouth bass and channel catfish in abundance at the Coffeen Lake State Fish and Wildlife Area. The lake serves as cooling water for the Coffeen Power Station. Boat fishing, bank fishing and picnic area are in designated areas. (217) 537-3351.

❦ Farmersville

Visit the Historic Thomas Manor, the Mansion Antique Mall and come in time for lunch at the Mansion Tea Room in Farmersville (tea room open from 10:00am until 4:00pm daily).

❦ Hillsboro

Located along the Lincoln Trail, Bluegrass and Country Music Muzzleloaders and Wildlife Sanctuary. The lakes offer boating and fishing. You are invited to tour by car, bike or the Volksmarch route past three homes on Mainstreet plus the Old Courthouse, with "The World Needs God" sign — listed in the National Register of Historic Places. An open invitation is extended to enjoy our hospitality. (217) 532-3711 or (217) 532-6332.

❦ Nokomis

War Memorial Park

Located in Memorial Park is one

of the nicest War Memorials in the midwest. Made from seven vertical black granite stones, the memorial provides a background for the dedication stone and flag display.

Bottomley-Ruffing-Schalk Baseball Museum

The museum was founded in 1981 to honor Montgomery County's three Hall of Fame baseball stars, "Sunny Jim" Bottomley, Charles "Red" Ruffing and Ray "Cracker" Schalk. (217) 563-7573

❦ Raymond

Raymond boasts the Governor's Hometown Award for two of its country restaurants, plus an exclusive dining facility for evening meals in Veteran's Memorial Park. Enjoy the Shoal Creek Golf Course a public facility. (217) 229-4516

❦ Waggoner

This is an active residential village settled in 1886. There is a newly renovated park and railroad depot.

❦ Witt

Site of the Montgomery County Farmers Institute has many unique antique shops.

Annual Events

Call for dates, times and a complete schedule of events and activities.

May

• Customer Appreciation Days — 3,000 people are expected to attend; the Gold Wing Road Riders host vendor booths and there are music, games, refreshments and entertainment. Handicap accessible. (217) 324-6565

July

• International Chili Society District Cook Off —See spirited competition for winners with chili cooked by former winners of State International Champions. (217) 324-2533

November

• Holiday Walk — Enjoy a festive stroll through the district, lighted and decorated for the Christmas season. Visit businesses offering refreshments, ornament displays and entertainment.

Fairs and Festivals

January

• Antique Shopper Month

February

• Wolf Pack Mid-Winter Cruise In, *Hillsboro*

March

• The Promise, a passion play based on the life of Christ
• Dinner Theater, *Waggoner*

April

• Shoal Creek Muzzleloaders Rendezvous, *Hillsboro*

May

• Gold Wing Road Riders Motorcycle Appreciation Days Celebration, *Litchfield*

June
- Irish Days Celebration, *Farmersville*
- Illinois Route 66 Motor Tour, *Litchfield*
- Wolf Pack Car Show, *Litchfield*
- Montgomery County Fair, *Butler*
- Train Show, *Waggoner*

July
- Independence Day Celebration, *Litchfield, Hillsboro and Raymond*
- Homecoming Celebration, *Nokomis*
- Bluegrass Festival, Hillsboro
- Ethnic Festival, *Waggoner*
- Party In the Park — International Chili Society District Cookoff

August
- Illinois Country Music Fair, *Hillsboro*
- Homecoming Celebration, *Butler*
- Old Settlers Celebration, *Hillsboro*
- Fly-In, *Hillsboro*
- Farmer's Institute, *Witt*
- Town Yardsale, *Waggoner*

September
- Spinal Cord Midnight Bike Ride

October
- Nine Fingers Muzzleloaders Rendezvous, *Litchfield*
- Chocolate Temptations, *Hillsboro*
- Historic Home Tours, *Hillsboro*

November
- Holiday Walk, *Litchfield*
- Christmas Parade, Litchfield
- Hillsboro for the Holidays, *Hillsboro*
- Craft Show, *Waggoner*

December
- Christmas Light Tour throughout Montgomery County.

Tips

✔ If you want to get back to nature camp in Montgomery County. You will find some very good campgrounds.

Conclusion

For further information contact:
Litchfield Chamber of Commerce
P.O. Box 334
Litchfield, Illinois 62056
(217) 324-2533 or website
www.litchfield.il.us

66 Fields of wheat and corn, rolling hills, sleepy hollows and stands of mighty oak trees . . . that's Montgomery County. Bordered on the West by Interstate 55, crossed by Illinois Route 16, the county is a melting pot of commerce, tourist attractions, small villages and farms.

Swim in cool blue waters, soak up the sun on sandy beaches, fish in quiet lagoons. Feel the thrill of skiing across the wake of a speeding motor boat. Visit historic buildings, homes, roadways and parks.

Experience the excitement of fun filled celebrations, festivals, and Fourth of July fireworks. Take a scenic drive through the countryside abounding with fall colors. Stop at the many unique antique and craft shops along the way.

Play golf, dine, camp or just relax — let Litchfield be your destination **99**

—*Charlene Pigg*

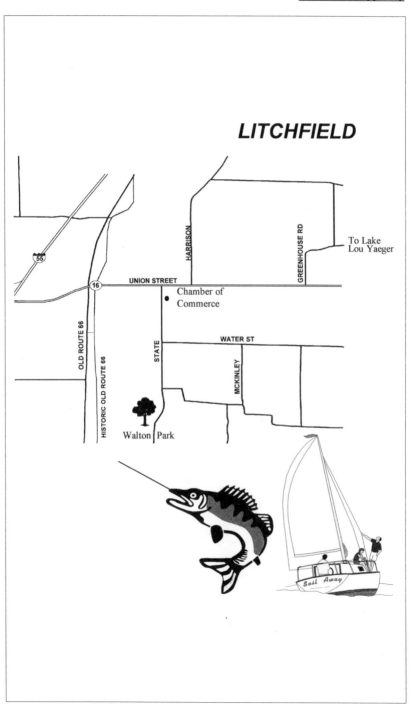

Springfield
The City Lincoln Loved

Location

Springfield, the capital of Illinois and the seat of Sangamon County, is located at the intersection of Interstates 55 and 72.

History

"My friends, no one not in my situation can appreciate my feeling of sadness at this parting. To this place and the kindness of these people I owe everything. Here I lived for a quarter of a century, and have passed from a young to an old man . . ." So said Abraham Lincoln as he boarded the train that took him from Springfield to Washington, D.C., as president of the United States. His footprints around the city are still highly visible.

Ironically, Springfield did not even exist in 1818, when Illinois was admitted to the Union. That year witnessed the arrival of Elisha Kelly, a North Carolinian, to the area. Finding the land fertile and the game plentiful, the rugged pioneer returned to the Tar Heel State and persuaded his father and four brothers to return with him to the valley along the

Lincoln Home National Historic Site

Sangamon River. That first Kelly cabin soon enticed others to plant roots in the neighborhood, and soon a small community was formed. Sangamon County was formed in 1821. Because Kelly's settlement was the largest in the area, it was chosen to house the county officials. That year the town was named Springfield after nearby Spring Creek. John Kelly was commissioned to construct a courthouse and the roots of government for the county took hold. In 1825 the choice between Springfield and nearby Sangamo Town for the county seat was biased when Andrew Elliot, a local woodsman, led a party of officials through swamps and swollen creeks to the rival village. After the journey, the officials were unanimous in their decision to make Springfield the new county seat of government.

Though a hardy steamboat named the *Talisman* was able to venture the Sangamon River from St. Louis in 1832, its inability to turn around in the narrow river kept Springfield a landlocked city.

The 1830s witnessed a great influx of settlers looking to farm the fertile land around the state of Illinois. A movement was started to relocate the capital from Vandalia to a more centrally located site. Led by the formidable Abraham Lincoln, a delegation from Springfield was successful in securing a sufficient number of votes in 1837 to bring the state legislature to the growing community of 1,500 inhabitants. Though it became a capital, Springfield was not incorporated into a city until 1840. By the time Lincoln left the city in 1860, it had grown to more than 9,400.

Other events promoted city growth. Railroads brought profit-minded industries, and in 1853 the city held its first state fair. The commencement of coal mining operations in 1867 increased the opportunities for workers.

In 1865 a movement was started to relocate the capital to Peoria. Though the bill was tabled, the citizens of Springfield overwhelmingly allocated funds to build a new capitol building that started in 1868. Though the legislature moved into the building in 1874, appropriation wrangling held up the building's completion until 1887.

➽ Getting Started

Start by stopping by the Lincoln Home Visitor Center 426 South 7th Street (217) 492-4150 It is recommended you phone 1-800-545-7300 to verify site hours before planning your trip. Write or call for brochures.

Attractions

Lincoln Home National Historic Site
(217) 492-4150
8th and Jackson
A good place to get started, the home is a restoration of the residence of Lincoln from 1844 until 1861.
✪ Free admission

Lincoln-Herndon Law Offices
(217) 785-7289
6th and Adams
The office above the Tinsley store was Lincoln's legal office from 1843 until 1853.

Old State Capitol
(217) 785-7961

Downtown Mall
This restored building is where a young Lincoln got his governmental feet wet from 1837 until 1858.
✪ Free admission

Lincoln Depot
(217) 544-8695
10th and Monroe
The Depot was Lincoln's departure point on his way into infamy as he left his childhood home to take the reigns of the Presidency. Open April-Sept.
✪ Free admission

Lincoln Tomb
(217) 782-2717
Oak Ridge Cemetery
The final resting place for

New State Capitol

President Lincoln and his family.
✪ Free admission

Lincoln Ledger
(217) 525-9600
Bank One
6th and Washington
You can read the famous family's ledger at this bank in downtown Springfield.
✪ Free admission

Lincoln Pew
(217) 528-4311
First Presbyterian Church
7th and Capitol
You will enjoy the architecture at the church where the Lincolns worshipped.
✪ Free admission

Illinois State Capitol
(217) 782-2099
2nd and Capitol
The building has served the people of Illinois since 1877 and its immaculate furnishings represent the successful wealth of the state. You can watch the legislature when they are in session.

Dana-Thomas House
(217) 782-6776
301 East Lawrence
The home of Susan Lawrence Dana, a local socialite and activist. The home is considered one of Frank Lloyd Wright's finest Prairie style houses.
✪ Admission charge

Dana-Thomas House

Edwards Place
(217) 523-2631
700 North 4th
Enjoy history and an art gallery in this restored 1833 mansion where Lincoln once addressed a crowd.
✪ Free admission

Vachel Lindsay Home
(217) 524-0901
603 South 5th
The birthplace of native Springfield artist and poet Vachel Lindsay, born in 1879. This 1840s home was built by the designer and builder of the Lincoln home. This site is closed indefinitely for restoration. Contact the Visitor Center for an update on a completion date.

Executive Mansion
(217) 782-6450
5th and Jackson
The third-oldest continuously occupied governor's home in the nation. Seven presidents of the U.S. have been received there, including Lincoln. The mansion is closed during official state functions.
✪ Free admission

Springfield Children's Museum
(217) 789-0679
619 East Washington
Enjoy learning about everything from archeology to weather with your children.   .
✪ Admission fee

Oliver Parks Telephone Museum
(217) 789-5303
529 South 7th
The history of telephones is depicted with more than 117 antique phones to see.
✪ Free admission

Washington Park Botanical Gardens
(217) 753-6228
Washington Park
An excellent place to enjoy flowers, tropical foliage, and a variety of plants in a domed conservatory.
✪ Free admission

Henson Robinson Zoo
(217) 753-6217
Visit more than 300 exotic and native animals, many in open display.
✪ Admission fee

Lincoln Memorial Garden
(217) 529-1111
2301 East Lake Drive
Explore five miles of wooded trails along the shores of Lake Springfield and seek out Lincoln's favorite spots.
✪ Free admission

Adams Wildlife Sanctuary
(217) 544-5781
2315 Clear Lake Avenue
You will find a sense of peace and

serenity at this centrally located park.

❂ Free admission

Thomas Rees Memorial Carillon

(217) 753-6219
Washington Park
Visit the world's third largest (three stories) bell tower. An excellent view of Springfield awaits you there.

❂ Free admission

Illinois Vietnam Veterans Memorial

(217) 782-2717
Oak Ridge Cemetery
Located near the Lincoln Tomb in Oak Ridge Cemetery this is a powerful granite monument with an eternal flame. The monument pays tribute to the 2,972 Illinois residents who served, died or are still missing in the Vietnam War.

❂ Free admission

Illinois Korean War Memorial

(217) 782-2717
Oak Ridge Cemetery
The names of 1,744 Illinois veterans killed in action are engraved on the granite walls of this breathtaking monument. Surrounded by 400 Rose of Sharon bushes, the memorial is located near Lincoln's tomb.

❂ Free admission

Illinois State Military Museum

(217) 789-9364
1301 N. MacArthur
Military exhibits portray the lives of veteran Illinoisans and the state's military heritage.

❂ Free admission

Grand Army of the Republic Memorial Museum

(217) 522-4373
629 South 7th
A variety of Civil War-era memorabilia is on display

Daughters of Union Veterans of the Civil War Museum

(217) 544-0616
503 South Walnut
Books and photos from the Civil War period might assist you in your genealogical search.

Amusements

Knight's Action Park and Carribbean Adventure Waterpark

(217) 546-8881
South Bypass 36 and Chatham Roads
Rides, games, giant water slide, lazy river rides, pedal boats, batting cages and miniature golf highlight this family fun park.

❂ Admission fee

Lake Springfield Marina

(217) 528-9207

7100 Woodland Trail
Six acres of water and land fun for the whole family on the shores of Lake Springfield.
✪ Free admission

Adventure Village
(2170 528-9207
Sangamon Avenue and Peoria Road
Children's entertainment is the specialty of this amusement park that caters to families on a budget.
✪ Admission fee

Satellite Attractions

✎ **Clayville**

Clayville Stagecoach Stop
(217) 626-1132
Route 125
An 1850s stage stop as well as several other buildings.

Special Tours

Mr. Lincoln's World
Take an 1850s style tour of the Old State Capitol on weekends during the summer months.

Annual Events

Many events take place during the year. For continual listings and updates call 1-800-545-7300 or (217) 789-2360.
February
• Lincoln's Birthday—At the Lincoln Home National Historic Site, celebrate with the Lincoln family.
✪ Free admission
May
• International Carillon Festival — Special events where bell ringers are showcased every evening throughout the week.
✪ Free admission
June
• Old Capitol Art Fair — The largest fair in central Illinois features more than 200 nationally celebrated artists.
✪ Free admission
• Bloomington Gold/Corvettes USA—You'll want to catch this "Vette" extravaganza at the Illinois State Fair grounds.
✪ Admission fee
June-August
• 114th Reactivated Regiment Flag Lowering Retreat Ceremony — Tuesday evenings in the summer are occasions to conduct military ceremonies at the Lincoln Tomb.
✪ Free admission
July
• Nineteenth Century Children's Festival — The Old State Capitol is the backdrop for a gala filled with games, entertainment, crafts, and good food.
✪ Free admission
• Lincoln Family Festival — Period re-enactors bring to life the Lincoln Home Site. Fine arts

and music accentuate the festivities.

✪ Free admission

- Summer Festival — Lincoln's New Salem recreates the 1830s in this event filled with early American crafts, costumed interpreters, and fun for the whole family.

✪ Free admission

- Springfield Air Rendezvous — Aeronautical acrobatics, aircraft displays, and hangar parties highlight this popular event.

✪ Admission fee

August

- Illinois State Fair — Ten days of memorable fun with livestock programs, rides, races, and headline entertainment.

✪ Admission fee

- New Salem Prairie Tales — Literature, drama, and music are performed by nationally acclaimed storytellers.

✪ Free admission

Labor Day

- Ethnic Festival — African-American, Asian American, German, Italian, Irish, Greek, Spanish are all represented in this celebration of ethnic foods.

✪ Free admission

September

- Bluegrass Festival — Lincoln's New Salem musically recreates the heritage that tamed the land. You can even dance to the same music that entertained your great- greats.

✪ Free admission

October

- Candlelight Tour — Another adventure at Lincoln's New Salem, this one is at night.

✪ Free admission

- Edwards Place Fine Crafts Fair — Shop for handmade original crafts from artisans from around the Midwest.

✪ Free admission

- Indian Summer Festival — Lake Springfield serves as the backdrop for this seasonal gala filled with arts, crafts, food, entertainment, and children's activities.

✪ Admission fee

November

- Harvest Feast — Lincoln's New Salem recreates one of the most anticipated events for the 19th century pioneer. Lots of activities and fun for all ages.

✪ Free admission

- Holiday Market — Lincoln Memorial Garden craft workers provide the atmosphere for this holiday gift and decorations opportunity.

✪ Free admission

- Festival of Trees —The Illinois Building at Illinois State Fairground, becomes filled with trees and trimmings during this Yuletide program.

✪ Admission fee

December

- Christmas in Mr. Lincoln's Neighborhood — Fanfare and

special seasonal events take place at the Lincoln Home.

- Dana Thomas House Christmas — This beautiful Frank Lloyd Wright home is bedecked in holiday splendor throughout the month.

✪ Admission fee
- Old State Capitol Christmas — The Old State Capitol is decorated with fir trees decorated by area school children. Every December 3rd marks a special holiday tribute to Illinois' statehood anniversary.

✪ Free admission
- Edwards Place Christmas — Each year this Victorian mansion is decorated on a selected theme for the year.

✪ Free admission
- First Night Springfield — Hundreds of performers at dozens of sites in downtown Springfield ring in the New Year with a celebration of the arts topped by a spectacular midnight fireworks display over the capitol building.

✪ Admission fee

Shopping and Dining

In the shopping arena Springfield offers adventure and a little bit of everything from one-of-a-kind antiques to the latest in fashion. It is Christmas all year long in the specialty vintage shops. You will find a gift shop at almost every historic site or local attraction More than 30 antique shops await the treasure hunter (write for an antique guide). Springfield also boasts the largest enclosed shopping center in central Illinois.

You will find an abundance of restaurants dispersed throughout the Springfield area—Family restaurants, pubs, pizza parlors, seafood restaurants, ethnic foods, tea rooms as well as the major franchised restaurants. You can write for a restaurant guide.

Conclusion

For further information contact:
Springfield Illinois Convention & Visitors Bureau
109 North Seventh Street
Springfield, Illinois 62701
1-800-545-7300 • (217) 789-2360
http://www.springfield.il.us/visit

Tips

✔ 30 public parks for you to enjoy.
✔ Other fun things to do — horseback riding, ice skating, roller skating and miniature golf courses are available.
✔ Our attractions are easy to find and many within walking distance.
✔ Trolley tours or open-air carriages drawn by horses are available. Call Illinois Convention and Visitors Bureau for more information. Fee charge for tours. Trolley stops at all major attractions.

66 To truly describe Springfield, perhaps no better words have ever been spoken than those uttered by Abraham Lincoln as he left here to take his place in history.

". . . To this place and the kindness of these people, I owe every-thing . . ."

Still today, it's the kindness of Springfield's people and the city's love of tradition that brings our history to life. Springfield was even selected as the second friendliest city in America in a recent national "manners poll."

Each year, nearly one million friends from around the globe make Springfield part of their vacation tradition. As you walk the historic streets and visit the sites of our city, you can really feel the past come to life. There's no other place on earth where you can experience Abraham Lincoln's 19th century firsthand at fifteen different Lincoln-era historic sites. And, then, once you have had your fill of history, you can easily step into the 20th century with exciting possibilities including everything from wonderful restau-rants and unique shops to four-diamond hotels . . . from top-name entertainment to local musical and theatrical performances that rank among the very best. If it's outdoor recreation you are look-ing for, don't miss our top-flight golf courses, water sports on Lake Springfield, and miles and miles of hiking in our many parks and nature preserves. For the kids, and the kids art, you'll find every-thing from waterparks to ferris wheels.

No matter what you and your family choose, you'll experience a wonderful mix of the old and the new in Springfield . . . hosted by the warmest, friendliest people you'll find anywhere. **99**

—Director of Tourism
Springfield Convention & Visitors Bureau

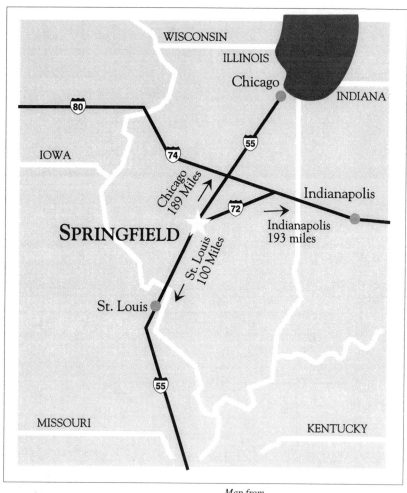

Map from
Springfield Convention and Visitors Burean

Daytrip Illinois
Interstate 57

Cairo
See It To Believe It

Location

Located along Highway 37 in Alexander County and accessed by Interstate 57, exit 1.

History

The little town between the shipping lanes of the Ohio and Mississippi Rivers was first settled in 1818 by John G. Comegys, who envisioned the site as resembling the ancient city in Egypt; thus came the name. After his death in 1820, the site was referred to by many as Egypt, but it was not permanently settled until 1837. That year a Bostonian, Darius B. Holbrook, presided over the Canal Company in Cairo, and enticed English settlers to the region to build levees, shops, and houses. The venture failed in 1840, but a few hundred hearty settlers remained in the area. A famous early visitor to Cairo was Charles Dickens, who docked there in 1842.

Cairo became the focal point of a travel route to both the South and the North in 1846. The plans called for the town to become a depot for boats heading south to the Gulf and for trains to link to Chicago to the north. By 1855, trains were running along that very route. By 1857 the city's population increased to nearly 2,000.

Cairo's importance as a trade route suffered irreparably during the Civil War. Goods from central Illinois began to move up to Chicago.

The Civil War had other impacts on the small river town. General Ulysses S. Grant established his headquarters there in 1861. The city became the starting point for the successful campaign to take the Mississippi and sever the Confederacy. The population continued to grow following the war, and by 1867 there were more than 8,000 citizens employed in the area.

➡ Getting Started

Cairo is one of several cities in the Southernmost Illinois Region. The Southernmost Illinois Tourism Bureau is located at Exit 18 of Interstate 57.

Attractions

Church of the Redeemer — Episcopal
(618) 734-1819
6th and Washington
This 1888 building is open for advance notice tours.
✪ Free admission

Fort Defiance State Park
Route 51
From this historical vantage point, see the convergence of the Mississippi and Ohio Rivers.

Magnolia Manor
(618) 734-0201
2700 Washington Avenue
The 14 room brick structure built in 1869, was the home of Charles Galigher, a friend of President Grant.
✪ Admission fee

Safford Memorial Library
(618) 734-1840
1609 Washington Avenue
This 1883 red brick building is an outstanding example of Queen Anne Gothic. The library houses a valuable collection of Civil War documents and interesting antiques are on public display.

The Hewer Statue
Ninth and Washington
This statue by George Grey Barnard was exhibited at the St. Louis Worlds Fair and presented to Cairo in 1906.

U.S. Custom House
(618) 734-1019
14th and Washington Avenue
This 1872 office houses several historical items, including a desk used by General Grant.

Satellite Attractions

🌿 Alto Pass
Union County

Alto Vineyards
(618) 893-4898
Route 127
Tours and tasting are available at this popular working vineyard.

Bald Knob Cross
(618) 983-2344
Route 127
This white porcelain monument to peace stands 111 feet tall.

🌿 Cobden
Union County

Cobden Museum
(618) 893-2067

Walton's Lamb Farm—Anna, IL

206 Front
Civil War and Indian artifacts along with memorabilia from the two World Wars are on display.

🐑 **Metropolis**
Located in Massac County, the only town so named in the United States. The city has maintained its wide streets and graceful homes of an earlier time. The city adopted Superman as its favored son. You are welcome throughout the year.

The Curtis Home
(618) 524-5210
405 Market
This 1870 museum was once home to Major Elijah P. Curtis.
✪ Free admission

Fort Massac State Park and Museum
(618) 524-9321
1308 East 5th Street
The first state park in Illinois contains a reconstructed 1794 American fort. Along with this history are, miles of hiking trails. Living history weekends accent this part of early America. You can see a statue of George Rogers Clark.

Merv Griffin Theater and Riverboat Casino
1-800 929-5904
East Front
Music shows, comedies, and family-style acts are featured at this facility.

Superman Square—Metropolis, IL

Superman Statue
Superman Square and Market Street
Don't miss the opportunity to see a 15 foot Superman while you're in his hometown.

Super Museum
(618) 524-5518
611 Market Street
The super hero's legend is related in memorabilia in this super attraction.

⚜ Mound City
Pulaski County
Mound City National Monument and Cemetery
Highway 51 and 36

Several thousand Civil War soldiers, both North and South, are buried in this historical location.

⚜ Tamms

The Old Depot
(618) 747-2343
This 1890 Chicago and Eastern Illinois Railroad Depot is today a restored museum.
➊ Free admission

⚜ Thebes

Thebes Courthouse
(618) 764-2587
Route 3
The hand-hewn 1845 courthouse

overlooking the Mississippi witnessed the Lawyer Abraham Lincoln and was an overnight resting place for Dred Scott. Tours are given with advance notice.

Natural Attractions

This region is covered by natural beauty in every direction. Rolling wooded hills with breath taking river views await the energetic hiker.

Shawnee National Forest

1-800 699-6637
Proclaimed a National Forest by President Roosevelt in 1939, this park contains nearly 270,000 acres of woodland, creeks, rivers and caves. Hiking and equestrian trails will conveniently take you to most points of interest.

Special Tours

Tours can be arranged by contacting the Southernmost Illinois Tourism Bureau which serves five counties: Alexander, Johnson, Massac, Pulaski and Union. Enjoy the romantic history and beauty of any one of the communities by calling 1-800-248-4373 or (618) 845-3777, Fax (618) 845-3303 and arrange the tour of your choice.

Agri Tours:

• Apple and Peach Orchards

• Vineyards & Winery
• Lamb Farm
• Holly Garden and Arboretum
• Herb Farm and Greenhouse
• Christmas Tree Farm

Historic & Architectural Tours

• Ft. Massac Park & Museum
• U.S. Custom House, 1872
• Magnolia Manor, 1869
• Thebes Courthouse, 1845
• Safford Memorial Library, 1883
• Stinson Memorial Library, 1914
• Mounds City National Monument and Cemetery
• Former Secretary of State Paul Powell Home and Museum
• Civil War Major, Elijah P. Curtis Home and Museum

Annual Events

March

• Re-enactors demonstrate the lifestyle of the 1700s at Ft. Massac State Park Living History Weekend (each month).

April

• Easter Sunrise service is held atop Bald Knob Mountain at the base of the 111 ft. cross.

May

• Herb Fest at Fragrant Fields in Dongola has a huge selection of herb plants & unusual flowers.

June

• Superman Celebration in Metropolis: Superman drama, car show, arts & crafts, and contests.

July
- Cobden Backyard BBQ contest features live entertainment, crafts, flea market and car show.

August
- Cobden Peach Festival has carnival, games, bingo, queen contest and lots of peaches!

September
- Johnson County Heritage Festival at Veinna, IL, features a parade, games, car show, arts and crafts.

October
- Riverboat Days Festival, Cario, IL
- Union County Fall Colorfest, Union County, IL.
- Ft. Massac Encampment, Metropolis, IL.

November
- November 25-December 31: Massive Lighting Display at Ft. Massac State Park (5-10pm).

December
- Holiday House at Magnolia Manor in Cairo.

In Conclusion
For more information contact Cairo Chamber of Commerce 222 Eighth Street, Cairo, IL 62914. (618) 734 2737.

Tips
✔ Winter is varied in Southernmost Illinois — come prepared for heat, cold, rain, or snow.

66 Welcome to Southernmost Illinois with its rich historic heritage, the Shawnee National Forest, and two great rivers: the Ohio and Mississippi with their confluence at the southern tip of the state at Cairo. The hills turn pink and white in early spring with the blooming of the apple and peach orchards, and autumn brings spectacular fall colors. Try your luck on Players Riverboat Casino, have your picture taken with Superman, and visit a Fort dating back to the 1700's all in the same day. We can 'theme' your trip with birding, antiquing or hiking. Southernmost Illinois is full of fascinating things to do and see. 99

—Cairo Chamber of Commerce

∽∾

Carbondale
State of Being . . .
A Comfortable Way of Life

Location

Located on Interstate 57 Carbondale is in Jackson County bordered by the mighty Mississippi River, rolling hills, towering sandstone bluffs, and acres of beautiful lakes.

History

This south central Illinois city at the foothills of the Illinois Ozarks became associated early on with the coal industry. Carbondale's founder, Daniel Harmon Brush, stood beside his newly finished railroad freight pavilion and awaited the first Illinois Central train on July 4, 1854. Its selection as a division point on the Illinois Central System ensured industrial growth in the area. In 1879 Southern Illinois Normal University was establlished.

Getting Started

Set your cruise control for Carbondale and start your tour at the Carbondale Convention and Tourism Bureau located at 1245 Main Street, Suite A-32, University Mall, Carbondale, IL 62901. (618) 529-4451or 1-800-526-1500 Fax (618) 529-5590 Website: www.cctb.org

Historic Attractions

Plan to visit the historic sites which have been listed on the National Register of Historic Places or the Carbondale Register of Historic Places.

Old Railroad Passenger Depot
111 South Illinois Avenue
The depot was built in 1903 by the Illinois Central Gulf Railroad.

Town Square Pavilion
When the first train came to Carbondale in 1854, the Pavilion was the site for a large public Fourth of July celebration.

Woodlawn Cemetery
405 East Main Street
On April 29, 1866, the first Memorial Day observance in Illinois was held. General John a Logan, a Civil War hero, gave the commemorative address.

Attractions

West Walnut Historic District
Located between Springer and
Maple Streets in the heart of
Carbondale you will find examples of 19th and early 20th
century homes — mansard-roofed,
colonial revival, Queen Anne and
square Italianate. Known for their
architectural design, many are
private residences and are not open
to the public.

Babcock Allyn House
505 W. Walnut Street
Built in 1848 for Edwin Babcock.

Bradley House
308 W. Walnut
A beautifully preserved bungalow
with broad side gables and wide
overhanging eaves.

Commercial Block
100-106 E. Jackson Street
The block was built in three stages
with ironclad oriels, carved
sandstone lintels and pressed metal
cornices. In 1900 the buildings
were rebuilt as one after a fire.

Dixon House
511 W. Walnut Street
The roof angle of this house is like
many homes built by the French
along the Mississippi River.

Driggs Houses
200 and 202 N. Poplar

Two Gothic revival cottages have
central steep gables and double-
pointed windows.

Dunaway House
409 W. Main Street
This Italianate house originally
was built with three bay windows
and a side entrance hall. It was
later expanded to five bays and a
central entrance hall.

Etherton House
500 S. Poplar Street
The Queen Anne style home of the
1890s has vertical massing,
multiple gables and a profusion of
wooden ornaments.

Felt's House
The Queen Anne home was built
in 1870 and in 1890 a Queen Anne
porch and tower were added to
bring the home into fashion.

*George Washington Smith/
Whitlock Home*
605 West Walnut
An SIU professor and noted
Lincoln historian, George Washington Smith, built the home in
1901. It is an example of transi-
tional Queen Anne/colonial revival
architecture.

Hundley House
601 W. Main Street
J.C. Hundley, a turn of the century
Carbondale businessman, built a

square two-story home featuring a red tile hip roof built of glazed tile with wide overhanging eaves.

Lightfoot House
520 S. University Avenue
Built in 1884-85 the square Italianate brick house has the original porch and roof with paired brackets intact.

Ogden House
323 W. Walnut
This is an excellent example of colonial revival architecture with intersecting gambrel roofs, Palladian windows, federal door lights and trim derived from pre-1800 styles.

Prickett Building
127 N. Washington Street
Built in 1903 this Queen Anne home features a corner bay window with an eight sided roof forming a turret.

Reef House
411 S. Poplar Street
A circa 1892 home built by A.M. Etherton for William A. Reef.

Smith House
605 W. Walnut
The Queen Anne asymmetrical east facade and patterned shingles combine the colonial revival era with its colonial railing and square massing.

Stotlar House
705 W. Main
Built of stucco and wood, this home combines prairie and craftsman styles.

Winnie House
204 S. Maple
The Italianate house has a three-bay sidehall with a low hip roof and eave brackets. The front facade has tall arched windows typical of the style.

Walking Tour of the Historic Town Square
Take a walking tour through Carbondale's Historic Town Square. Write or call for a brochure listing all locations in more detail — map included:

Carbondale Convention and Tourism Bureau
1245 E. Main St. Suite A-32
University Mall
Carbondale, IL 62901
(618) 529-4451 • 1-800-526-1500
Facsimile (618) 529-5590

Satellite Attractions

💮 **Alto Pass**

Alto Vineyards
(618) 893-4849
On Illinois 127 — A variety of award-winning wines.
✪ Tours by appointment

Bald Knob Cross

One of the most famous southern Illinois attractions, this 111-foot cross tops Bald Knob Mountain. The view from the top is spectacular. Thousands attend Easter sunrise services that have been conducted since 1937.

General John A. Logan Statue

2125 Spruce Street
The marble and bronze statue of John A. Logan was built in 1928.

☙ Gorhan

Fountain Bluff Indian Carvings

On the rock walls of Fountain Bluff at the north end Big Hill you will find carvings of prehistoric dwellers in the rock walls of Fountain Bluff.

☙ Grand Tower

Devil's Backbone
Devil's Bake Oven

- Devil's Backbone is an unusual rock ridge running along the Mississippi River.
- Devil's Bake Oven is at the north end of the park. The Oven is pitted with caves that once harbored river pirates until a U.S. cavalry troop drove them away in 1803. Legend has it that the ghost of a young girl who died of a broken heart — can be seen on quiet moonlit nights.

☙ Makanda

Boomer the Faithful Hound Dog's Monument

There is a Civil War legend in Makanda about a faithful, three legged hound dog named "Boomer." He died in the 1850s while trying to put out a flaming hot box on his master's speeding train. While running down the tracks, the dog was so pre-occupied with what he was trying to do he did not see a bridge abutment until it was too late. The monument stands in the heart of Makanda by the railroad tracks.

☙ Murphsboro

General John A. Logan Museum

1613 Edith Street
The museum features the life of General John A Logan, who was born in 1826. He was an early educator, lawyer, congressman, spokesman for southern Illinois, and served in the Civil War. The museum also depicts life as it was in the mid-19th century. Periodically special programs are held.

Jackson County Historical Society Museum

224 South 17th Street
You will find vintage clothing for women and more than 160 files for research dating to the 1800s.

Natural Attractions

Crab Orchard Lake
(618) 997-3344
Built in 1936 between Marion and Carbondale, Crab Orchard Lake is known for its hunting, fishing, camping and boating opportunities. It is a sanctuary to some 170,000 geese each year and famous for its large mouth bass.

Kinkaid Lake
(618) 684-1722
This 2,850-acre spring-fed impoundment was built in 1968 and is located northwest of Murphysboro. Known for its fishing, Kinkaid Lake, is the only southern Illinois lake where muskie can be found as a result of the cooler water temperature. Deer, wild turkey, rabbit, quail and squirrel hunting are for the taking.

Annual Events
Write or call the Convention & Tourism Bureau for continual updates on annual events.
(618) 529-4451 •1-800-526-1500

February
• Orchids, Trains, Planes and Stamp Show — A winter orchid show also has exhibits of model trains, planes and collectible

Kincaid Lake

stamps. Fills Hillside Nursery in Carbondale attracts 7,500-10,000 people annually.

March

• St. Patrick's Day Festival includes an Irish Stew Cookoff and a parade. Held in Murphysboro annually on the weekend prior to St. Pat's day.

April

• Spirits of the Midwest Powwow will be held for the first time at the Southern Illinois University Arena on April 5, 1997. This event will include Native American dancers, storytellers, artisans and cuisine.

May

• Makandafest is a folk festival held near Makanda, Illinois, in the midst of the Giant City State Park and the Shawnee National Forest. It is complete with crafts, music and food.

June

• Jackson County Shriner's Club Rodeo is held in Grand Tower along the Mississippi River and draws approximately 7,000 people.

July

• A Blues Festival held at Murphysboro's Riverside Park on the same weekend annually features regionally and nationally known rhythm and blues artists.

September

• Cascade of Colors Balloon Festival fills the air with approximately 40 balloons. Held at the Southern Illinois Airport, outside of Carbondale, it includes balloons, music, food and festivities and is attended by approximately 30,000.

• Apple Festival, one of the oldest events in Illinois, held in Murphysboro's downtown and includes a carnival, parade, crafts, entertainment, music and great food. Same weekend annually—second weekend of the month.

October

• *Midwest Harvest of the Arts* and *Arts in Celebration* are events held in alternate years on the same weekend. Both events feature arts activities which include hands-on activities for children, music, and art exhibits.

December

• Lights Fantastic is a lighted evening holiday parade held the first weekend in December each year in Carbondale's downtown with marching bands, floats, food and festivities.

In Conclusion

Carbondale Convention &
    Tourism Bureau
1245 East Main Street
Suite A-32 • University Mall
Carbondale, IL 62901

66 The residents of the City of Carbondale . . . and all of Jackson County . . . extend a huge welcome and friendly invitation to you! We want you to visit our region and enjoy the things we enjoy every day.

In 1996 the Carbondale Convention and Visitors Bureau was hailed as "Best of Show" by the Illinois Conference on Tourism. They competed against 85 other entries.

Jackson County Illinois isn't just a place to visit or a place to live. Jackson County is a special *state of being* and *a comfortable way of life.* Ranging from the rich German heritage prevalent in the rural communities to the varied international population located in the university community of Carbondale, over 64,000 residents live and work in Jackson County . . . and they play in Jackson County, too! . . . a hassle-free center of natural magnificence.

Scenic lakes combined with the spectacular beauty of state and national park sites further support the appeal of Jackson County to visitors and newcomers alike. The Shawnee National Forest extends into Jackson County and provides even additional opportunities for hiking, biking and picnicking in the midst of the most magnificent woodland in the world.

The tiny rural communities are just as important as the big university town. "As far as the eye can see" corn and soybeans are no more colorful than the mega shopping mall filled with thousands of shoppers from a five state region. Doctors still make housecalls, while Jackson County boasts the largest hospital and medical community in all of southern Illinois. In 1990 Carbondale was cited as the "Number one city in Illinois as an alternative to metropolitan hassles" in *Life in America's Small Cities* by G. Scott Thomas.

You'll definitely want to "Set your cruise control for Carbondale" and visit beautiful Jackson County . . . where it is the *people* who create that special *state of being . . . a comfortable way of life!* **99**

—*Debbie Moore*
Executive Director

Champaign-Urbana
Twin Cities

Location

Located at the intersections of Interstates 74, 72 and 57.

History

The two towns are separated by a street. Urbana was settled in 1822 by Willard Tompkins. In 1833 it became the county seat of Champaign County. When the Illinois Central came through the area, they chose a site some two miles west of Urbana to lay their tracks. Urbana chose to remain in its location, but soon the town of West Urbana spang up. Early local designations were the "Depot" and "Old Town." When Urbana was incorporated in 1855, they tried to annex the Depot territory. Outraged inhabitants of Depot were successful in 1860 in forming their own town which they called Champaign. In 1867 Urbana became home to the University of Illinois.

➨ Getting Started

The Champaign-Urbana Convention and Visitors Bureau is the place to get started. We are located at 1817 S. Neil Street in Champaign.

Attractions

You will find a large diversity of attractions in this community along with many cultural and educational opportunities.

Champaign County Historical Museum
(217) 356-1010
709 W. University

Champaign
The Wilber Mansion houses the Historical Museum. Step back in time while visiting the museum and listen to music provided by an old victrola. The museum was founded in 1974 with the purpose of preserving the county's history through objects depicting its development.

Curtis Orchard
(217) 359-5565
3902 S. Duncan Road
Champaign
Located 2 1/2 miles south of Springfield Avenue.
For great family fun from August

until early December you can pick apples from the approximately 4,000 trees located there. Kids can pick pumpkins, tour the working farm that produces corn and soybeans, play in the hay-filled barn, pet the goats, bunnies and chickens in the petting farm. There is a Market Store filled with pottery, baskets, wreaths and produce from the grounds. Hours Mon-Sat 9am-5:30pm and Sun 12 noon-5pm.

✪ Free admission

Parkland College
(217) 351-2200
2400 Bradley Avenue
Champaign
Drive through the beautiful 233 acres of Parkland College. The college was cited as an outstanding example of late 20th century architecture in 1979.

Prairie Farm
(217) 398-2550
Centennial Park
W. Kirby Avenue
Champaign
Another family experience is feeding and petting farm animals located in the petting area. Traditional farm animals such as sheep, horses, goats, pigs, cows, chickens, ducks and geese can also be found. Have fun crossing a footbridge as well as having a picnic in the facilities provided.
✪ Free admission

The Discovery Place
(217) 352-5896
Groups call 217 352-5895
Orpheum Theatre
Champaign
Listed in the National Register of Historic Places, the historic theater is home to the Discovery Place, a hands-on children's science museum. Exhibits include a water tornado, an eye magnifier, angular momentum, colored shadows, a human torso model, a giant lever, bending light, a PVC pipe organ, and a Bernoulli blower.

The Olympic Tribute
(217) 398-2550
N. Mattis Avenue
Champaign
The Olympic Tribute is located on the community college campus. You will find a granite platform inscribed with Champaign County residents who have participated in the Olympic Games. Along with the names are some inspiring words of James Russell Lowell and the Olympic symbol of linked rings.
✪ Free admission

The William M. Staerkel Planetarium
(217) 251-2200
2400 W. Bradley Avenue
Champaign
Through the latest state of the art audio-visual equipment, visitors can view 5,000 stars on a 50-foot

overhead dome. Part of Parkland College Cultural Center, this is the second-largest planetarium in Illinois. Special children's shows are scheduled as well as special seasonal presentations.

University of Illinois
(217) 333-4666
General Information
As a state-supported land-grant institution, the University of Illinois was chartered in 1867. A variety of cultural opportunities are open to the public.

John Philip Sousa Library and Museum
(217) 333-3025
1003 S. 6th Street
Champaign
The museum houses John Philip Sousa's personal band music library. Period band uniforms and musical instruments are on display. The museum is a tribute to a true music man.

Krannert Art Museum & Kinkead Pavilion
(218) 333-1860
500 E. Peabody Drive
Champaign
This is the second largest art musuem in Illinois. It houses a collection of over one thousand works of art ranging in date from the fourth millennium B.C. to the present.

Krannert Center for the Performing Arts
(217) 333-6280 or
1-800-KCPATIX
This magnificent showcase for the performing arts, is a professional laboratory for theater, opera, dance and music. The center hosts internationally known artists and is home to the Champaign-Urbana Symphony. The Krannert Center houses three indoor theaters, an amphitheater and a concert hall.

Memorial Stadium
(217) 333-3630
200 E. Florida Avenue
Champaign
Home of the "Fighting Illini" football team. Write for schedule.

The Museum of Natural History
(217) 333-2517
1301 W. Green Street
Urbana
Exhibits cover the fields of anthropology, botany, geology and zoology. The entire bird collections from Chicago's Columbian Exposition is housed there. It is listed on the National Register of Historic Places.
❍ Free admission

Rare Book and Special Collections Library
(217) 333-3777
346 Library
Urbana

1408 W. Gregory Drive
First edition of James Audubon's,
"The Birds of America" is housed
in the Library.
○ Free admission

World Heritage Museum
(217) 333-2360
484 Lincoln Hall (4th Floor)
702 S. Wright Street
Urbana
The musuem highlights man's
development from prehistoric
times to the present with 25,000
items.
○ Free admission

Satellite Attractions

Allerton Park
(217) 762-2721
Rural Route 2, Box 135
25 miles Southwest of Champaign-Urbana
This 1,768-acre country estate was
donated to the University of
Illinois in 1946. The park contains
an outstanding collection of
sculpture and statuary from
Cambodia, Thailand and China.
You will find the statuary placed
among beautiful flower gardens on
the grounds.

**Early American Museum
and Mabery Gelvin
Botanical Garden**
1 mile north of I-74
North Route 47
Mahomet

(217) 586-2612—*Museum*
The museum has two floors of
exhibits depicting 19th and early
20th century life in east-central
Illinois. Children are offered hands
on opportunities in a special
Discovery Room.

(217) 586-3360—*Garden*
The gardens are some of the most
beautiful and diverse in east
central Illinois. A display garden
features the newest and best
bedding plants and vegetables.

**Wabash Depot and Monticello
Railway Museum**
(217) 762-9011
Located at I-72, exit 63
Monticello
The restored Wabash Depot was
originally built in 1899 and serves
as the departure point for rides to
the Monticello Railway Museum.
Train rides are available from the
first weekend in May until the last
weekend in October. Display cars
are open 10am-6pm weekends
only.
○ Museum free
Admission charge for train rides

**Octave Chanute Aerospace
Museum**
(217) 893-1613
2 Aviation Drive, Rantoul
The aerospace museum is the
largest in Illinois. You will find
126,000 square feet of display

space depicting the history of Chanute Air Force Base.

Theaters

Contact one of the theaters listed below for seasonal productions from live theater and musicals to a classical experience:

Parkland College Theatre
(217) 351-2528
2400 Bradley Avenue
Champaign

The Station Theatre
(217) 384-4000
223 N. Broadway Avenue
Urbana

The Sunshine Dinner Playhouse
(217) 359-4503
1501 S. Neil Street
Champaign

The Virginia Theatre
(217) 359-1483
210 W. Park Street
Champaign

Art Galleries

International Galleries
(217) 328-2254
Lincoln Square Mall, Urbana

Kanfer Photography Gallery
(217) 398-2000
2503 S. Neil Street Champaign

Old Vic Art Gallery
(217) 355-8338
11 E. University Avenue, Champaign

Street Michael's Studio
(217) 359-8504
125 W. Church Street, Champaign

The Studio Fine Arts & Crafts
(217) 352-5333
1723 W. Kirby Avenue, Champaign

Parkland College Art Gallery
(217) 351-2200
2400 W. Bradley, Champaign

Annual Events
January
- Boat Show
  Marketplace Shopping Center
February
- Winterfest
  Kaufman Lake
- Illinois High School Association Boys' Wrestling Tournament, *Assembly Hall*
March
- Home Show, *Assembly Hall*
- Illini Cat Club show
  National Guard Armory
April
- Annual Model Railroad Show and Swap Session
  Lincoln Square Mall
- University of Illinois Mom's Day
May
- Junior Academy of Science
  Assembly Hall

- University of Illinois Commencement
  Assembly Hall
- Market at the Square (June-October)
  Lincoln Square

June
- Aerospace Open House
  Rantoul
- Stravinsky Awards International Piano Competition
  Smith Music Hall

July
- Freedom Celebration
  Memorial Stadium
- Annual Bluegrass Festival
  Crystal Lake Park
- Gus Macker 3-on-3 Basketball Tournament
- A Day in the Park
  Hessel Park
- Champaign County Fair
  Champaign County Fairground

August
- Annual Sweetcorn Festival
  Downtown Urbana
- Annual Cultural Arts Festival and a Taste of Champaign-Urbana
  West Side Park

September
- Rantoul Festival of the Arts
  Wabash Park

October
- Apple Harvest Days
  Early American Museum
- Pet Masquerade
  Lincoln Square Mall
- Prairie Settlers Day
  Anita Purves Nature Center

November
- Christmas Past
  Early American Museum
- Chris Cringle Craft Show and Sale
  Assembly Hall

December
- Annual Carol Concerts
  Krannert Center for the Performing Arts
- Christmas Walk Main Street
  Mahomet, Illinois
- Candlestick Lane
  Urbana, Illinois
- Christmas Open House and Florists Showcase
  Champaign County Historical Museum

Shopping and Dining

With fine dining to please every palate, eating establishments and shops are adequately dispersed throughout Champaign-Urbana

Tips

✔ If you enjoy the outdoors you will find 80 parks within Champaign County. There is something for everyone. Those who wish to visit parks in the area contact:
Champaign Park District
(217) 398-2550
706 Kenwood Road
Urbana Park District
(217) 367-1536

✔ Champaign-Urbana is located three hours from Chicago, two hours from Indianapolis and three hours from St. Louis.

In Conclusion

For further information contact:
Champaign-Urbana Convention
& Visitors Bureau

1817 S. Neil Street, Ste. 201
Champaign Illinois 61824-1607
(217) 351-4133 • 1-800-369-6151
www.cvpartnership.org

Chamber of Commerce
(217) 359-1791
(217) 359-1809 (fax)
www.ccchamber.org

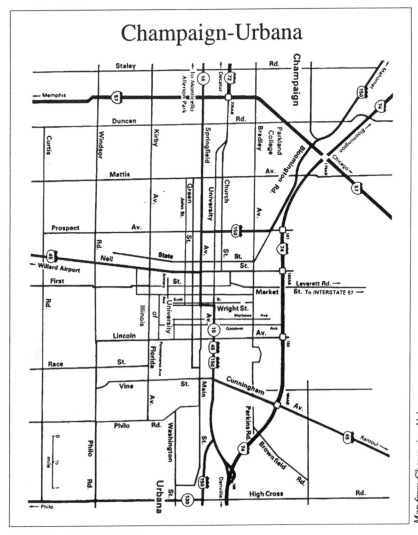

Champaign-Urbana

Map from Champaign-Urbana Convention & Visitors Bureau

66 Champaign-Urbana truly is a community with big ideas, solid midwestern values and old-fashioned fun. What a great place to visit for your weekend escape!

With one of this country's leading universities in its midst, it's hardly surprising that Champaign-Urbana is the premiere midsize community in Illinois. Residents hail from all over the country, indeed from all over the world, and their diversity is evident in many world-class recreational and cultural activities.

Yet Champaign-Urbana never forgets its roots in the rich prairie soil. Participants won't be disappointed by the rural heritage reflected in the local farmer's markets and summer festivals, such as "Apple Harvest Days" and the "Annual Sweetcorn Festival."

The University of Illinois is home to a number of fine museums, including the World Heritage Museum, which houses 25,000 historical artifacts from around the world. Here guests can see a reconstructed Egyptian tomb, one of the earliest passages from the Biblical book of *John* on a papyrus fragment, and a collection of paintings from Old Masters to modern sculpture, photography, and even ceramics and glass.

Champaign-Urbana enjoys a variety of cultural and recreational activities rarely found outside major metropolitan areas. The University of Illinois' Krannert Center for the Performing Arts regularly hosts world renowned performing artists and musicians in its five theatres. For entertainment from Shakespeare to Kabuki, opera to experimental theatre, Krannert is the place to go.

Marvel at the 5,500 stars and planets reflected in the dome of the William M. Staerkel Planetarium at Parkland College. Here visitors may view elaborate programs orchestrated with state of the art projectors, special effects, and automation.

The Sunshine Dinner Playhouse offers "Professional Dinner Theatre" at its best, offering a wonderful mix of old and new musical comedies and shows with a full buffet dinner for evening performances and a luncheon for matinees.

For a special treat and a change of pace, try Champaign-Urbana for your next weekend escape. Centrally located, inexpensive and loads of fun for the entire family, you'll be wondering why you didn't think of it sooner! **99**

Eldorado
City of Antiques, Arts, Crafts, and Specialty Shops

Location

Located off Interstate 57. Take Highway 13 to Harrisburg and then pick up Highway 45 to Eldorado.

History

The area around Eldorado (pronounced El-do-ray-do) was first settled around 1800. Soon other settlers moved in. With news of a railroad coming, Joseph Read and Samuel Elder decided to lay out a village. The plat was made August 22, 1857. From the names of these two men, Elder and Read, the name of Eldorado was formed. The village was incorporated in 1873. A city charter was granted in 1894. The center of business developed around the intersection of State Street and Locust Street. But with the coming of the railroad, businesses began to move toward the rail line and eventually the center of town was at Locust and Fourth Streets.

➠ Getting Started

Start your visit by coming to the Visitors Center located in the Old City Hall at 1604 Locust Street. Located here are the offices of the Chamber of Commerce and Project BOUNCE.

The Visitors Center offers brochures and maps of the city as well as public restrooms. You may reach BOUNCE at (618) 273-7109 or the Chamber of Commerce at (618) 273-3119.

Attractions

Old City Hall

City Hall was erected in 1924. City business was carried on there and the city court was held . Housed in the lower part was the fire station and fire engine. Eldorado's first Library was located on the third floor. Project BOUNCE leased the building from the city in 1991 when the city officers were moved. BOUNCE, with the aid of grants, began renovating the building. They were instrumental in having the building placed on the National Registry of Historic Places.

Cheese Factory

On March 1, 1933 the Cheese Factory began operation located at Crockett and Organ. The building is now occupied by Gibson Supply Co.

Ice House

Behind the Water Company building at Locust and Veterans Drive was a turn of the century poultry business and ice house. Eldorado was a principal shipper of dressed poultry, which was a boon to the farmers of the area. The business was located next to the railroad for ease of shipping poultry in ice. Chicago was the main destination.

T.G. Mitchell Building

Many stores occupied this building at the corner of Locust and Organ. The wooden building which faced Organ Street burned in 1910 and was replaced with a brick building facing Locust Street. Due to so many fires in the old wooden buildings, the town council declared all new buildings be made of brick.

Kuntz Building

John Kuntz erected a "two front" building in the 1300 block (north side) of Locust Street. He operated a tin shop and sold stoves. The second section was occupied by several people and was the site of Eldorado's first hospital.

Theaters

Before the theaters there was an Opera House in Eldorado located on the upper floors of a two story frame building at Locust and Fourth Streets. It burned, was rebuilt of brick and was at one time called the Grand Theater. An open-air theater enclosed by a high board fence was next to the Casino Theater on Fourth Street where the first movie house was located. It was destroyed by fire in 1915 and rebuilt. It was destroyed again in 1927, rebuilt and consumed by fire within three months. It was again rebuilt and renamed the Orpheum Theater. Silent movies were shown there accompanied by hired piano players. The Nox Theater on Locust Street was built in 1936, and the Grand Theater, across from the Orpheum was constructed in 1936. None of the theaters are in operation now.

Latham Building

The Latham building, set on the alley in the 1300 block of Locust Street, was built by Dr. Samuel Latham for his offices. A building behind was built for Dr. Latham's stable and later occupied by the *Eldorado Daily Journal*. This building was destroyed by fire in 1918.

Burnett Buildings

C.P. Burnett erected a large brick

building in the 1000 block of Fourth Street. It housed Burnett's Bank and Burnett's Big Store which included groceries, shoe store, men's store, dry goods, ladies fashions and furniture. The post office was also located in this building from 1903 to 1913. It was later renovated and housed a funeral home, and is now a doctor'office. Next to this building was the tin warehouse for the hardware store. It was razed and a modern dental office was constructed by Dr. William Johnson.

Eldorado Water Company

The historic building was built on the corner of Locust Street and Veterans Drive by Gar Slow and leased to the interurban railway. The railway ran between Eldorado through Harrisburg and on to Carrier Mills. It closed in 1931. The building is now occupied by the Eldorado Water Company.

Cox Building

Built in 1920, this two story brick building at the corner of Third and Locust served as a hardware store and buggy shop. After World War I it became a furniture store. In 1933 a five story building was attached to house an elevator and warehouse. It is the tallest building in Eldorado.

Cummins Building

O.D. Cummins built a brick one story building at Fourth and North Railroad streets to house a Ford agency and garage. He later needed more room and hired local house movers to add a second story. They inched the roof up as they constructed the second story. It is now the home of the Illinois Power Company.

Bramlett Building

A two story brick building was erected just north of the Union Station and tracks to serve as a grocery wholesale building. Its location next to the tracks permitted access to rail traffic. It later served as a garment factory.

IOOF Building

The two story building at Walnut and Locust was built in 1922. The second floor served as the IOOF headquarters and the lower floor was rented. A grocery store was here for many years.

Factory Building

In 1926 a group of businessmen constructed a brick building at Grant and Webber Streets and worked to bring a factory to Eldorado. A dress factory operated here for a time. When it closed, the Federal Wholesale purchased the building from the city. They operated here for many years until they moved to the outskirts of Eldorado. At that time they deeded the factory site back to the city. In 1990 the city offered the property to the Eldorado Memorial Library for a new building. On January 22, 1992 the library opened its doors at the new location.

Annual Events

Each third Wednesday of the month Project BOUNCE has a fund raiser dinner in the dining room at Old City Hall. For continual updates on events, call Project BOUNCE (618) 273-6188 or the Chamber of Commerce (618) 273-3119

January
• Chicken 'n' Dumpling Dinner
February
• Chili Cook-Off
March
• Lasagna Dinner
April
• Quilt Show
• Springfest and Beauty Contest
May
• Pork Chop Dinner
June
• Cook Book Dinner
• Bridal Show
July
• Steak Dinner
• Appreciation Dinner
August
• Rummage Sale
• Salad Bar

September
•Town and Country Days
October
• Dinner Theater
November
• Ham and Bean Dinner
December
• Christmas Fest

Shopping and Dining

For the avid shopper there are over 60,000 square feet of antiques, arts, crafts and jewelry shops. Three malls are located here with one-hundred dealers and many individual shops. There are a number of eating establishments in the community.

Conclusion

For further information contact:
The Eldorado Chamber of Commerce
1604 Locust Street, Eldorado
(618) 273-3119 or
Project BOUNCE
1604 Locust Street, Eldorado
(618) 273-7109
http:\\www.sirin.lib.il.us\doc\bus\ms-index.html

Tips

✔ The city of Eldorado welcomes individuals, car loads and bus loads to visit us. We are ever-changing, so come back and you will see different things each time.

66 Like many Illinois towns, Eldorado continues to be a shopping center for the surrounding farms. Very early in the 19th century the town was fortunate when the railroad was routed through the town. The railroad facilitated the shipping of dressed poultry to Chicago from the town plant which had an ice house that was a necessity before refrigerated cars. Earlier in this century two factories began shipping cheese and dresses.

Local needs are met by downtown stores and three malls. Of special interest, however, is Eldorado's center for antiques and crafts.

A sense of community is fostered by Project BOUNCE. Note the list of monthly community dinners to which everyone is invited, both resident and traveler alike. **99**

—Eldorado Chamber of Commerce

Golconda
Land of Great Wealth

Location

Golconda is located in Pope County on the beautiful Ohio River in extreme southeastern Illinois off Interstate 57 to Interstate 24 to Route 146.

History

The history of Golconda begins with the arrival of Revolutionary War Major James Lusk and wife Sarah who established a ferry at what is now Golconda, in 1798.

After Lusk's death, Sarah married Thomas Ferguson, one of the original settlers. He gave the name "Sarahsville" to the town when he donated land for the courthouse in 1816. In 1817 the name was changed

Burden Falls

to "Golconda," a word meaning "land of great wealth." Ferguson later was a member of the First and Second Territorial Legislatures, and he, together with Robert Lacy and Benoni Lee were commissioned as judges of the County Court.

Sarah Lusk was granted a ferry license in 1804 by Governor William Henry Harrison of Indiana Territory. The ferry house, constructed of keelboat timbers, stood until 1833, the same year the Dr. Alexander Sim house was built where it still stands on east Main Street.

The post office was Ferguson's Ferry from 1812 until 1825 when it became Golconda.

In 1838-39 the Cherokees crossed the Ohio on the ferry on their Trail of Tears. The Buel family witnessed the event and their log home still stands on South Columbus Avenue.

The *Golconda Herald* has been published continuously since 1858. Another organization with a continuous history is the First Presbyterian Church, organized in 1819 by Sarah Lusk Ferguson and fifteen other residents. It is the oldest Presbyterian congregation in Illinois.

Getting Started

We invite you to stop by the Chamber of Commerce located on Main Street or the Main Street Golconda office located on the corner of Illinois and Market. We will provide brochures, maps and information to help you get started.

Attractions

Buel House
Located at the end of Columbus Avenue is a log house in its original condition. It was built in 1840 by A.H. Buel, a tannery owner. It is now part of the Illinois Historical Preservation Agency, with the Society as caretakers.

Chocolate Factory
(618) 949-3829
The factory prides itself in offering quality gourmet chocolates, in a wide variety of mouth-watering flavors. They use only the finest ingredients and boast irresistible silky smooth blended chocolates.

Davidson Cabin
This is an original homestead that has been restored and relocated at the end of Columbus Avenue.

Pope County Historical Museum
The original museum was a home built in 1858 by William Lowth, an early merchant in the town. A fire destroyed the museum and its entire contents in 1987 because of an explosion of a neighboring house. Society members would

Davidson Cabin

not be defeated. Within a year they began the job of collecting memorabilia again. The museum today is located in a 1896 home located on Main Street, which was formerly used as a Presbyterian manse. Again it is brimming with treasures depicting the history of Pope County. Hours are Saturday 9am-11am and Sunday from 2:00pm 4:00pm.

Satellite Attractions

◈ Dixon Springs State Park

This is one of several state parks in the Illinois Shawnee Hills. Dixon Springs is located on a giant block of rock that drop 200 feet along a fault line extending northwest across Pope County. The park consists of 787 acres about 10 miles west of Golconda on Illinois Route 146 near the junction of Illinois Route 145.

The area was once occupied by various tribes of Indians. One of their favorite camping grounds was called "Kitchemuske-nee-be" named for the Great Medicine Waters. One of the better named trails known as the "Grand Trace" is located off Illinois Route 145. This is one of the most scenic highways in the state. It runs nearly all of its length south from Harrisburg through the Shawnee National Forest.

One Horse Gap Trail Ride

The park was named after William Dixon, one of the first white settlers to build a home in this section. For more information about park facilities call (618) 949-3394.

ꆛ Dixon Springs Agricultural Center

Established in 1934 by the University of Illinois, the center researches agricultural problems of Southern Illinois on its 600 acres, as well as on 4500 acres of Forest Service land.

ꆛ Smithland Locks and Dam

Located on the Ohio River 18 miles below Golconda, this is the world's largest twin navigational locks system.

Recreation

Golconda Marina
(618) 683-5875
Located in Golconda, the 80 acre site is a full-service boat marina with 206 slips. It is the gateway to the Smithland Pool area of the Ohio River. The marina is host to many fishing tournaments. Courtesy transportation is provided by several businesses in Golconda, or you might enjoy walking the short distance from the heart of Golconda.

One Horse Gap Trail Ride
(618) 683-RIDE
Experience a trail ride in the

Shawnee Forest. Ride your horse through some of the most scenic areas of the Midwest. The rides are 16 miles northwest of Golconda. Trails are safe for the experienced rider, they will still find a variety of challenging events that will be challenging. After a trail ride you can enjoy some real downhome cooking and live entertainment.

Walk About Wilderness Hikes
(618) 672-4396
Walk through the Shawnee National Forest with a guide to lead you through the Wilds of Illinois Down Under. This is one of the richest biologically and geologically diverse areas to be found in Illinois. Enjoy scenic vistas, wildflowers, songbirds, ferns, caves, fossils, natural bridges and more.

Annual Events

For a complete listing of current events and additional events call: (618) 683-MAIN • FAX (618) 683-5021

March/April
• Easter Egg Hunt — The courtyard is the focus of the annual Easter Egg Hunt. Over 2,000 candy Easter eggs are hidden for children ages 0-12. The Bunny will be on hand to greet participants. Held Easter Sunday 2:00 every year.

April
• River to River Relay — Golconda is the finish line for the annual relay event. The race begins each year on the west side of the state near the Mississippi River. The run is 80 miles long over rough terrain to the Ohio River. At the conclusion of the race the Main Street merchants support the event with a food booth.
• Quilters Welcome — This event is in conjunction with the National Quilters Convention held in Paducah, Kentucky. Quilt displays, local tours and activities.

June
• Spring Bass Tournament — Sponsored by the Chamber of Commerce the third Saturday in June.

May-September
• Farmers' Market — Every Saturday 8:00-noon. Produce, plants, baked goods, livestock, craft items, games, contests, and entertainment.
• Civil War Days — Civil War memorabilia and displays in conjunction with Farmers' Market.
• Concert in the Courtyard — Each 3rd Thursday evening a free outdoor concert is held on the Pope County Courthouse Lawn. Refreshments are available.

September

• Tour deShawnee — A two-day Bicycle tour which features rides of 35, 62 and 100 miles passing through some of the most beautiful country in Southern Illinois.

October

• Chamber Bass Tournament — Second Sunday in October. (618) 683-9702

• Fall Festival held the 2nd Sunday of October features arts, crafts, food and fun!

November

• Deer Festival — Three day event coincides with the first shotgun deer season. Crafts, exhibits, famous barbeque, parade and much more. Held annually the weekend before Thanksgiving.

December

• Annual Christmas House Tour — Tour of historic homes decorated in Christmas finery. Sponsored by the Chamber of Commerce.

Shopping and Dining

You will find a number of antique, specialty shops and restaurants located on or near Main Street in Golconda.

Conclusion

For further information contact:
Main Street Golconda
Box 482
Golconda, Illinois 62938
(618) 683-6246
FAX (618) 683-5021
or
Chamber of Commerce
P.O. Box 688
(618) 683-9702

Tips

✔ Bed and Breakfast accommodations are available as well as motels, cottages, ranch, or lodges. Write or call for a comprehensive list.

✔ Plenty of campgrounds and stables in the area. Write the Chamber for a list of facilities. Box 688—(618) 683-9702.

Welcome to Golconda

❝ Let us invite you to historic Golconda on the scenic Ohio River. Our village is rich with river heritage and abundant with warmth and hospitality. There is something for everyone here in our corner of Southern Illinois. Just a fifteen minute drive from Interstate 24 lies a sportsman's paradise and a shopper's haven amid the awesome natural beauty of the Shawnee National Forest.

You may choose to stay in one of our charming Bed and Breakfast inns. Or you may prefer the historic Mansion of Golconda where fine dining and luxurious accommodations are a way of life.

You can spend a day or a week visiting our friendly, distinctive shops. Genuine antiques, original art, gourmet foods and unique crafts are all within walking distance of your lodging.

Golconda is more than a place. It is a year around experience. The bustling farmers market is held on the courthouse lawn every Saturday from May to October. The Fall Festival, held during the height of the seasonal color change in October, features artisans and craftsmen from throughout the region. The world famous Deer Festival in November brings an estimated 15,000 to 20,000 visitors for the parades, entertainment and barbecue. Take the fun way home. Through Golconda.

Hope to see you soon! **❞**

—Jim Roper, Mayor
Charlotte Anderson, Program Manager, Main Street Golconda
Bill Altrman, President Pope County/Golconda
Chamber of Commerce

MAIN STREET
Golconda

Harrisburg
Northern Gateway to the Shawnee National Forest

Location
Harrisburg is on Highway 13 off Interstate 57 in the extreme southern tip of Illinois on the northern edge of the Shawnee National Forest.

History
Harrisburg, once known as "Crusoe's Island," was plotted upon 20 acres of land. Harrisburg began functioning as a county seat with the convening of court for the April term in 1859. The community was chartered as a town in 1861. It became a city with aldermanic government in 1889 when the population was about 1,500. Residents of Harrisburg raised $1,000,000 toward railroad construction costs for a line to be built by the Cairo & Vincennes Railroad Company. The line was put through Harrisburg in the 1870's. This paved the way for one of Harrisburg's greatest industries—coal mining. By 1906 Saline County was listed as producing a half a million tons of coal a year with a labor force of 1,000 men. But from the beginning of railroad service, Harrisburg enjoyed continuous growth. The availability of freight service to markets stimulated agricultural production.

➠ Getting Started
Start your visit by stopping by the Harrisburg Tourist Information Center located at the south end of Parker Plaza on Route 45. There you will be able to get maps and brochures of the area.

Attractions
Mitchell-Carnegie Library
The Library is located at 101 E. Church Street in Harrisburg. The building was funded by a grant from the Carnegie Foundation.

Muddy Post Office
The Post Office is the second smallest post office in the United States and is located northeast of Harrisburg.

Saline County Area Museum
(618) 253-7342
1600 South Feazel Street
The museum complex covers three acres. Start your tour at the central museum known as the old Pauper Home. Around the central museum are five authentic log

buildings that were moved from their original site in the hills and restored. Several families from Galena came to Saline County to take a break from lead mining, and some of them remained in the area and built log cabins. Open throughout the year with guided tours from Thursday through Saturday 9 a.m. to 4 p.m. and Sundays from 1 to 4 p.m.

Saline County Genealogical Library

Located on the first floor of City Hall in the old fire department office for seekers of family roots. The library is open on the fourth Tuesday of each month from 9 a.m. to 3 p.m.

Camel Rock—Garden of the Gods

Natural Attractions

Harrisburg is known as the "Northern Gateway to the Shawnee National Forest" which totals 265,000 acres. In the forest you will find many scenic and recreational attractions, some created during prehistoric upheavals in the region. You will find beauty, tranquility and a peaceful lifestyle in the area.

Eagle Mountain

From Harrisburg you can see the crest of Eagle Mountain to the southeast, the range stretches from Horseshoe Gap at the Saline-Gallatin County line to Womble Mountain on the south. It intersects with the main east-west range of the Shawnee Hills

Equality Cave

Spelunkers are welcome to explore the approximately 2.5 miles of passage located in the cave. The passage in the cave ranges from clay-filled crawl space to 30 foot high places just wide enough to walk comfortably. If you are not familiar with the cave, it is advisable you do not explore alone. For more information contact the Shawnee National Forest.

Garden of the Gods

The Shawnee National Forest is located at the southeast corner of

Devil's Smoke Stack—Garden of the Gods

Saline County. Shawnee Hills is a 320 million year old mountain range originally covered by a giant inland sea. Visitors will find a variety of interesting rock formations with names such as Camel Rock, Anvil Rock and Devil's Smokestack. The one-quarter mile long Observation Trail is a must for hikers. Use caution as some of the cliffs are high and the trail has some short, steep grades, but it is

"Old Stone Face" near Rudament in Saline County.

not tiring. Scenic picnic and camp-grounds are available. Motorized vehicles are not allowed. For more information contact the Elizabeth-town Ranger District at (618) 287-2201.

Old Stone Face

East of Harrisburg, one mile east of Somerset on Route 145 is Old Stone Face. Old Stone Face is on the west side of Eagle Mountain 730 feet above sea level.

River to River Trail

From Battery Rock on the Ohio River to Grand Tower on the Mississippi is an equestrian lover's dream. For more infor-mation contact River-to-River Trail Society at 11432 Winkleman Road, Harrisburg, IL 62946 or call 618 252-6789.

Saline County Conservation Area

Fishing enthusiastists will find 2.7 miles of shoreline with a water depth of approximately 33 feet. The lake contains a variety of fish including largemouth bass, bluegill, redear sunfish, crappie and channel catfish. Boats are allowed and boat rentals are available. On the premises you will also find a two-acre pond stocked with rainbow trout. Four five mile hiking and equestrian trails are designated in the area.

Shawnee Hills on the Ohio National Scenic Byway

South of Harrisburg on Route 34 and Route 145. This scenic 70-mile byway is the 91st scenic byway to receive national designation by the United States Forest Service.

Williams Hill

This is the second highest point in Illinois and the highest-elevation in southern Illinois at 1,065 feet above sea level. It is located south of Harrisburg and three miles west of Herod.

Satellite Attractions

❧ Equality

The Old Slave House
"The House that Salt Built"
South of Route 1 and 13
The John Hart Crenshaw House was built in 1827 when slavery was legal at the Salt Works and on the Reservation.

General Michael Kelly Lawler Monument
Civil War hero.

❧ New Haven

Joseph Boone's Mill
The Mill was built in 1814 six miles south of New Haven. Joseph Boone operated the ferry and fort on the premises.

Old Green House or Stage Coach Inn

Built in 1840 the inn served as a hotel on the Shawneetown-Vincennes Trail.

🍂 Gallatin County

A neighborhood of small towns and 7,000 friendly people. Gallatin County is full of history and "Firsts" —post office, bank, published book by a woman, industry, and the first Masonic Lodge. You will find great fishing in small cyprus-lined lakes, ponds and the Ohio River. Natural resources are coal, oil, natural gas, fertile soil and wild game. This is a great place to visit or just sit a spell, take in a festival, or enjoy the beauty of the county.

🍂 Junction

Gold Hill Ratite Farm

A real working ostrich and emu ranch is located at 7800 Island Riffle Road. Tours on request by calling (618) 269-2419.

🍂 New Shawneetown

Court House Mural

Located in the court house is a large painting depicting prominent historical figures and early life in Gallatin County. A molasses mixture was used to apply the mural to the wall.

🍂 Old Shawneetown

John Marshall House

This is the site of the first territory bank established in Lafayette in 1818.

Lafayette Landing

This is both the newest and the oldest establishment in Old Shawneetown. The historic hotel is known for its fine dining overlooking the beautiful Ohio River.

🍂 Ridgeway

Ridgeway Park

Camping, picnicking and children's playground.

Comstock Fruit Company

Home of "Pops-Rite" popcorn.

St. Joseph Church

A French Gothic Catholic church features beautiful stained glass windows, a marble altar and a pipe organ.

🍂 Shawnee National Forest

A must for the biking enthusiasts, the biking trails on the country roads in the national forest are among the best to be found anywhere.

Annual Events

July

- Fourth of July Parade — A parade of a variety of groups and organizations. Bands, floats, and much more.
- Fourth of July Fireworks — Saline County Fairgrounds, beginning at dusk.
- Local County Fair — A great family day. You will find rides, livestock, horse and auto races, horse shows, bands. During the last full week of July.

September

- Past to Present Festival — At this large attraction crafters and exhibitors display their skills—soap making, broom making, weaving, glass blowing, candy making, blacksmithing, and much more.

November

- Heritage Days — One of the largest craft shows in the area, this is held at Southeastern Illinois College. Crafts, food, and entertainment.

Shopping and Dining

Shopping opportunites will not leave you disappointed.

There are many eating establishments from fast food to relaxed dining.

Conclusion

For more information contact:
Harrisburg Chamber of Comerce
303 South Commercial
Harrisburg, IL 2946-2125
(618) 252-4192
1-888-844 TOUR (8687)
E-Mail: hcoc@sic.cc.il.us

66 If you are looking for a relaxing, good time, Harrisburg is the place to come and visit. Harrisburg is located in the extreme southeastern part of Illinois. It is noted for being the "Northern Gateway to the Shawnee National Forest." Being the last large community that one will pass through on the way south to the Shawnee Forest, there are many things available for all.

The Saline County Museum holds many items from the past, including an old one room school house complete with an old wood stove. The Harrisburg City Park will please anyone with its ballparks, picnic areas, shelters, playgrounds, tennis courts, basketball courts, and swimming pool, not to mention the lake in the center of the park fully stocked with fish.

Harrisburg is also the home of Southeastern Illinois College. The newly constructed theater on campus promises to bring a wide variety of theatrical and musical entertainment to the area.

Just south of Harrisburg you enter the Shawnee National Forest. There is something here to please anyone that enjoys nature. From hiking to biking to horseback riding — there are trails for you. At any of the numerous types of campgrounds, you will find a trail leading to the many wonders of the area. The Garden of the Gods is a large attraction with majestic rock formations along with scenic beauty. Bed and Breakfasts are nestled among the hills and along the beautiful Ohio river.

Along the Ohio river, there is a marina that could please any fisherman. The Shawnee is a hunter's delight. Whether you hunt deer, pheasant, geese, or turkey — there are hunting areas for you. Hunting guides and lodges are readily available.

If you prefer to rock climb or rappel — it's here! Old fashioned swimming holes with canoeing and paddle-boating are available. If your interests lean toward antiques, this is the area for you.

Wanting to get away for a weekend? Come down to Southeastern Illinois — "God's Country." There's something here for the entire family, young and old alike! **99**

—Harrisburg Chamber of Commerce

Kankakee County
The Fun Starts Here

Location

Located off Interstate 57 at exits 308, 312 and 315.

History

The Kankakee River, once thought to be the upper Illinois River, was called the Theatiki by the Pottawatomi Indians who lived in the area. Through variations in the pronunciation of Theatiki, Kankakee evolved.

Some of the meanings of Theatiki are Wolf, Swampy Place, and Wonderful Land. The Kankakee River Valley's beautiful land and rich natural resources are a result of debris and minerals left by three massive glaciers that came down from Canada thousands of years ago, thus accounting for the beautiful area that tourists, re-locators, and community members now enjoy.

Settlers came to Kankakee County in March of 1853. The city of Kankakee grew in the shadow of Bourbonnais, a French settlement nearby. Kankakee nonetheless became the eventual seat of government for Kankakee County, and in 1855 it became the site of a depot on the Illinois Central Railroad. Its population had grown by 1900 to about 13,500. Kankakee County's population is currently 101,290 and growing.

➦ Getting Started

Start your visit by dropping by the Kankakee County Convention and Visitors Bureau located on 1270 Larry Power Road Bourbonnais, IL 60914-4494

Attractions

Bennett-Curtis House
815 465-2288
302 West Taylor Street, Grant Park
Enjoy dining in this 17 room mansion built in 1900. The mansion is surrounded by 100-year old maple trees. Open for lunch and dinner with a full menu selection.

Exploration Station . . . a children's museum
815 935-5665
Children are encouraged to explore their world in a "Please Touch" setting. They can enjoy a space shuttle simulator, a fairy-tale

castle, a post office, sailing ship and much more.

✪ Admission Charge $1.50.

Castle Antique Mall
(815) 936-1505
1789 Route 50, North Bourbonnais. This antique lovers paradise has 86 dealers under one roof.

Fall Color Walks
(815) 933-1383
Start your walk at the Kankakee River State Park where guided tours are available through the beautiful fall foliage of the Kankakee River and Rock Creek Canyon.

Hidden Cove Family Fun Park
(815) 933-9150
Enjoy miniature golf, fun jungle, batting cages, paddle boats, arcade, driving range and go-karts located behind Northfield Square.

Indian Oaks Antique Mall
(815) 933-9998
Find bargains galore with over 165 dealers to see under one roof located on Route 50 and Larry Power Road, Bourbonnais.

Kankakee Antique Mall
(815) 937-4957
145 S. Schuyler, Kankakee
This is the largest antique mall in the state with three floors of collectibles and treasures from over 225 dealers.

Kankakee County Historical Society Museum
(815) 932-5279
8th and Water Street
The museum is opened 10-4, Monday-Thursday, 1-4 Saturday and Sunday. It is closed during the months of November and January. The special Gallery of Trees is in December.

Kankakee County Speedway
(815) 932-6714
Route 45/52, 1 mile south of I-57, Exit 308. Stock car racing every Friday night.

Kankakee River State Park
(815) 933-1383
Family fun for everyone—you will find horseback riding, canoeing, fishing, camping, picnicking, biking, walking or hiking.

Kankakee Valley Theatre
(815) 935-8510
Theater productions throughout the season, call the above number for listings.

Meadowview Shopping Center
(815) 939-4790
Kennedy Drive, Kankakee
A very large shopping complex is filled with special stores and theaters.

Canoeing on the Kankakee River

Northfield Square Mall
(815) 937-4111
Route 50 North, Bradley
At this large mall you will find department and specialty stores and a food court. For more information on events throughout the year at this location call for event listings.

Perry Farm
(815) 933-9905
Kennedy Drive, Bourbonnais
This 170 acre farm is full of history and beauty with its rich tapestry of woods, river and canyon. Cyclists, runners, cross country skiers and walkers can enjoy four miles of paved paths all year long.

Strickler Planetarium
815-939-5395
Located on the campus of Olivet Nazarene University, Bourbonnais. Visitors can enjoy the planetarium shows on the 1st Friday of every month at 7 and 8 pm except when closed in June, July and August. There is a $1 charge.

Annual Events
Kankakee County has many annual events every year. Write for continual updates and more information on what you can see and do. Call 800-74-River.

April
• Kankakee Area Business Showcase

—area industrial displays show what the area business community offers. It is held at Kankakee Community College. KACC (815) 933-7721.

- Annual Flower Festival — 1695 S. Schuyler, Kankakee. Listen to beautiful music while relaxing in the greenhouse atrium with its scenic water fall and many flowers. Call (815) 933-7848 for more information.

May

- Annual Women in Business Seminar & Trade Show. Call (815) 933-7721.
- Armed Forces Day—Pause for Patriotism. See Black Hawk helicopters, Navy amphibious vehicles in and out of the river, demolitions on the river bank. Great family fun with picnic facilities available. For more information call (815) 939-8327 or (815) 932-1281.
- Spring Herb Festival in Momence, Il. Exit 1-57, 7 miles east on Route 17. Two full days feature lectures, cooking and craft demonstrations, display gardens on seven acres, garden tours. (815) 472-2572.
- "Roaring on the River" Momence Drag Boat Races — 3360 Vincennes Trail. Boat races on a 1/4 mile course reaching up to 160 mph. (815) 472-6663.
- Annual Manteno Watercross Challenge —This is a ski world

championship qualifying event. Call (815) 468-8471.
- Pembroke Rodeo — St. Anne Rodeo Park, featuring the largest traveling rodeo in Illinois. This picnic and rodeo features bare back riding, steer wrestling, calf roping, relay races, barrel racing, flag races and bull riding. May 27-28. For more information call (815) 427-6384.

June

- Kankakee Valley Strawberry Festival — Memorial Park 8th and Water Streets. Strawberries and strawberry treats are sold. For more info call (815) 932-4470.
- 2000 Kankakee River Valley Fishing Derby — Kankakee River and its tributaries. One of the nation's richest fishing competitions, offering over $315,000 in cash and prizes. 1-800-74-RIVER.
- Annual Arts and Crafts Fair — Courthouse Lawn in Kankakee. See demonstrations of butter making, weaving, caning, spinning and much more —a day for all ages. (815) 933-1603.
- Bourbonnais Friendship Festival — Friendly family entertainment for all ages includes parades, a carnival, fireworks, dance bands, battle of the bands, karaoke, Lip Sync, 5-K run, volleyball, craft shows and much more.

Call 1-800-74-RIVER.
- River Valley Fishing Derby — One of the richest fishing competitions offers over $315,000 in prizes. Call 1-800-74-RIVER.

July
- Fourth of July Celebrations — Popular and patriotic music is performed by the Kankakee Valley Symphony Orchestra. Evening fireworks follow the concert.
- Thee Olde Time Farm Show — Early farm life is depicted through actual working tractors, threshers and steam engines from the past. (815) 932-7531.
- A Gathering on the Theatiki — Experience a reenactment of life in the 1700s when trappers traded furs for goods. Enjoy authentic entertainment, battles, 17th century foods of all kinds. History is brought alive at the gathering. (815) 468-6963,

August
- The Kankakee County Fair — Route 45/52, south of I-17, Exit 308. Traditional and modern ways meet at this county fair.
- Momence Gladiolus Festival — Featuring over 200 exhibits there are flower shows, flea markets, antique car show, and unlimited carnival rides.
- 1/4 Mile Canoe Drag Race — Great family fun. Entry fee— spectators free. (815) 472-2408.

September
- Kankakee River Valley Regatta-River Festival — Powerboat racing with 200 drivers competing for the National Championships at speeds up to 160 mph. Small admission fee. Call 1-800-74-RIVER.
- Herscher Hare and Tortoise 5K and 2 Mile Fun Walk — (815) 426-2211.
- Astrofest 17 — Chicago Astronomical Fair —One of the largest astronomy fairs in the country is held at Camp Shaw-Waw-Nas-See in Bourbonnais. For more information call (312) 725-5618.
- Bradley/Bourbonnais Business Expo — Call (815) 932-BBCC.
- Good Shepherd Manor's Annual Fall Festival — Good Shepherd Manor Campus in Momence. Enjoy delicious ethnic foods — Italian, Irish, German, Mexican, American and more as well as children's entertainment. Call (815) 472-6492.
- Rusty Weybright Fishing Derby — Momence Anchor Club 3360 Vincennes Trail, Kankakee River. Fish from shore or boat. Call (815) 472-2408 for more information.
- St. Anne Pumpkin Festival — Downtown St. Anne. (815) 427-8466 for more information.
  ✪ Free Admission
- St. Anne Pumpkin Festival 5K

Power Boat Racing

Run/Walk — (815) 427-8312.

October

• Kankakee Valley Arts Festival —Small Memorial Park, 8th & Water Streets. Take in live music, drama, art exhibits, and crafts. (815) 935-1115

• Governors 10 Mile and 5K Run —Bourbonnais. (815) 933-9255.

• A Night in Sleepy Hollow — Perry Farm on Kennedy Drive, Bradley — Enjoy the retelling of the legend of Sleepy Hollow and watch for the headless horseman. Other activities include a movie in the barn, pumpkin decorating, games, music and more. (815) 933-9905

✪ Admission $4.00 for adults and $2.00 for children

November

• Vana's Fall Celebration — Visit live reindeer getting ready for Christmas, the craft house, and enjoy homemade goodies from the "Soon to be Famous Fudge Shoppe". (815) 935-1700.

• Les Artesen Arts and Crafts Fair — BBCHS, Bradley. Over 170 booths of arts and crafts are on display. Call (815) 933-2535.

December

• Christmas Evening Fantasy Parade — Bradley on Broadway. The parade begins at 6 p.m. Be delighted by this Fantasy Parade, where every float in the parade is lit with Christmas lights (815) 935-1500.

• Ebony Fashion Fair — Kankakee Junior High School, 2250 E. Crestwood, Kankakee. The world's most prestigious Fashion Show. Showing clothes from top designers. 7:30-11:00 p.m. Admission (815) 933-0469.

• Vana's Country Christmas — Fresh cut trees, wreaths, country gift shop with gifts and decorations. Enjoy a horse drawn sleigh ride. (815) 935-1700.

• Gallery of Trees — Kankakee Historical Society, 8th and Water Streets. A wonderful opportunity to mix history and art. You will have the opportunity, to vote for your favorite tree out of thirty decorated trees. Call 800-74-RIVER.

• Historical District Luminaries — Riverview Historical Society hosts the annual luminaries display on Christmas Eve. (815) 939-4007.

Shopping and Dining

Along with shopping and dining at its best, Kankakee County boasts many fine antique shops and malls. There are more than 534 antique dealers in the county. Write or call the Convention and Visitors Bureau for a complete listing of shops and malls.

Chose from over 150 restaurants in Kankakee County, featuring everything from fine or casual dining, specialty food restaurants, pizza parlors, and fast food restaurants. Banquet facilities are also available. Call 800-74 RIVER for more information on dining in Kankakee County.

Tips

✔ When you enter Kankakee County, tune your radio dial to WTKC91.1 FM for tourism information on events, attractions, accommodations, restaurants, gas stations and more.

✔ Stop by the Kankakee County Convention and Visitors Bureau when you arrive in town for county brochures, directions and ideas.

✔ The spring and summer are busy with graduations and sporting events. Be sure to call ahead and book your hotel early.

✔ Kankakee County has 18 yearly festivals. Call or write for a complete Visitors' Guide.

✔ Call for a complete restaurant guide for your choice of dining experiences. (Fast food to fine dining).

Conclusion

For further information contact:
Kankakee County
Convention & Visitors Bureau
1270 Larry Power Road
Bourbonnais, IL 60914-4494
800-74-RIVER (7390)
FAX: (815) 935-5169
email: kccvb@keynet.net
website:
www.visitkankakeecounty.com

Welcome to Kankakee County!

 Whether you like antiques, fishing, festivals, county fairs, stock cars or the excitement of powerboat racing, there's something here for everyone! Kankakee County is home to 18 Festivals as well as the beautiful Kankakee River. Just one hour south of Chicago, Kankakee County is a great place to take your family or yourself for lots of fun and relaxation. **99**

Marion
Hub of the Universe

Location
Marion is located on Interstate 57 in Williamson County.

History
Founded in the 1820s, Marion became the eventual seat of Williamson County. Two famous citizens, Robert G. Ingersoll and John A. Logan, Colonels of regiments they had formed.

Getting Started
Begin your visit by stopping by the Crab Orchard Refuge Tourism Bureau located at 8588 Route 148 South. Brochures, maps, tour information and other general information will be available for you. Call before coming and we will send information to help you plan your trip. (618) 997-3690 or 1-800-GEESE-99.

Attractions

Goddard Chapel
The chapel in Marion's Rose Hill Cemetery, was built in 1918 by Leroy Goddard, is built of Bedford stone and features beautiful art glass.

Marion Cultural Center
(618) 997-4030
The majestic theater in downtown Marion was built in the 1920s as part of the renowned Fox Orpheum movie and vaudeville circuit. It was closed in 1971 and reopened in 1972 after extensive renovations. Today it features gospel shows, reruns of classic movies, a patron series and childrens' performing arts programs. Tours are available.

Veterans Affairs Medical Center
(618) 997-4152
Main Street just off Interstate 57
The landmark serving veterans for 50 years was built in 1914. The beautiful tree lined drive welcomes visitors to the center which features an Egyptian architectural motif. Call for tour information.

Williamson County Museum
(618) 997-5863
105 S. VanBuren
You will find 17 rooms full of exhibits featuring artifacts, antiques, records and a school.

Willis Allen House

514 S. Market

The oldest house in Williamson County was where General John A. Logan, a Civil War hero, studied law under Senator Willis Allen. The house is listed on the National Register of Historic Places.

Satellite Attractions

🍃 **Carterville**

John A. Logan College

The school was named after Civil War General John A. Logan. At the Museum and Art Gallery of the Conference Center you will find memorabilia from the general and his wife Mary. General Logan is remembered as a founder of May 30 as Memorial Day.

🍃 **Herrin**

Egyptian Drive-In

Located south of Herrin on Illinois Route 148, just off Illinois Route 13, the Drive-In is the only active outdoor theater in Illinois outside of Chicago. It boasts the world's largest screen towering 12 stories high. Take your family on a nostalgic visit for a family outing with first-rate movies and old-fashioned prices. When it opened in 1948, the first showing was that of Frank Capra's classic, "Lost Horizon," starring actor Ronald Coleman.

Harrison House

(618) 942-7112

Located about one-half mile west of Herrin just off the Herrin-Colp blacktop is the home of David Ruffin Harrison, one of Herrin's founders. The brick structure was built in 1868 and is furnished with period furniture which includes a grand piano made in 1874.

Herrin Civic Center

(618) 942-6115

Downtown Herrin

This modern facility is a multi-purpose building with a 350 seat auditorium and five conference rooms. A list of scheduled activities can be obtained by calling the above number.

🍃 **National Wildlife Refuge**

The Refuge offers free guided wildflower walks on the Rock Bluff trails that twists some three quarters of a mile through native woodland areas north of Devils Kitchen Lake and along the banks of Grassy Creek. There is an offering of eleven walks with a limit of 16 people per walk. The walks take approximately two hours and reservations are required. Walks include identification, description and historical uses of wildflowers of the area. This is truly a spectacular time to enjoy spring for the horticulturalist. Write or call for a schedule of events (618) 997-3344.

- Harbinger-of-Spring Walk — Harbinger-of-Spring flowers are some of the first blooms to be seen in the spring, but look for bloodroot, spring beauties and toothwort.
- Spring Beauty Walk — Look for the spring beauty along with rue anemone, wild ginger and goldenseal.
- Trout Lily Walk — Along with the trout lily, other flowers to view are the mayapple and jacob's ladder.
- Celandine-Poppy Walk — The transition of spring allows many of the previous months' flowers to still be in bloom. New arrivals are spiderwort and waterleaf.
- Blue-Belle Walk — The peak of springs brings the spectacular blue-bells as well as the jack-in-the-pulpit to finish out the April season. Look for the ox-eye daisy and wild geranium to usher in May.
- Trillium Walk — Enjoy spring at its peak when the forest floor is exploding with violets, dandelions and trilliums.

🌿 **Pittsburg**

Old Squat Inn
(618) 982-2916
Route 7 northeast of Marion in Pittsburg
The 1800s original log cabin now serves as a quaint bed and breakfast.

Rocky Bluffs Trail

Annual Events

Williamson County offers many enjoyable family events throughout the year. For continually updated events call (618) 997-3690. Brochures are available upon request.

April
- Southern Illinois Earth Science Gem Show — Carterville. Gem and mineral show, Indian artifacts, arts, artists fossil demonstrations, wire wrapping of gems, lapidary work.
  ✪ Free admission
- River to River Relay Race — A

foot race from the Mississippi to the Ohio through the Shawnee National Forest.

May

• Herrinfesta Italiana —Herrin. An annual festival featuring Italian heritage. Delicious Italian food, parade, entertainment, carnival, and pasta sauce cook-off.

June

• Williamson County Fair — Marion. The fair is Illinois' oldest continually running fair. Livestock judging, harness races, tractor and horse pulls, carnival, queen pageant, entertainment.
✪ Admission charge

July

• Family Fun Day — Caterville.

Pancake breakfast, fun run and walk, softball tournament, parade, family games, entertainment and fireworks.

September

• Annual Wonder Water Reunion — Creal Springs. Parade, queen crowning, gospel singing, quilt and art shows, entertainment.
✪ Free admission

• National Hunting and Fishing Days — John A. Logan College, Carterville. This is a celebration of the out-of-doors with displays, seminars, exhibitors, a wildlife art show, kids' activities, a taxidermy show, and world class turkey, duck and goose calling.
✪ Free admission

• Carterville Free Fair

Gone Fishing

- Women's Health Conference, John A. Logan College, Carterville.

October
- Marion Oktoberfest — Beauty pageant, children's parade, bluegrass jamboree and gospel music, arts and crafts.
- ✪ Free admission

November
- Autumn Fest — John A. Logan College, Carterville. Pre-holiday arts and crafts show, featuring more than 100 skilled craftsmen.
- ✪ Free admission

Hunting

The county is known for the hundreds of thousands of geese that migrate along the Mississippi Flyway route. You will find many public and private areas for hunting. The Refuge is a popular white tailed deer hunting area in Illinois.

Recreation Lakes and Parks

Four major lakes are located in Williamson County where fishing is abundant. Call the Refuge headquarters for information on laws, licenses, services or tournaments. (618) 997-3344

✹ Lakes

Crab Orchard Lake — Covers 7,000 acres filled with a variety of game fish. You will find camping facilities, picnic areas and two full-service marinas.

Little Grassy Lake — The 1,100 acre lake is popular for bass and crappie. Channel catfish are stocked annually. The lake is adjacent to Devil's Kitchen.

Devil's Kitchen Lake — The lake is an 810 acre lake located nine miles south of Carterville. It is one of the top trophy bass lakes in all of southern Illinois. Rainbow trout are stocked annually. It is an ideal family camping, hiking and horseback riding facility.

Lake of Egypt — The 2,300 reservoir offers both public and private recreational opportunities. Bass fishing tops the bill.

✹ Parks

Giant City State Park — The scenic state park covers 3,694 acres in the Shawnee National Forest. It is famous for an abundance of plants, wildflowers, flowering trees and its unique rock formations. It has become a popular recreational area for fishing, hiking and horseback riding. There is an extensive network of trails for hikers and trailriding.

Ferne Clyffe State Park — South of Marion on Illinois Route 37 is a beautiful park packed with unusual plant life and geological formations of the Shawnee Hills.

Shopping and Dining

Williamson County is a storehouse of interesting shops, offering a wide variety of antiques and collectibles. You will find a shopper's delight in the Illinois Centre located in Marion on Illinois Route 13, just west of Interstate 57. The marketplace opened in the fall of 1991 and features major retail stores. It is the newest and largest shopping mall in southern Illinois.

You will find many eating establishments in the area.

Conclusion

For further information contact: Williamson County Tourism Bureau, P.O. Box 1088 Marion, IL 62959 (618) 997-3690 1-800-GEESE-99 http:\\sivirtual.com\wctb

Tips

✔ Group tours may be planned by calling the Tourism Bureau 1-800-433-7399. Pre-planned itineraries, maps, and other information are also available.

✔ Golf courses are scattered throughout the county. Call or write for a listing.

❝ Come to Williamson County, Illinois, the HUB of Southern Illinois, located between the Ohio and the Mississippi Rivers. Williamson County, with 19 motels, over 1,000 beds, 90 plus restaurants available is the best place to stay to see all of Southern Illinois. You can do several daytrips from Williamson County and never see the same thing twice.

In Williamson County you can tour the Historical Museum, many antique shops, Illinois Center Mall, Crab Orchard National Wildlife Refuge or fish our lakes — Crab Orchard, Devils Kitchen, Little Grassy and Lake of Egypt.

When you are in Williamson County you are 50 miles in any direction from most of the attractions in Southern Illinois.

To the south you have the Shawnee National Forrest, the largest and most diverse natural treasure in Illinois and the most beautiful scenery in the Midwest. Cache River State Natural area is home to a cypress tree over 800 years old. Fern Cliff State Park has the largest shelter bluff in Southern Illinois. Fort Massac State Park features a replica of the fort built in 1794 and is the oldest state park in Illinois. Fort Defiance State Park is where the Ohio and Mississippi River meet.

To the east is Cave In Rock, a 55 foot wide cavern overlooking the Ohio River, Garden of the Gods with bluffs and unique rock formations dating back 300 million years. Ridgeway is the popcorn capital of the world. Old Shawnee Town was once the banking center of Illinois. The John Marshall Bank and home built in 1818 served as the first bank in Illinois.

To the west are Bald Knob Cross, the tallest Christian Monument in North America, Giant City State Park which tells a geologic tale 315 million years old and LaRue-Pine Hills, a diverse ecological area, Pomona Natural Bridge, the largest natural bridge and Alto Vineyards producing award-winning wines, are all worth a visit.

North is Rend Lake, the second largest man-made lake in the state. Southern Illinois Arts and Crafts Market Place has more than 25 categories presented by more than 700 Illinois artisans. Our newest attraction is the National Coal Museum, which presents the story of coal mining and coal consumption past, present, and future in various exhibits. Coal mining could not be a real experience for the public without hard hats, miners lights and a trip into a real underground coal mine. That is exactly what happens when you venture over 600 feet underground to see what goes on in a real coal mine. To be able to tour a museum of this caliber is an opportunity one would not want to miss.

A trip to Southern Illinois can give you all this and much more. ❞

Mattoon
A Good Place to Visit;
A Great Place to Live!

Location

Located in East Central Illinois on Interstate 57 and Routes 16 and 45. Exit 190B and 184.

History

In 1830 a charter was granted for organizing Coles County twelve years after Illinois was admitted into the Union. The county was named in honor of Governor Edward Coles. The community grew on the prairies of east central Illinois and was originally known as "Pegtown" because of the pegs or stakes that marked lots sold at public auction. In 1855 a crowd of 3,000 gathered to give the town the new name of Mattoon. The town was renamed for William Mattoon who helped construct the Terre Haute and Alton Railroad. The projected junction of this rail line with the Illinois Central in 1854 convinced local settlers that the land was an ideal site for a community. Swamp grass and prairie would give way to steel rails, homes and businesses.

Mattoon prospered and grew at a surprising rate. The first churches, schools and businesses were established, and by 1856 there were more than 100 buildings. In 1857 the officials of the growing community started to incorporate and in 1861 the final charter was adopted.

Between 1857 and 1858 the Essex House hotel was built, one of the most famous of the early hotels in the area. In 1858 a relatively unknown lawyer and politician, Abraham Lincoln, addressed a crowd from an east window of the hotel. One of history's famous debates between Abraham Lincoln and Stephen Douglas took place in Coles County later in 1858.

Mattoon prospered and by 1870 the population had reached 4,500. Coal mining became a prominent industry.

Throughout its development, a key to Mattoon's prosperity has been its location in the great midwestern farmbelt. The rich black farmland around Mattoon is abundantly productive and today corn is the number one grain produced with soybeans second.

⇥ Getting Started

Much of Mattoon's history lies in the Peterson House which serves as the Mattoon Welcome Center located at 500 Broadway. A visit or a call will start you on your way to an eventful stay in Mattoon. The way we look and act says a lot about who we are. So does our past. To know us, it is best to know where we have been.

Attractions

Church of the Immaculate Conception
2018 Richmond Avenue
The church was built in 1887 and is one of the two oldest churches still standing here. Over 40 churches of all denominations speak to the religious needs of the community.

George Curyea Home
5 Lafayette Avenue
The brick residence of George Curyea was built in 1892 in the elegant style derived from the French and known as Second Empire. Curyea was one of the original owners of the land upon which the town of Mattoon developed. Curyea was born in Pennsylvania in 1812 and came to Coles County in the late 1840s. In 1849 he bought hundreds of acres of land in Sections 13 and 18 of Mattoon and Lafayette Township,

Church of the Immaculate Conception

and raised cattle and wheat. In 1849 he married Melvina Tipton, a daughter of a pioneer Coles County family. They had eight children, of whom only three survived to maturity. In 1855 Curyea refused to let the founders of the town of Mattoon include his land in their plat and instead platted his part of Section 13 himself. The area south of Lafayette Avenue, between 9th and 16th Streets, is still referred to as "Curyea's Addition."

Lake Mattoon
Owned by the city of Mattoon, it is located in the counties of Coles, Shelby and Cumberland. The 765

acre lake is fed by the Little Wabash River and is a popular recreation spot for boating, fishing and camping. There is also a marina with launching ramps.

Mattoon Public Library
1600 Charleston Avenue

Located in front of the library is a flagpole commemorating the only remnant of Camp Grant where Union soldiers received training. The camp was originally named Camp Goode but later renamed after Colonel Ulysses S. Grant, after he administered the oath of allegiance to the Union soldiers. One member of the regiment said, "the boys like the silent Grant in his rusty civilian clothes going about military matters with quiet

efficiency and as he left camp they named their camp for him." The flagpole was rescued from destruction by Dr. S.D. Campbell, a civil war veteran from Mattoon, and placed in front of the U.S. Grant Hotel in 1928. Later it was relocated again and stands in front of the Mattoon Public Library.

—reprinted with permission from Mattoon . . . a Pictorial History

Oblinger-Record House
3205 Western Avenue

This Queen Anne Revival style home was built in 1887 and to date has only been occupied by three families. A solitary tree called the Lone Elm stood at the corner of Western Avenue and 32nd Street for about 140 years. When the tree was a seedling, there were no

Oblinger-Record House

avenues, no streets, nor any town, only a grassy ridge on the prairie. As the elm grew, it became a guidepost for Indian and settler alike. The tree was a memorable sight, standing alone in the midst of tall waving blue stem, and it was the subject of many stories. Pioneer farmers grazed cattle nearby and families crossing the prairie rested in its shade. When the railroads came, a town was born on the ridge and the graceful elm watched it grow. In 1934 the Daughters of the American Revolution placed a commemorative marker under it. When the old tree died in 1950, it had served not only as a landmark, but as a symbol of the strength and self-sufficiency of our forebearers.

Peterson House
500 Broadway Avenue
Built in 1880 by a notable resident of Coles county, Judge Abner M. Peterson, the house is a simple, symmetrical Italianate structure renovated in keeping with that architectural style. The project is being done by the Friends of Peterson House. Today the Peterson house houses the Mattoon Welcome Center.

Peterson House

Satellite Attractions

∿ Arthur

Amish Settlement
Twenty miles to the north, the communities of Arthur and Arcola are recognized as the heart of Illinois' Amish settlement. Approximately 300 Amish families live there and have created a thriving enterprise of cottage industries, marketing their superb craftsmanship worldwide.

∿ Lake Shelbyville
Located on Highway 16 west of Mattoon, the lake covers nearly 11,000 acres with 250 miles of unspoiled shoreline, 640 camp sites and 15 public boat ramps. The entire family can enjoy the baseball diamond, picnic facilities, and playground equipment.

∿ Sullivan

The Little Theatre on the Square
16 E. Harrison
(217) 728-7375
Try the Little Theatre on the Square in Sullivan, the area's only equity theater, offering the best of Broadway's musicals every summer.

Lincoln Log Cabin State Historic Site
Southeast of Mattoon is the living, historical farm surrounding the cabin that was once the retirement home of Abe Lincoln's parents. Thomas and Sarah Lincoln lives are depicted at the site through first person interpreters who recreate life in the 1840s. Watch them prepare daily meals, plant gardens and tend to chores and livestock of that period.

Annual Events
Mattoon boasts many special events held throughout the year. For continual updates on event listings call 1-800-500-6286.

April
• Herb Festival — a good reason to spend a weekend in Mattoon and learn about the art of herb gardening. Call (217) 235-5661 for more information or if interested in exhibiting.

June
• Pow Wow — Native American Indian enthusiasts recreate an authentic Native American Indian Pow Wow at Peterson Park. There are crafts for sale and authentic dances for prize money.

July
• Bagelfest — A family oriented festival in downtown Mattoon features free bagel breakfast, entertainment and booths of all descriptions. The first *Bagelfest* was held in 1986 when the Kraft plant in Mattoon began pro-

Murray Lender Points to the World's Record Bagel — 563 pounds.

ducing Lender's Bagels. The first breakfast held was for more than 12,000 people. It was such a success that it has become an annual event serving 60,000 bagels to 40,000 people and has evolved into a five-day festival. The "Biggest Bagel" ever baked weighed in at 563 pounds and was submitted to *Guinness World Book of Records.* Call 1-(217) 235-5661 for more information.

• Fourth of July Celebration — Held in Peterson Park all day, there's food, fun and entertainment. After dark there will be a huge fireworks display.

October

• Halloween Special — Fireworks, pet parade, kiddie costume parade and much more.

November

• Christmas Open House and Artist Walk —Hosted by Mattoon Antique and Craft Association. All the joys of Christmas will be featured. Antique and gift shops will be filled to the brim to help you choose the perfect Christmas gift.

• Christmas Marketplace — Christmas Treasures and Holiday Pleasures are at the DeMars Center and Peterson House in Peterson Park.

✪ Free admission

December

• Mattoon Lightworks — Held from mid-November to late December, a major contributor to the Starflake Trail, this is the largest themed outdoor lighting event in the United States. Bus tours and groups are welcome by appointment.

Visit • Call • Write
Chamber of Commerce
1701 Wabash
(217) 2335-5661

Shopping and Dining

You will find shopping at its best when you visit the Cross County Mall, Good Neighbor Shopping Center, Midtown Mattoon, and the East Route 16 Retail Complex. People come from all over Illinois and bordering states to enjoy the more than 20 antique, craft and gift shops.

Eating establishments include fine dining, sports pubs, fast foods, donut shops or the all-time favorite pizza parlors.

Conclusion

For further information contact:
Mattoon Welcome Center
500 Broadway Avenue
P.O. Box 431
Mattoon, IL 61938
(217)-258-6286
1-800-500-6286 or the
Mattoon Chamber of Commerce
1701 Wabash Avenue
(217) 235-5661 or FAX: 234-6544
website: www.mattoonchamber.org

Tips

✔ Amtrak availability at 1718 Broadway Avenue, (217) 235-3220.

✔ Coles County Airport Reservations 1-800-241-6527 A-1 Rent-A-Car 1-800-245-7515 432 Airport Road

✔ Checker Top Cab, 1904 Broadway (217) 234-7474.

66 Mattoon is rich in history. It is also a place of progress where the quality of life attracts many people every year. People who are looking for a place where they feel good about their neighborhood, their schools, the places they go to church and shop, the health care they receive, and the job opportunities available to them.

Mattoon is a prime example of a small progressive area supported in its many facets by warm and friendly people. It offers, all within minutes, excellent educational facilities, a church of your choice, recreational facilities, cultural activities including the arts, concerts, lectures, and theater, modern medical facilities, a library, restaurants, and other necessities that one looks for and needs to maintain a full and satisfying living experience.

The Mattoon area is centrally located between Chicago, St. Louis and Indianapolis, three of the country's largest metropolitan centers. All are reached within three hours via interstate highways. This excellent location places the community in the hub of our nation's population, industry and commerce and surrounds it with comprehensive transportation systems with links to the entire world.

New residential additions are continually being developed and expanded in and on the perimeter of the city. In the already established areas of the city, there is a restoration surge to renovate many of the older homes which are of many styles, designs and periods. These renovations have caused the existing areas to increase in value and offer an appeal to the residents and newcomers who prefer the charm of broad avenues (some of which are still brick-paved), big shade trees and a blend of the old and new in home styles.

There's always something to do in Mattoon. Whether it is visiting one of the annual festivals like **Bagelfest, Native American Pow Wow, Chocolate Harvest, Herb Festival,** or the dazzling **Mattoon Lightworks** holiday display in Peterson Park; or by shopping Mattoon's many fine retail stores, or craft and antique shops; or simply enjoying everyday life . . . Mattoon is a good place to visit. It is an even better place to live and call home! **99**

—Valerie Mullens, Director

Mattoon is located in East Central Illinois on Interstate 57 at Routes 16 and 45 and has many fine motels, restaurants, and shopping areas.

Map from Mattoon Chamber of Commerce

Mt. Vernon
Heartland of Hospitality

Location

Mt. Vernon is conveniently located in the heart of Southern Illinois at the juncture of Interstates 57 and 64.

History

The town was chosen in 1819 to become the seat for Jefferson County. The original settlers were predominately Southerners who were content to allow the agricultural community to grow slowly. The entry of the railroads changed all of that as Mt. Vernon joined many Illinois cities in growing with the Industrial Age.

➡ Getting Started

When you arrive, stop by the Mt. Vernon Convention and Visitors Bureau located at 200 Potomac Blvd., Mt. Vernon, IL. 1-800-252-5464 or (618) 242-3151

Attractions

Appellate Courthouse
(618) 242-3120
Main and 14th Streets
This building was constructed in 1857 as the southern division of the Illinois State Supreme Court. Abraham Lincoln successfully argued a famous tax case here in 1859. Clara Barton used the building as a hospital in 1888. Tours are available, but please call in advance.

Appellate Court House

Brehm Memorial Library
(618) 242-6322

101 South 7th Street
Visitors are welcome to research

local history and genealogy as well as with the more typical library fare. It houses the Illinois State Organization of the National Society of the Daughters of the American Revolution library. Other materials reflect the general migration patterns of people to Southern Illinois, who came primarily from Virginia, North and South Carolina, Tennessee and Kentucky.

Cedarhurst

(618) 244-6130
Richview Road
Enjoy the nationally renowned Cedarhurst Craft Fair held on this 80 acre estate. Visitors will find hiking paths, a bird sanctuary, the Cedarhurst Art Center and the Cedarhurst Braille Trail for the sight impaired. The outdoor Sculpture Park is a must see for our visitors. Featured on the cover of *A Guide to the Sculpture Parks and Gardens of America,* Cedarhurst could well be the model for a new kind of contemporary sculpture parks. Since much of the sculpture is on loan for a two-year period, the collection is always changing.

Mitchell Museum

(618) 242-1236
Richview Road
8,000 square feet of 19th and 20th century art is located on the

Mitchell Museum

grounds of Cedarhurst at the Mitchell Museum. Art exhibits, special event and musical programs are scheduled throughout the year.

Wheels Through Time

(618) 244-4118
Veterans Memorial Drive
This is a 13,000 square foot museum that houses a collection of vintage motorcycles and automobiles. Over 90 motorcycles and thousands of items of art work and memorabilia are on display Monday through Saturday 9am-5pm
✪ Wednesdays by appointment only.

Historical Village

(618) 246-0033

North 27th Street

See historic buildings and memorabilia from the pioneer days. The village consists of a former log calaboose used from 1820 to 1937, the log Mount Olive Church which dates back to 1873, the Hickory Hill one room school, and a blacksmith shop. The other two buildings on the grounds are a General Store full of antique tools, display counters, harness and many other items and a modern building housing an antique printing press and other associated materials. The Historical Village hosts the Pioneer Days in October.

Satellite Attractions

❧ Rend Lake

I-57, (618) 629-2320

19,000 acres of water surrounded by 21,000 acres of public lands give our visitors plenty of room for their favorite pastimes. Fishing, hunting, watersports, and camping are just a few of the attractions at this beautiful man-made lake.

❧ Southern Illinois Artisan Shop

(618) 629-2220

Located at Rend Lake on I-57, just west of Exit 77, the 15,000 square foot facility houses the Illinois Artisan Shops and galleries where visitors will find an exciting variety of southern Illinois' finest crafters. Expansive grounds with

Wheels through Time

an outdoor stage provide ample space for spring and summer programs of art and craft events, demonstrations and exhibits. Open seven days a week 9:00am to 6:00 pm.

Annual Events

February
• Midwestern Herb Show — For the novice, the beginner and the small scale herbalist, this three day event features many guest speakers and classes about herbs.

July
• Salute to Freedom — Usually scheduled around the 4th of July, this event celebrates our freedom and includes fireworks.

August
• Sweetcorn and Watermelon Festival — During this celebration of summer, the week is packed with activities ending with a parade and flea market on the last day.

September
• Cedarhurst Art and Craft Fair — This two day juried art and craft show of over 160 exhibitors includes many fine craftsmen of semi-precious stone jewelry, pottery, furniture, sculptures of brass and iron, and much, much more. There is special art for children with hands-on fun and creativity.

October
• Pioneer Days — On the grounds of the Historical Village, the early settlers' lifestyles are recreated.

Shopping and Dining

Times Square Mall, King City Square, Jent Factory Outlet, Antiques, and the areas largest craft supply store provides an assortment of specialty shops for your shopping delight.

Mount Vernon offers more than 60 restaurants with something for every taste and budget.

Conclusion

Group tour arrangements can be made by contacting:
Mt. Vernon Convention and Visitors Bureau
P.O. Box 2580
Mt. Vernon, IL 63864
1-800-252-5464 Toll Free
(618) 242-6849 Fax
Website:
www.southernillinois.com

Tips

✔ An excellent location to enjoy cultural offerings, recreation, golf, shopping, restaurants, accommodations and travel services usually found in large cities.
✔ We're on your way.

66 Location is our main attraction. We're on your way when you travel through Southern Illinois and we have something for everyone. Business people enjoy our central location since almost one-third of the nations top fifty metropolitan areas are within 500 miles of Mt. Vernon. Our big-city professionalism with hometown hospitality is always appreciated. Travelers and tourists find shopping, golf, historical attractions close, easily accessible, and fun. The new winery has a gift shop, as well as, award winning wines and the new antique mall has over eighty-five vendors to delight the most avid collectors. So, slow down, relax, and enjoy your time with us. 99

—Mt. Vernon Convention and Visitors Bureau

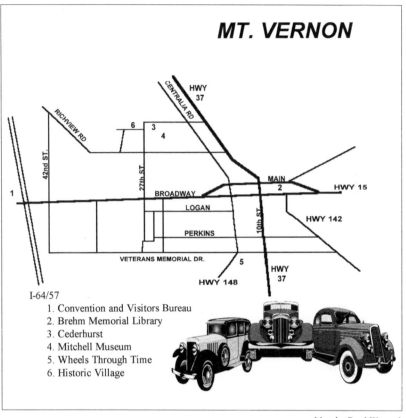

MT. VERNON

HWY 37

CENTRALIA RD

RICHVIEW RD

42nd ST.

27th ST

6 3
   4

1

BROADWAY

LOGAN

PERKINS

VETERANS MEMORIAL DR.

10th ST

MAIN
2

HWY 15

HWY 142

5

HWY 37

HWY 148

I-64/57

1. Convention and Visitors Bureau
2. Brehm Memorial Library
3. Cederhurst
4. Mitchell Museum
5. Wheels Through Time
6. Historic Village

Map by Paul Wentzel

Rantoul
Discover Rantoul!

Location

Located on I-57 just 15 minutes north of Champaign-Urbana.

History

The first white man to settle on the site that is now Rantoul was Archa Campbell. In 1848 he built a 14 foot square, one story, split log cabin and a stone-walled well near Mink Grove. The Indian name for Mink Grove was "Nipsquah, Neepswah or Neipswah" meaning "abounding in mink." This was one of the few groves not situated on a body of water.

Other pioneers, mostly farmers, joined him in migrating to northern Champaign County traveling by horseback and wagons. They journeyed over unmarked buffalo and Indian trails which provided the most direct route from grove to grove and offered safest passage when fording rivers. The terrain was hard to travel due to tall prairie grass and few navigable rivers. This slowed the migration of the white man to this part of central Illinois until the coming of the railroad.

Entrance to Rantoul

Robert Rantoul, for whom the town was named was an early member of the board of directors for the Illinois Central Railroad. Mr. Rantoul obtained the first land grant for a railroad in the United States and a preliminary survey started in 1851.

Hundreds of laborers laid the tracks by picks, shovels and sledge hammers. The railroad was completed from Chicago to Urbana on July 24, 1854. After the completion of the line, Mr. William F. Burrell, president of the railroad, suggested the station at Gaynor's Crossing be named in honor of Robert Rantoul.

Getting Started

Stop by the Rantoul Area Chamber of Commerce office located at 117 N. Garrard for brochures and more information to help you in Rantoul, or call (217) 893-3323.

Attractions

Octave Chanute Aerospace Museum
(217) 893-1613 • fax (217) 893-3970
http://www.cu-online.com/~leonhard/chanute/

The Chanute Air Force Base closed in 1993 after being an economic force in the community for 76 years. It was the major employer in Champaign County. After the devastating announcement that the base would close, the Economic Development Office knew the best thing to do was to redevelop the base. It is now known as the Rantoul Aviation and Development Center. The airport is open to the public and is a general aviation facility featuring a full service operation providing storage, instruction, fuel, maintenance, charter, and passenger services. The runways are 5,000 feet and are capable of supporting all general planes and most cargo aircraft.

The Octave Chanute Aerospace Museum is located on 2,000 acres formerly known as Chanute Air Force base where over 2,000,000 service men and women trained, lived and died for close to eighty years of aviation history, you will find a large collection of the fastest and most famous U.S. planes used in our country's defense. Of the six remaining B-58 Hustlers in the world, one is located in the museum, along with World War I's Jenny replica and World War II's famous P-51 Mustang.

You will have the opportunity to climb into the cockpit of a B-52 or check the payload on a B-25. You will be reminded of Jimmy Doolittle's secret squadron on one of their low-level bombing runs or catch a glimpse of a recon-

Octave Chanute Aerospace Museum

naissance plane on high-altitude surveillance.

You will have the opportunity to explore a one-of-a-kind training silo for the deadly accurate Minute Man intercontinental ballistic missile. You will feel the Cold War tension of not so many years ago, when our country stood eyeball to eyeball with the Soviet Union. Remember living on the brink of destruction as huge C-133 Douglas Cargomasters transported ICBMs and their nuclear payloads to launching sites around the midwest. Catch a glimpse of aviation history spanning World Wars I and II, Korea, Vietnam and Desert Storm. The museum houses uniforms, squadron patches, flags, authentic barracks, rare artifacts and memorabilia of its famous officers and aviators who were aviation pioneers.

The museum is open year round. Groups and bus tours are welcome! Guided tours can be scheduled in advance. Open weekdays 10am to 5pm, Saturday 10am to 6pm and Sunday noon to 5pm. Closed Tuesday.

Satellite Attractions

🌿 Gifford

Central Region Championship Rodeo Finals and Cowboy Trade Show
5 miles east of Rantoul on US Route 136. Held in November.

Gordyville USA Flea Market & Auction
Write for a yearly update — The auction arena is located 5 1/2 miles east of Rantoul on Route 136 or 7 1/2 miles east of Interstate 57 on Route 136. You will find antiques, collectibles, vintage items, art, crafts, etc.

Flea Market Hours
Friday 4pm-9pm, Saturday 9am-6pm, Sunday 9am-4pm

Auction Hours
Saturday 11am • Sunday 11am

Annual Events

Call or write for dates and continual updates of annual events.

June
- Rantoul Air Festival — a two-day air festival with acrobatic air show, ground static displays, food and entertainment vendors.

June-October
- RACC Farmers Market — In the heart of the downtown area you will find the freshest fruits and vegetables, the tastiest baked goods and the prettiest plants and flowers available.

July
- Independence Day in Rantoul —The week of July 4th ushers in a four-day carnival and vendor celebration culminating on the 4th with all-day activities such as live entertainment, a parade, baseball, volleyball, and fireworks.

August
- Rantoul Monster Truck Rally — A two-day, three-show event with Monster Truck competition, Tuff Truck competition and ugly truck competition as well as souvenir and food vendors.
- Rantoul Fall Fest — A Saturday event consisting of flea market, a quilt show, a car show and live entertainment.

November
- Downtown Christmas Parade is held the day after Thanksgiving with a Christmas theme, the parade kicks off the Christmas season with the first appearance of Santa.

Shopping and Dining

Great shopping in Rantoul offers upscale children's and women's wear and bridal boutiques. For the antique lover stop by the largest auction house in the area.

Rantoul is home to a variety of lodging and eating establishments offering light snacks, for people on the go, to sit-down all-you-can-eat buffets. There is something for everyone.

Conclusion

For further information contact:
Rantoul Area Chamber
of Commerce
117 N. Garrard
Rantoul, IL 61866
(217) 893-3323
Fax (217) 893-3325

For more information see the homepage on the internet at: www.rantoulchamber.com

Tips

✔ Visitors are welcome with almost 200 hotel rooms. Hotels that can also accommodate large gatherings.

✔ For the golfing enthusiasts two 18-hole public golf courses are available.

✔ Campers will find a year-round camping facility with water, sewage and electric hookups on level, shady campsites located just minutes from the downtown area.

✔ The fitness enthusiast will find everything needed at the state-of-the-art Forum Fitness Center.

Discover Rantoul!

❝ That slogan might seem a little strange at first glance. Most people would say, "I know where Rantoul is—right there on Interstate 57 a few miles north of Champaign/Urbana." Other folks might say, "I know about Rantoul—that's where Chanute Air Force Base was." While both of these statements are true, Rantoul is much more than that.

If you really "Discover Rantoul," you will see that we are a community of approximately 15,000 with a thriving industrial complex, unique shopping opportunities, excellent schools, high quality housing, recreational opportunities that out-shine all other communities of similar size, an aerospace museum that is the largest of its kind in the state and a quality of life that can't be beat.

We are proud of our community and are constantly striving to make it even better. If you are stopping for an hour, a day or a lifetime, take time to "Discover Rantoul." ❞

Rantoul Area Chamber of Commerce

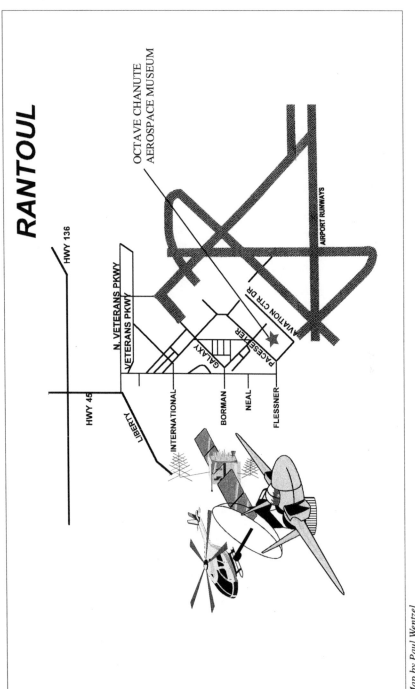

RANTOUL

HWY 136

HWY 45

LIBERTY

INTERNATIONAL

BORMAN

NEAL

FLESSNER

N. VETERANS PKWY

VETERANS PKWY

GALAXY

PACESETTER

AVIATION CTR DR

OCTAVE CHANUTE
AEROSPACE MUSEUM

AIRPORT RUNWAYS

Map by Paul Wentzel

Daytrip Illinois
Interstate 64

Belleville
Beautiful City

Location

Belleville is located 20 minutes from downtown St. Louis, just south of I-64. From I-70, take exit 20 for I-55 South; 5 miles to Exit 15 for Rt. 159 South at Maryville; 15 miles south to downtown Belleville.

History

Chosen in 1814 as the site to succeed Cahokia as the county seat for St. Clair County, Belleville quickly became an early milling and political center for southern Illinois. Because Illinois was settled in the south, Belleville was well established before many northern towns were barely platted. By 1830 political unrest in Germany forced many educated and mechanically trained Germans to emmigrate. Belleville and the surrounding area became the center of the largest German migration to the state of Illinois. Their inventiveness propelled Belleville to the forefront of Illinois manufacturing by 1870. They began the Belleville Philharmonic Orchestra, the second oldest in the nation, and the Belleville public library, the oldest subscription library in Illinois continue to this day to reflect Belleville's cultural heritage. In the library's archives it has original German book collections that are noted for its extensive genealogical research materials.

➡ Getting Started

Begin your visit by stopping by the Belleville Illinois Tourism office located at 216 East "A" Street. We will help you plan your visit to Belleville or help you set up group tours. There is plenty to do in our "Beautiful City."

Attractions

Cathedral of St. Peter
(618) 234-1166

The 1852 Gothic cathedral in downtown Belleville was modeled after the cathedral of Exeter in England. Short organ concerts are played for visitors.
✪ By arrangement only

Eckerts Country Store and Farms
(618) 233-0513
3101 Greenmount Road
Located on Route 15 East and Greenmount Road just 10 minutes

from downtown Belleville, this fifth generation fruit and vegetable farm is in a unique country setting. It is a great place to bring a family to enjoy "picking-your-own-fruit," petting animals or taking a wagon tour. Special events and festivals are planned throughout the year. Just write or call for a listing.

Emma Kunz House Museum
(618) 234-0600
Located in Belleville's Historic District is an 1830 German "street house" it is furnished with period furniture. Meeting rooms are available and a candlelight house tour is held in December. During December a special event is held depicting the "Secret Lives of Teddy Bears." Write for date, time, and admission fee.

Historic District Tours
1-800-677-WALK (9255)
In downtown Belleville special tours are available of the Historic District. You will learn about the history of the area and architectural descriptions will be explained. The tour includes two museum homes, the cathedral of St. Peter, other historic churches and the architecturally significant German street houses. The tour can be customized to fit your needs. There is a charge. Groups are welcome by appointment.

Carriage Ride

**National Shrine of
Our Lady of the Snows**
(618) 397-6700
442 S. DeMazenod Drive, Rt. 15
9500 West IL Highway 15 at
Route 157 South—ten minutes
from downtown St. Louis and two
miles from Belleville is the
nation's largest outdoor shrine
located on 200 acres of rolling
hills. Tram tours are available with
a guide to show you through the
entire complex and the new shrine
church. This is a beautiful place
of tranquility for people of all ages
and denominations. A drive
through the "Way of Lights" is a
holiday event held each year
✪ Write or call for date.

Scott Air Force Base
(618) 256-4241/4206
375th Airlift Wing
The base is located on Illinois
Routes 158 & 161 off I-64 just 15
minutes from downtown Belleville.
You have your choice of different
areas to tour with a step-on-guide to
provide understanding of the base.
The different areas include Military
Working Dogs, C4 Agency,
Parachute/Survival Equipment
Shop and Windshield Tour. Each
tour lasts about one half hour.
✪ Advanced reservation required

Lincoln Theatre
(618) 233-0123
103 East Main Street
The 1920 Lincoln Theatre was
home to silent movies and vaudeville acts. Once again you can see
silent movies and enjoy the
renovated mighty pipe organ.
✪ Write for date, time and admission fee.

**The Gingerbread House/Aunt
Elsie's Treasures**
(618) 624-8455, *Swansea*
4932 Benchmark Centre Drive
If you are interested in craft
demonstrations, this is the place to
go. You can make and take your
craft home. There is a large
collection of quality handicrafts,
gifts and holiday decorations. A
wide variety of events take place.
✪ Call for an updated listing.

Victorian Home Museum
(618) 234-0600
This home, located in the downtown Belleville Historic District,
is a beautiful example of a
Victorian adaptation of the earlier
Greek revival style. There is a
special Candlelight House Tour in
December.
✪ Write for date, time, and admission fee.

Annual Events

**Belleville Philharmonic Society
and the Belleville Masterworks
Chorale**
(618) 235-5600
Belleville Philharmonic Society
100 N. Jackson Street

A variety of concerts is held throughout the year including Winter Pops, World Premiere , The Nutcracker, and Christmas concerts.
✪ Write or call for dates, times and admission fees.

Flea Market
(618) 233-0052/235-0666
Held in the Exposition Hall, Belle-Clair Fairgrounds, the 3rd Saturday and Sunday of each month. The market has better than 500 booths.
✪ Free admission

May
• Eckert's Farm Strawberry and Craft Festival — Come pick strawberries and enjoy a variety of desserts. Children will enjoy the petting farm, pony rides, face painting and the kiddie corral. (618) 233-0513

June
• Fountainfest — The annual spring street festival downtown, offers entertainment, food booths and crafts. (618) 233-2015
• Scott Air Force Base Air Show This two day show features flight demonstrations and aircraft displays. (618) 256-4241.
✪ Free admission

July
• Annual Doll, Toy and Miniature Fair — Teddy bears, dolls, toys and miniatures, both antique and modern, are for sale.

(618) 233-0940/233-0052
✪ Free for children
   Admission for adults

August
• Optimist Rodeo — Come enjoy a real live rodeo with all the happenings. Belle-Claire Fairgrounds. (618) 233-0052
• St. Claire County Fair — Six days of carnival fun, animal judging, music, crafts and special performances at the Belle-Clair Fairgrounds (618) 233-0052

September
• Annual Arts and Crafts Fair — Along the first four blocks of E. Main Street in downtown Belleville, enjoy the annual fall arts and crafts fair. Private exhibitors and plenty of food booths.
(618) 233-2015
FAX (618) 235-8769

October
• Annual Chili Cook-Off — Chili, other food booths and entertainment are along the first four blocks of downtown Belleville. (618) 233-2015
✪ Free admission

November/December
• Secret Lives of Teddy Bears — Visit over 300 teddy bears and their cousins, the dolls. Emma Kunz House Museum (618) 234-0600.
✪ Admission Fee
• Annual Gingerbread Walk — "Don't Miss It" Try your hand

Annual Way of Lights

at creating prize-winning gingerbread creations. These will be displayed in merchants' windows in the first four blocks of downtown Belleville. For more information call:
(618) 233-6769/800-677-9255
✪ Free admission

• Annual Way of Lights — The National Shrine of Our Lady of Snows is the place to come to remember the birth of Christ. A display of nearly one million white lights creating a path leading to the traditional crib. Children's village. Free
(618) 397-6700/800-533-6279

• Annual Santa Claus Parade — Santa lands in Belleville to usher in the Christmas season.
(618) 235-7141
✪ Free admission

Shopping and Dining

For the antique lover shopping opportunities are unlimited. You will find many eating establishments in Belleville to suit the palate of everyone from adults to children. Restaurants in the area have motorcoach parking facilities. Write or call for the Group Tour Planner, which lists restaurants and lodging facilities and their telephone numbers.

Tips

✔ Belleville has four distinct seasons. Summers are generally warm; spring and fall are moderate; winters are brisk. Plan your wardrobe accordingly.

✔ Belleville is an excellent overnight center for lodging, meals and other activities.

✔ Belleville has many churches of different denominations and of historic importance. Allow 30-45 minutes to tour each church.

✔ When on the Gingerbread Walk allow two hours for walking and shopping in the downtown area.

Conclusion

For further information contact:
Belleville Illinois Tourism
216 East "A" Street
Belleville, Illinois 62220
1-800-677-WALK (9255)
or
Southwestern Illlinois
Tourism Bureau
10950 Lincoln Trail
Fairview Heights, IL 62208
1-800-442-1488
www.illinoissouthwest.org

---

66 The City of Belleville, Illinois invites you to visit and explore our German historic city at any time of the year.

Just 20 minutes from downtown St. Louis, Belleville's German heritage sets the stage for your exploration of our city and the surrounding area. From our National Shrine of Our Lady of the Snows to our 175-year-old Historic District and area attractions such as Cahokia Mounds World Heritage Site, quaint German Maeystown, Swiss Highland, and Riverboat Casino gambling, we can keep your groups busy for days!

Come to Belleville during the holiday season to experience the Annual Gingerbread Walk, the Secret Lives of Teddy Bears, and the Annual Way of Lights and much more. For an overview of the many different events, attractions, dining and lodging facilities the Belleville area has to offer, contact our office for a continual update of listings and dates.

So what are you waiting for? Give us a call today and we'll help to plan your trip! 99

—*Cathleen Lindauer*
Belleville Tourism

BELLEVILLE AREA

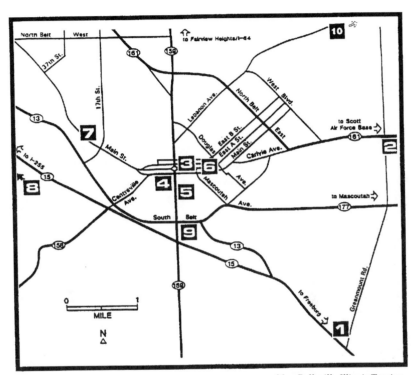

Map Belleville Illinois Tourism

1 Eckert's Country Store

2 Belleville Area College

3 Gingerbread Walk

4 St. Peter's Cathedral

5 Town House Motel

6 Historic District

7 Hyatt Lodge

8 National Shrine of Our Lady of the Snows

9 Belle-Clair Fairgrounds

10 The Gingerbread House

Southwestern Illinois
The Other Half of St. Louis

Location

Roads leading to Southwestern Illinois are west of Interstate 70, 55, 64, and 255. This is the largest certified bureau in the state covering most of eight counties.

History

Southwestern Illinois, rich in cultural and textbook history, is a tourist's dream. The area holds the stories from the largest population of American Indians in one area to the story of one of a few all-German Volunteer Infantry Units to fight in the Civil War and the seat of government for "New" France and all stories inbetween.

Cahokia Courthouse

➡ Getting Started

Begin your visit by stopping by the Visitors Center where you can obtain brochures, tour information, maps, annual events and much more. We welcome you to 10950 Lincoln Trail Fairview Heights, IL 62208

Attractions

CLINTON COUNTY

❧ Carlyle Lake

The largest man-made lake in Illinois was created to control flooding from the Kaskaskia River and to create a local water supply. Today the 26,000 acre lake serves equally as a regional recreational attraction with public boat ramps and marinas. The Visitor Center at the lake invites you to come and browse through its educational exhibits and to receive further information as to the many opportunities available there. The center is open 10am-6pm daily from Memorial Day weekend through Labor Day weekend.
Visitor Center
(618) 594-LAKE

❧ City of Carlyle

Come explore hidden treasures in Carlyle as you journey back in time.

Clinton County Historical Museum

This visit is a must for the history buff.

Sailing Carlyle Lake

Supreme Court
Justice Breese Home

This is the residence of former Supreme Court Justice Breese. On display in this historic home is a charming collection of antique wedding gowns, furniture, handmade quilts and children's toys.

General Dean Suspension Bridge

Listed on the National Register of Historic Places is the 130 year-old General Dean Suspension Bridge. The bridge is located right outside of the city.

✺ Centralia

Enjoy a rare opportunity in Centralia by listening to an hour's concert on the 165-ft, 65 bell Centralia Carillon. This is one of the few such instruments remaining in the country. The chimes sound on the hour and quarter hour as well.

Fairview Park

Located in the park is a 225-ton locomotive, one of the last locomotives produced by the Illinois Central Railroad. The railroad established its rail yard in the city during the 1850s.

FAYETTE COUNTY

✺ Vandalia

Vandalia is part of Southwestern Illinois Tourism and is home to some prominent landmarks. See page 182 for more information about this unique community and learn why Fayette County entices so many visitors.

MADISON COUNTY

Come to Madison County and discover its many riches. The county was named for President James Madison.

✺ Edwardsville

The seat of Madison county was chartered in 1816 by Governor Ninian Edwards. It is the state's third oldest city and boasts of being the birthplace of seven of its governors.

Madison County Historical
Museum in Weir House

Built in 1836 the museum houses many exciting remnants of that period. You will find furniture, maps, Indian artifacts, historical documents and children's toys.

✺ LeClaire Village

The village was annexed to Edwardsville in the 1930s and is on the National Register of Historic Places. Many original structures remain of the 19th century homes which Edwardsville is known for. Walking tours are recommended to truly enjoy the ambience of the village homes.

🍂 Highland

One of the oldest and largest Swiss communities in the United States, it was renowned for milk and beer.

Latzer Home

Louis Latzer founded the Pet Milk Company in Highland. He developed what he called Helvetia Milk from his cow, Pet.

✪ Tours arranged by appointment

Wicks Organ

The nation's second largest pipe organ factory is located in Highland.

Today the 100,000 copies of the Midwest Edition of the *Wall Street Journal* are still printed in Highland.

Dr. Albert Kaeser Memorial Park

Today a beer bottle museum is in a building which in the past served as a stage coach stop.

🍂 Maryville

Maryville was founded in 1902 when 300 residents came to take part in the coal mining boom in the area. After the coal was depleted, the town became a professional baseball players' training ground.

🍂 Tri-City Speedway

Join the crowds and thrill to the thunder of circle track auto racing at the speedway. Premier events take place on the one half mile dirt oval.

St. Clair Square

✦ Fairmount Park Race Track

Experience the excitement of watching thoroughbred and harness racing year-round.
○ Group packages (618) 345-4300.

ST. CLAIR COUNTY

✦ Belleville

The city of Belleville has been a thriving community for over a century. See page 139 where you will read more about the largest historic district in the state.

✦ Fairview Heights

The city of Fairview is less than 30 years old but is the fastest growing retail community in Southwestern Illinois. People flock there each year for the "Midwest Salute to the Masters Festival of Fine Arts." This is one of the leading art fairs in the country with over 100 artists, selected by jury from thousands of entrants.

Kinsella Log Cabin

The cabin, located in Pleasant Ridge Park, was built by early settlers and is used by the city to host many events and activities.

St. Clair Antique Mall

Visiting 110 booths across from St. Clair Square is a must for the antique collector. St. Claire Square— This is the metro area's largest shopping mall, featuring 140 exciting stores and "The Square Meal" food court.

✦ O'Fallon

Named for Colonel John J. O'Fallon who served as an assistant Indian agent to his uncle, William Clark of the Louis and Clark Expedition fame. He later became president of the Ohio and Mississippi Railroad, and the first railroad station outside St. Louis was named for him. The city is gaining a reputation as one of the fastest growing housing markets.

✦ Scott Air Force Base/Mid America Airport

This is the headquarters for the U.S. Transportation Command, the Military Airlift Command, and the Air Force Communications Command. Each summer brings tours, aircraft exhibits and an air show. Tours of the base are available by appointment.

✦ Lebanon

Emerald Mound

This is a satellite of the Cahokia Mounds World Heritage Site. The mound is almost as large as the famed Monks Mound of that ancient city.

Mermaid House

This is the home that Charles Dickens stayed in when he was inspired to write "*A Jaunt to*

Looking Glass Prairie and Back." Today there is a community theater named "The Looking Glass Playhouse" where productions include both plays and musicals.

❧ East St. Louis

Casino Queen on the Riverfront

Eads Bridge
The bridge, built between 1867 and 1874, has carried travelers across the Mississippi River into East St. Louis. It is regarded as an engineering marvel. Today it is used as the MetroLink light rail system connecting Illinois and St. Louis.

Gateway Geyser
This is the tallest fountain in the world. It shoots 650 feet in the air between 12 noon and 1pm, weather permitting.

Katherine Dunham Museum
The museum is named for its founder, Katherine Dunham, a world-famous dancer, choreographer and exponent of Caribbean cultural arts.

❧ Gateway International Raceway
Thrill to the excitement of automobile road racing, drag racing and motorcycle racing. This is one of the region's largest attractions.

Peterstown House

MONROE COUNTY

❧ *Historic Maeystown*

You will find an entire village designated as a historical district with St. John's United Church of Christ as the focal point of Maeystown. Buildings dating back to the 1800s still exist and many annual events are held there.

❧ Waterloo

Peterstown House

Visit Peterstown House, the only stagecoach stop still intact along the historic 60-mile Kaskaskia-Cahokia Trail. Originally built by Emery Peter Rogers in the 1830s, it has now become a charming, fully-restored home that houses a country store and museum. In 1975 two log cabins originally lived in by early pioneer families, were moved to the site. The house and cabins are on the National Register of Historic Places and welcome visitors.

Belle Fountaine

This 18th century settlement is located in southern Waterloo. You will find a fountain and cemetery from the Revolutionary War era. There is a local Historical Society.

New Design

Site of the first English speaking school and the first Protestant church in Illinois. While there take a walk along the original Kaskaskia Trail.

❧ Columbia

Gundlach-Grosse House

Built in 1867 for the Gundlach brothers who were owners of the local brewery, the house is on the National Register of Historic Places. The home is not open to the public.

❧ Illinois Caverns

Visitors have access to 14 miles of underground walkways. The caverns are known as the "Mammoth Cave of Illinois."

❧ Churches in Monroe County

The county boasts a number of architecturally significant churches. The most interesting ones can be found in Wartburg, Tipton, Renault and Maeystown.

RANDOLPH COUNTY

❧ Kaskaskia Island and Fort Kaskaskia

This is the site of Illinois' first capitol. The early citizens built a wooden stockade to protect themselves from Indian raids. Later, during the French and Indian War, they built Fort Kaskaskia to protect against British attack. The townspeople later destroyed the fort to prevent the British from using it. Today the only thing that remains is the earthwork. Visitors are welcome to come and view the

St. John Evangelical Church of the United Church of Christ — Maeystown

breathtaking panoramic beauty overlooking the Kaskaskia Island and the Mississippi River.

✤ Pierre Menard Home

The home exemplifies upper-class French-American life during the late 1700s and the early 1800s. This is a beautiful example of southern French Colonial architecture. An interesting feature of the home is the exposed stone basement known as "raised cottage." The structure is a one-and-a-half story clapboard frame with a spacious porch wrapping the front and sides, lending easy access to rooms on the main floor.

Many of the original pieces of furniture are still in the home. It has been designated as a National Historic Landmark and is listed on the National Register of Historic Places.

✤ Sparta

Misselhorn Art Gallery

Housed in the old train depot is a gallery for an artist known as the Norman Rockwell of the Midwest. Misselhorn contributed a great deal to tourism efforts in the state of Illinois and received the Illinois Governor's Award. You will find more than 4,000 of his sketches of steam locomotives, historical buildings, paddlewheelers, and the historical town of Ste. Genevieve are exhibited in the gallery.

Hunter Field

The field was used as a stop-over for Charles Lindbergh, the famous aviator.

✤ Chester

Popeye the Sailor Statue

The six-foot bronze Popeye statue and museum are popular stops for visitors. Each year an annual picnic is held honoring the creator of Popeye, native Elzie C. Segar. The event is held the weekend after Labor Day.

Sheriff's Office

The office houses the Railroad

Creole House

Museum where Chester Sheriff Ben Picou's extensive private collection of memorabilia is on display.

Evergreen Cemetery
The first governor of Illinois, Shadrach Bond, is buried here.

Mary's River Covered Bridge
The bridge was built in 1854 and now serves as a popular picnic area.

Charter Oak School
This is one of the only three remaining octagonal school houses remaining in the U.S.

Rockwood
Home of the Tuthill Chair Factory, which during the Civil War was used as an entrance to the historic Underground Railroad.

❧ Prairie Du Rocher
Founded in 1722 Prairie Du Rocher is the oldest town in Illinois. It was also known as "Prairie by the Rock." The early French farming community produced large amounts of grain. The grain was then shipped to New Orleans and on to the Caribbean islands which were controlled by the French. The community celebrates New Year's eve by touring and singing LaGuianne, an old French custom.

Creole House
The 1755 house, listed on the National Register of Historic Places, ushers in autumn with an annual Apple Fete event.

❧ Fort De Chartres
Located near Prairie du Rocher is

a fort, built of wood, and later destroyed by a flood and rebuilt of limestone in 1753. The fort was surrendered to the British after the French and Indian War and was abandoned in 1772. In June and November a bi-annual Rendez-vous complete with period music, dance and food is held. Life is recreated with people in authentic costumes portraying fur trappers, Indians, craftsmen, soldiers and musicians. This is the largest flintlock rifle shooting contest in the Midwest. Call the Visitor Center for more information. (618) 284-3463

◈ Ruma

Convent of The Adorers
The village was home to five nuns martyred in Liberia, Africa, in 1992. The nuns' bodies were brought back and buried in the cemetery at the Convent. It is open to visitors and group tours are available by request.

BOND COUNTY

◈ Greenville
Greenville is the home of sculptor and artist Richard Bock. He gained fame as a collaborator of 20th century architect Frank Lloyd Wright, also a native of Illinois. Bock created furniture and stained glass panels for the world famous homes designed by Wright. His work was regarded by Wright as integral to his architectural designs

Richard Bock Museum
The Bock museum houses a large collection of intricate stained glass windows, lamps and detailed sketches and designs of both Bock and Wright. The classic style building was built in 1855 and is located on the campus of Greenville College, formerly known as Almira College. The building is listed on the National Register of Historic Places.

Hogue Hall
The second structure built on Almira College campus in 1857 was Hogue Hall. Today it is used for offices and classrooms.

Bond County Historical Museum
Located on the lower level of the public library is this museum for those interested in history. The museum holds a wide variety of pioneer household items, antique farming equipment and other artifacts. You will find a variety of Civil War and other military exhibits.

WASHINGTON COUNTY

◈ Okawville
The focal point of Washington County is located just 40 miles east of St. Louis' Gateway Arch.

Original Mineral Springs Hotel and Bath House

Started in 1867 the hotel continues its long tradition of baths, fine food and lodging. You will enjoy gracious hospitality.

Heritage House Museum

The Frank Schlosser home was built in 1800s. All the contents and furnishings remain as left by the family, down to a box of cigars and Mr. Schlosser's 1941 calendar. The family business was the local harness shop run by the men of the family while the women ran a laundry service for the town and hotel. The old-fashioned gasoline and hand-cranked laundry machines may be examined by visitors.

Front Street Cafe

A real treat to go back in time when you visit the cafe with its 19th century stools and photos of historic buildings.

✆ Nashville

You will find many historic homes, comfortable accommodations, the courthouse on the square and a unique roadside chapel. You will receive a warm welcome in this community.

Annual Events

June

• Fort De Chartres Annual Summer Rendezvous — Randolph County, Prairie du Rocher, held in the heart of the French Colonial Historic District.

Witness military and frontier camp life in the mid to late 1700s during the French and Indian War and the American Revolutionary War. Plenty of food and drink (618) 284-7230

• Schweizerfest — Madison County, Highland. Call for times. A two-day "Swiss Festival" features ethnic food, Swiss and German music, carnival rides, games of skill and chance and a parade each evening. (618) 654-3721
❂ Free admission

• Prairie State Games — St. Clair County—Fairview Heights is the host city. This is the largest amateur sports festival in the state. More than 20 different Olympic sports competitions are held. There is a kick-off dinner, torch relay throughout the local community and a gala opening ceremony. (618) 632-1002
❂ Free admission

August

• Pan American Baseball Championships for Juniors — St. Clair County, Fairview Heights. Top youth baseball teams tournament on this side of the world. Teams for 13-14 year olds from Cuba, United States, Mexico, Brazil, Venezuela, Nicaragua and other Pan American countries. (618) 236-1768
❂ Free admission

• Spassfest — Clinton County,

Germantown. This is a celebration of fun and music whose very name means "fun festival." Two days of continuous music, entertainment, games and plenty of food and drink are all in keeping with the German heritage (618) 523-4202.

✪ Free admission

• Midwest Salute to the Masters Art Festival — St. Clair County, Fairview Heights. This festival of fine arts consists of an exclusive show, the sale and competition by 100 master artists. All are winners of primary awards in national juried shows within the past three years. Huge tent galleries, live entertainment, an international food court and special activities. Fun for children includes workshops and a "for children only" gallery. (618) 397-9111.

✪ Free admission

• St. Paul Kirchenfest — Madison County, Highland. The parish major fund raiser features kids games, an auction, continuous live entertainment, food and drinks, 3 on 3 basketball, 2K & 5K walk/run and much more. (618) 654-2339

✪ Free admission

September

• Popeye Picnic — Chester in Randolph County. A community picnic honors city's best known citizen, "Popeye the Sailor Man,"

with lots of good old-fashioned family fun including a gigantic parade late Saturday morning and an extravagant fireworks display on Saturday night. Popeye Fan Club members from across the U.S. make this an annual event not to miss. Plenty of food and drink, music competitive races, volksmarch, car show, craft show and flea market, carnival rides. (618) 826-2667 or (618) 826-4567.

✪ Contestant entry fee

Shopping and Dining

You will find plenty of shopping and dining opportunities in Southwestern Illinois. Write or call for a list.

Conclusion

For further information contact:
Southwestern Illinois Tourism and Convention Bureau
10950 Lincoln Trail
Fairview Heights, IL 62208
(618) 397-1488 • 1-800-442-1488
FAX (618) 397-1945
www.illinoissouthwest.org

Tips

✔ You will find many recreational opportunities at the state and local parks from boating, fishing, canoeing, bicycling, hiking, swimming, camping, baseball and softball. Write or call for a brochure. 1-800-442-1488 or www.illinoissouthwest.org

66 One of the area's most popular overnight tours is the French Colonial District. The tour starts in Cahokia, then moves down to Prairie du Rocher, then on to Kaskaskia Island, the Chester Archives, Fort Kaskaskia and Pierre Menard Home at Ellis Grove. But the French influence does not stop there. Missouri also has a part of the French Colonial District. After seeing Prairie du Rocher, a short ferry ride takes you to Ste. Genevieve, and with a drive to St. Louis the tour is complete.

Fort de Chartres is the most famous stop on this tour, but it is also the most misunderstood. The primary use for the fort was not for defense, but to be the seat of government for "New France." The area in and around the fort was used to grow crops that would be used to feed the people in Louisiana and even in the homeland of France.

Southwestern Illinois also has the seeds of a heavy German influence. This is evident on the German Heritage District Tour. The tour begins in historic Maeystown, which is on the National Register of Historic places. We then move to Columbia, Waterloo, Wartburg, Madonnaville, Millstadt and Belleville. The Belleville area is where the German influence can most be felt. The tour can continue on to Clinton County and its German churches.

The city of Belleville grew heavily from an influx of immigrants directly from Germany itself. Some of the Germans to come over had just left a civil war in their own country and found themselves walking into our Civil War. Many of these men formed what is known today as the Bloody Ninth, one of the few all German fighting units to fight in the Civil War. Also, while in Belleville, don't miss seeing the largest cathedral in the state of Illinois, the Cathedral of St. Peter. The cathedral originally built near the end of the Civil War, and the interior of the church closely resembles the Cathedral of Exeter, England.

Those two tours are only just a glimpse of what Southwestern Illinois has to offer the travelers in our area. You can also see: The Historic Lebanon Tour, the Religious Pilgrimage Trail, the Clinton County Churches, the Kaskaskia Valley Country and Historic Okawville, plus much more. Visit Southwestern Illinois, the area that has it all. **99**

—Southwestern Illinois Tourism
and Convention Bureau

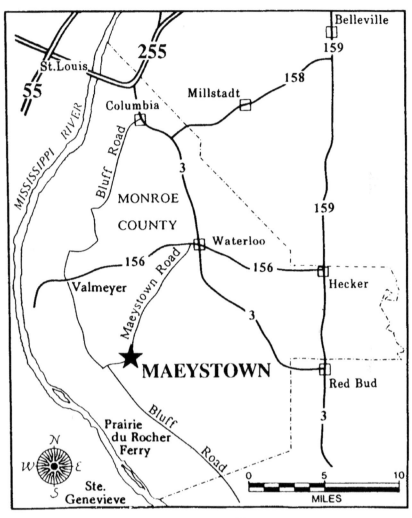

Map from Southwestern Illinois Tourism and Convention Bureau

Daytrip Illinois
Interstate 70

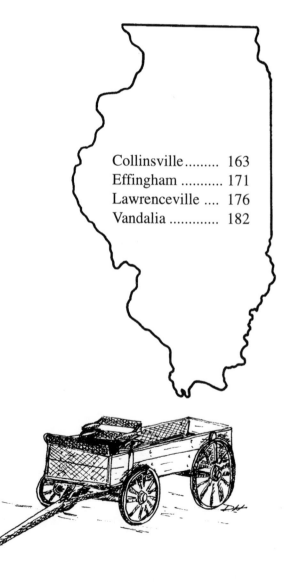

Collinsville

The Site of Cahokia Mounds State Historic Site, Illinois' Only United Nations World Heritage Site

Location

Collinsville is located off Interstates 55, 70 and 255 and five minutes from Interstates 64 and 270.

History

The city was named for William Collins who started a settlement here in 1817. Collins and his five brothers built a store, a blacksmith shop, a shoe shop, a wagon shop, a sawmill, a tannery, a distillery and a small church. Collinsville was incorporated in 1856. The first of many trains arrived in the village city in 1869, and three years later the community was incorporated into a city. Nearby coal deposits fostered the mining industry and a smelting furnace operation to assist in city growth.

Getting Started

Begin your visit by stopping by the Collinsville Convention and Visitors Bureau located at. One Gateway Drive, or call 1-800-289-2388.

You can pick up brochures that will help you tour the city and surrounding area, and find out about festival and special events dates.

Website:
www.collinsville.cvb.com

Brooks Catsup Bottle

Attractions

Brooks Catsup Bottle
The "Worlds Largest Catsup Bottle" is located on Highway 159. The towering steel water tank measures 170 feet. The landmark, representing "Roadside Architecture at its Best," was built in 1949 and restored in 1995.

Cahokia Mounds
(618) 346-5160

Located on a 2,200 acre site in Collinsville is the archaeological remnants of an ancient Indian city known as Cahokia. There you will find the remains of a prehistoric Indian civilization preserved in this State Historic Site. The city of Cahokia was inhabited from A.D. 700 to 1400. The city covered nearly six square miles at its peak, with a population of 20,000 in extensive residential sections. There you would have found houses arranged in rows around open plazas with the main agricultural fields outside the city.

The site is named for a subtribe of the Illini Indians known as the Cahokians. They occupied the land when the French arrived in the late 1600s. The city declined due to the depletion of its natural resources. Climate changes after

Cahokia Mounds State Historic Site

A.D. 1200 may have contributed to the decline in crop production needed to sustain plant and animal life. Around 1220 A.D. there was a gradual decline in population and by the 1400s, the site was abandoned.

The early inhabitants lived in compact villages, hunted, fished, cultivated gardens and gathered wild food plants. Another culture emerged between 800 A.D. to 1000, the Mississippians. They were industrious and developed an agricultural system, growing such things as corn, squash and several other seed-bearing plants. With their ingenuity in growing staple foods, and their hunting and fishing, they developed a highly complex community. They became a social, political and religious community with many outlying hamlets and villages.

The mounds themselves number over 120, but to date only 109 have been recorded. Modern farming and urban construction, altered or destroyed many mounds. Made entirely of earth, the mounds were built by people carrying soil in baskets to the site. More than 50 million cubic feet of earth were moved by the Indians in constructing the mounds. Three types of mounds were constructed,

Map of central Cahokia Mounds showing major site features and tour trails

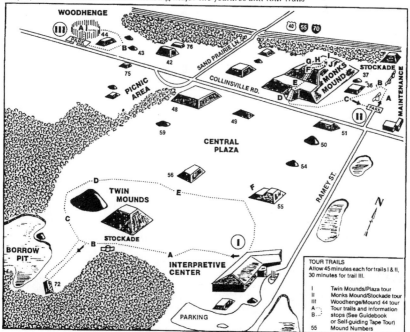

Map courtesy of Illinois Historic Preservation Agency

flat top mounds used for ceremonial buildings or residences of
the affluent, conical and ridgetop
used for burials or to mark
important locations. However
most Cahokians were buried in
cemeteries and not in the
mounds.

Monks Mounds

The largest Indian mound north
of Mexico is Monks Mound. This
is where the principal ruler lived,
conducted ceremonies and ruled
over the city.

Mound 72

This is a small ridge top mound
where ceremonial and sacrificial
burials took place. A male ruler
around 45 years of age was buried
there, along with a large cache of
grave offerings. He was surrounded by the remains of others
scarificed to serve him in the next
life.

The Stockade

Built for defense is a two mile
wall of posts set in trenches. The
stockade was built for defense,
serving as a social barrier, to
segregate the more sacred precinct
and the elite who lived there.

Woodhenge

Four calendars similar to those
found at Stonehenge in England
were uncovered. They were
probably used to determine
changing seasons and certain
ceremonial periods important to an
agricultural way of life. They were

constructed about 1000 A.D. and
are an impressive example of
Indian science and engineering.
For a listing of special programs
for equinox and solstice sunrise
dates and times contact:
Site Manager, Cahokia Mounds
State Historic Site,
30 Ramey Street
Collinsville, IL 62234
(618) 346-5160

Fairmount Park
(618) 345-4300
Located at 9301 Collinsville Road,
Highway 40. You can wager on
thoroughbred and harness racing
year round. Call (618) 345-4300
or write for schedule.

Annual Events

A large variety of festivals and
special events are held each year
at the Gateway Convention Center.
For an extensive list of events, call
the Gateway Center event information line at (618) 345-8998.
Popular annual festivals include
the following:

June
• **Horseradish Festival** — Held
in Woodland Park is the popular
International Horseradish Festival. People come from far and
near to share in this special
event. There is an array of
activities to choose from. Find
yourself hurling a freshly-dug
horseradish root in the Root

Toss. For the truly adventurous, participate in the Horseradish Eating Contest, where mounds of fresh horseradish are piled on hot dogs and quickly devoured by contestants. A recipe contest is held to discover new and unique ways to prepare this herb.

Many activities are available for the whole family — from a kiddie-tractor pull, a tot trot, a petting zoo, pony rides, a Little Miss Horseradish Contest, craft booths, live music and an abundance of food and drink. The festival is something for the family to enjoy together. Shuttle buses are available from the North Junior High School parking lot to Woodland Park.

September

• **Italian Fest** — Held on Main Street in downtown Collinsville the Italian Fest provides an educational and cultural experience focusing on the ethnic characteristics of the community and the region's large Italian descent population. Stroll down Main Street where you will find merchants and local business people dressed in festive attire, smell the mouth-watering aroma of ethnic foods while listening to wonderful music. Stop and taste Italian treats such as bagna caoda, canoli, salsiccia, polenta, garlic bread, spaghetti, pizza, meatball sandwiches, spumoni ice cream and much more.

Activities and entertainment include special sales, shopping, bocce ball tournament, pizza-eating contests, grape stomps and wine-tasting. Participate in the 10K Run and a Paisan Pedal Push which is a moonlight bicycle ride. There is something for everyone in the entire family to enjoy at this special event — two parades, food, drink, free entertainment, live music and a street dance.

• **Heritage America** — This festival is held annually at Cahokia Mounds celebrating the American Indian heritage from 1100 A.D. to present Indian cultures. Events include: Indian dances at the American Indian Center, Indian games and food demonstrations.Craft demonstrations, such as shell carving, cane basket making and blow gun construction are included. Traditional Indian foods and refreshments are served. Special exhibits will be on display in the Interpretive Center's gallery. At the Falcon picnic area, an Indian Dance will be held. The plaza area will have a display of traditional Indian crafts. Shuttle buses with tour guides will take visitors from the parking areas to the Plaza, Woodhenge, Monks Mound and the Interpretive Center.

Shopping and Dining

For shopping fun go to the Fancy Flea Funtiques located at 307 South Morrison Avenue in Collinsville or the Picket Fence at 119 West Main Street in Collinsville.

Dining at its finest includes contemporary dining, casual dining or fast food and pizzas.

Conclusion

For further information contact: Collinsville Convention and Visitors Bureau
One Gateway Drive
Collinsville, IL 62234
1-800-289 2388

Tips

✔ A listing of hotels, motels or bed and breakfasts can be obtained from the Convention and Visitors Bureau.

✔ Recreational opportunities — Parks and sports facilities include the Jaycees Sports Complex, Fletcher Gym at Collinsville High School, Glidden Civic Park, Van Fossan Fields and Woodland Park.

✔ *Field Trip Group Visit Guidelines for Cahokia Mounds State Historic Site.*

• To schedule a workshop or educational program, call the Scheduling Department at Cahokia Mounds at (618) 346-5160 on Wednesdays from 12:30-4:30pm. Regular tours can be scheduled by calling (618) 345-4999.

• Reservations must be made two weeks in advance for all group tours.

• The 15-minute orientation show, "City of the Sun," is shown daily on the hour.

• The minimum recommended time to tour the interpretive center after the film presentation is 45 minutes.

• Groups are limited to 70 persons per session. Larger groups will be assigned to consecutive sessions.

• Non-scheduled groups must wait their turn until there is room in the theatre and interpretive center.

• For school groups, it is recommended there be one adult for each 10 students.

• No writing materials, food, drinks, gum, smoking or flash photography are permitted in the interpretive center.

• The Museum Shop, which offers a large supply of resource books, slides and videos for classroom use, can only accommodate 15 students at a time.

• Pavilions in the Falcon Picnic Area are available to groups who bring their lunches. Reservations, available on weekends only, can be made by calling (618) 346-5160.

• Tapes for self-guided walking tours are available at the information desk.

• Tour booklets are available for purchase in the gift shop.

• Admission —none for education classes, scouting groups, day camps or organizations for persons with mental and/or physical disabilities. Suggested donations, $2.00 for adults and $1.00 for children.

66 Collinsville, served by Interstates 55, 70, 64, 255 and 270, has 13 hotel/motel properties and 50 restaurants. The city, located 12 minutes from downtown St. Louis, is 10 minutes from two MetroLink stations in East St. Louis that connect commuters to the St. Louis airport and most major St. Louis attractions.

Cahokia Mounds State Historic Site, the most important pre-historic Indian site in North America, is one of the city's major attractions. Visited by people from 78 foreign countries in 1996, it is one of only 17 United Nations World Heritage sites in America and the only one in Illinois.

The attraction features 65 man-made earthen mounds, 100-foot-high Monks Mound, a wooden sun calendar and the 33,000-square-foot interpretive center.

Another attraction is the one-mile Fairmount Park on Highway 40, a track that features year-round thoroughbred and harness racing, pari-mutuel wagering and simulcast wagering on major stake races across the country.

Roadside architecture at its best is the city's 170-foot-tall Brooks Catsup Bottle, the world's largest catsup bottle. The landmark, located on Highway 159 just south of the city, was constructed in 1949 and restored in 1995.

The Casino Queen, a floating river boat casino, offers slots, video poker and keno machines, craps, blackjack, roulette, baccarat and Caribbean stud poker. The attraction is only 10 minutes from Collinsville

Other area points of interest include the National Shrine of Our Lady of the Snows, Belleville, 10 miles; St. Clair Square Mall, Fairview Heights, 8 miles; and Southern Illinois University at Edwardsville, 8 miles.

Sports fans who come to St. Louis to see the Rams, Blues and Cardinals play can get to the three different sports facilities from Collinsville in about 20 minutes. Via MetroLink, riders can get to Busch Stadium, Trans World Dome and Kiel Center in 10 minutes. 99

—Sallie Jo Burton
Tourism Coordinator

Collinsville

TO MARYVILLE

270

270

157

255

40

66

55

159

STATE AID 35

4

KOEBLER ROAD

VANDALIA STREET

COMMERGE DRIVE

BLUFF ROAD

70

BELT LINE ROAD

PINE LAKE ROAD

EASTPORT PLAZA DRIVE

GATEWAY DRIVE

5

RAMADA BOULEVARD

3

CLAY STREET

MALL STREET

MAIN STREET

D E

LEBANON ROAD

BLUFF ROAD

DOWNTOWN COLLINSVILLE

B

C

COLLINSVILLE ROAD

ST LOUIS ROAD

B

1

CASEYVILLE ROAD

255

A

2

SOUTH MORRISON

159

157

A. Brooks Catsup Bottle
B. Cahokia Mounds State Historic Site
C. Fairmount Park
D. Historical Museum
E. Miners Theatre

Map Collinsville Convention and Visitors Bureau

Effingham
Crossroads of Opportunity

Location

Effingham is located at the intersection of Interstate Highways 57 and 70, U.S. Highways 40 and 45 and State Highways 32, 33 and 37. It serves as a hub for America's motoring public and brings vehicles through the area every day.

History

Effingham traces its roots back to 1814 when the first pioneers settled along the Little Wabash River. The next 40 years the isolated agricultural village witnessed little growth, adding population only when a farm family journeying west along the old Cumberland Trail stopped to work a living from the rich prairie soil.

The 1850s brought the coming of the railroad, bringing the area's first boom when stores and hotels opened up. The village was made a county seat in 1859. Once known as Broughton after a former governor, the town was renamed Effingham in honor of a British lord who refused to fight against the colonists during the American Revolution. In 1861 it was incorporated as a village. The community has a rich heritage from early German immigrants.

Getting Started

The Greater Effingham Chamber of Commerce & Industry office is located at 508 W. Fayette, U.S. Route 40, and is a good place to start touring our community. We invite you to drop by to pick up brochures, maps and a calendar of events for Effingham and its satellite areas.

Attractions

Effingham County Courthouse
Built in 1871, is the Effingham County Courthouse, it is one of the few courthouses in the state that has not undergone exterior remodeling.

Lord Effingham Marker
The marker is located on the northeast corner of the courthouse lawn. The Bicentennial project commemorates the English heritage

of the county. On the southeast corner of the lawn is the Veterans' Memorial dedicated to all Effingham County veterans who served in wartime and peacetime.

John Boos & Company

This is the oldest manufacturer of butcher blocks and metal tables in the country. Conrad Boos' blacksmith shop was where the first butcher blocks were made over one hundred years ago. The oneman operation now employs over one hundred and twenty people.

✪ Tours by appointment

Satellite Attractions

🌿 Altamont

Ben Winter Museum

The museum provides a unique look into history. You will find a steam engine purchased by Siemer Milling Company in 1894 and a threshing machine from 1881 along with steam and gas engines.

Altamont Living Museum

This unique museum is a testament to "Old Time Religion" with its luminous stained glass windows, curved oak pews and a sloped wooden floor that makes it possible to hear every musical note and spoken word. It is now a theater for live performances of music and drama. It is also a location for exhibiting crafts or fine art.

🌿 Bishop Creek

St. Aloysius Church

Built in 1894 the church is noted for its many statues and old-fashioned beauty. The church is 10 miles southeast of Effingham on Route 33, then 3 miles west.

🌿 Mason

Illinois Central Railroad Markers

The markers located about ten minutes southeast of Effingham on Route 37 commemorate the completion of the Illinois Central Railroad from Chicago to New Orleans.

🌿 Teutopolis

Teutopolis Monastery Museum

The museum displays a collection relics housed in a 32 room Franciscan Monastery founded in 1858. It is located 4 miles east of Effingham. The museum features approximately 2,000 antique items and many restored rooms, including a novice's cell and a library. Visitors come to relive the old days of the early pioneers and to learn more about the Franciscan friars.

St. Francis Church

Visit this beautiful Catholic

Teutopolis Monastery Museum

Church to see the outstanding stained glass windows.

Recreation

An array of recreational opportunities awaits you —golf courses, bowling alleys, parks and theaters. You can spend a day perfecting your swing at the batting cages or at the golf driving range. The YMCA and park district offer a variety of family opportunities.

❧ Lake Sara
(217) 342-4147
Just five miles northwest of Effingham is a man-made lake with 27 miles of beautifully wooded shoreline. For the avid fisherman there are black bass, bluegill, channel catfish, walleye and crappie. It is a complete outdoor paradise offering pavilions, a public beach, a waterslide, launching ramps for boats, campgrounds, cabins, picnic areas and a golf course. Call for a brochure.

Effingham Beach and Waterslide
(217) 868-2950
Something for everyone — picnics, reunions, company gatherings, social events and family outings.

Annual Events

Many festivals are held throughout the year including the county fair, state rodeo finals, German festival, herb festival. For a calendar of events contact the chamber office for dates and times by writing or calling.

June
• Illinois High School Rodeo Association State Finals — Everyone looks forward to this popular event. High school students from around the state saddle up to compete in the fun-filled event which is kicked off by a parade and other pre-rodeo events in Effingham. The rodeo stampedes over to the county fairgrounds in Altamont for an entertaining three day per-

formance. You will find bull and bronco riding, celebrity goat tying, steer wrestling, roping and much more.

August

• Effingham County Fair — Each spring residents and visitors begin looking forward to "Goin' to the Fair" in August. Held at the fairgrounds in Altamont, the fair features horse racing, entertainment, livestock judging and exhibits, contests and a complete carnival. "Come to the Fair."

September

• Effingham Transportation Celebration — The community's fall festival focuses on the transportation heritage of the area including a hot air balloon classic, carnival, craft show, parade, food and entertainment. The event is held in conjunction with the Corvette Fun Fest, which includes car shows, manufacturers' displays and museum tours.

Shopping and Dining

Effingham serves as one large shopping center for a trade population of 192,000. Smaller specialty shops, major department stores and restaurants make up the downtown business district.

Satisfy your appetite at one of the nearly 50 dining facilities offering everything from award winning restaurants to fast food establishments, your favorite pizza and catching the game with friends at a sports bar. No matter what time of day, you're sure to find a place to please your palette.

Conclusion

For further information contact:
Greater Effingham Chamber of Commerce & Industry
508 W. Fayette, P.O. Box 643
Effingham Illinois 62401
(217) 342-4147
EMail: Chamber@effingham.net
Fax (217) 342-4228
Website:
www.effinghamchamber.org

Tips

✔ Effingham is known nationwide as a great place to stop when traveling on 1-57 or 1-70. Facilities for both the motoring public and commercial truckers include 17 motels, 45 restaurants, four major truck stops, a convention center and numerous support facilities.

✔ We have 29 registered historical sites in the county.

✔ Effingham has a 9-hole and an 18-hole public golf course. Courses have professionally kept greens and fairways. The country club has the services of a golf pro as well. There is also a miniature golf course.

66 A place where fun, adventure and entertainment are combined with Midwestern Hospitality—That's Effingham! Seventeen motels featuring over 1200 motel rooms (from luxury to economy) offer comfortable lodging after a day packed with fun at beautiful Lake Sara, at one of our 9 or 18-hole golf courses, or on a tour of our many historic buildings and museums. Our stores, shops and malls are sure to satisfy your shopping needs, and annual events such as the Illinois High School Rodeo State Finals, Effingham Transportation Celebration and Balloon Classic, and Corvette Funfest are bound to put a smile on your face. Effingham, Illinois — Getting here is easy — we're right in the center of it all! 99

—Norma Lansing, President
Greater Effingham
Chamber of Commerce and Industry

Lawrenceville
Mid-American Living at Its Finest

Location

Lawrenceville is located off Interstate 70 at the Junctions of U.S. 50 and State Routes 1 & 33.

History

The earliest settlers to the region were French. One was a Captain Toussaint Dubois, who served in the Revolutionary War and settled in the area in 1780. The captain's youngest son, Jessie K. Dubois, served in the legislature and became a friend to Abraham Lincoln.

In 1821 the city along the west bank of the Embarras River became the seat of government for Lawrence County, named in honor of Captain James Lawrence who commanded the Chesapeake in the War of 1812 and uttered the famous words at his death, "Don't give up the ship."

The first circuit court was held in the county on June 4, 1821. The first female executed in Illinois was tried, convicted and hanged at

Photo by Bryan Stockinger, L'Ville, IL.

Lincoln Memorial between Lawrenceville Illinois and Vincennes, Indiana

Lawrenceville in 1845. Elizabeth Reed was found guilty of poisoning her husband to marry another.

In 1906 the first oil wells were brought into Lawrence County, making the county the first oil producer in the state.

Getting Started

Come by the Lawrence County Chamber of Commerce at 1112 Jefferson Street where you will receive brochures to help you get started on your visit to Lawrence County. (618) 943-3516
Fax (618) 943-4748
Email: lccc@midwest.net

Attractions

Lincoln Memorial Bridge and the Lincoln Trail Monument

State Route 250 commemorates the very spot where Lincoln's family first entered into Illinois in 1830.

Lawrence County Court House

The courthouse was built in 1889 and is a site of one of Lincoln's debates.

St. Francisville Log Cabin

(618) 948 2882
The reconstructed 1850s cabin now caters community activities,

Wabash Cannon Ball Bridge — One-Lane Toll Bridge in St. Francisville

Photo by Bryan Stockinger, L'Ville, IL.

for catering information call (618) 299-8921. The cabin is owned by the St. Francisville Women's Club which invites you to visit. Open by appointment. (618) 948-2882.

Bridgeport's Lanterman Park

You will find two buildings in the park. One is the office of Dr. John Frank Shader a small town doctor. The building is much the same as when he left it in 1944. The other is Pepple School a typical one-room school in use from 1907-1947.

Masonic Temple

This is the oldest building in Lawrenceville. It was erected in 1856 and has since been re-modeled. The timbers are all hand hewn and fastened with wooden pegs.

Historical Markers

George Field

Today known as the Mid-American Air Center, it was the site where pilots were trained for World War II overseas assign-ments in 1942.

Lincoln/Anderson Debate Marker

Located on the northeast side of the Lawrenceville Court House, the marker records one of Lincoln's 1854 debates.

DuBois Mill Stone

Located in front of the Lawrence-ville Public Library, the stone commemorates the saw mill built by heirs of Toussiant DuBois, a major financier of George Rogers Clark expeditions.

Small's Mill Stone

The marker on the southeast side of the Lawrenceville High School campus commemorates the water mill built by John Small in 1804, the first of its kind in the Embarras region.

Vincennes Track Indian Boundary Line Marker

In Red Hills State Park, this marker records the westernmost edge of the first land in Illinois ceded by the Indians in 1795 to the U.S. Government.

Recreational Areas

Red Hills State Park

(618) 936-2469

The park consist, of 948 acres of sanctuary and relaxation. The park is the highest point of land between St. Louis and Cincinnati. The park was ceded by the Indians to the United States by a treaty made in 1795 at Greenville, Ohio. The Indians relinquished all claims to the land northwest of the Ohio River and east of a specified line. A dam was constructed in 1953 creating a 40 acre lake with a depth of 30 feet and 2.5 miles of shore-

Stagecoach Rides at Old Settler Days at Red Hill State Park

line. Camping, game hunting and fishing.

Chauncey Marsh Nature Preserve
This 400 acres is a marsh nature preserve with trails.

Mid-American Air Center
Come join the fun for soaring and model airplane fun.

Annual Events
April
• Old Settler Days at Red Hill State Park, Sumner, 11:00am - 5:00pm on Saturday and 11:00 am-4:00pm on Sunday. Held the weekend of April 29-30.

May
• Memorial Day Weekend, Mike Harvey Super Gold, Lawrenceville Square (618) 943-3516.

July
• Independence Day Celebration/ Fireworks Display sponsored by Red Hills Settlers Association Red Hills State Park, Sumner. For more information (618) 936-2469.
• St. Francisville Fish Fry and Fireworks on the banks of the Wabash River, St. Francisville, call (618) 948-2837.

September
• Sumner Fall Festival on the streets in Sumner. Contact DeMova (618) 936-2212.
• Lawrenceville Fall Festival

around the square in Lawrenceville. Contact the Chamber Office, (618) 943-3516.

- Annual War Bird Fly-In at Mid-American Air Center, Lawrenceville, contact Joe Kremp, (812) 254-0017.

October

- Chestnut Festival on the streets in St. Francisville. Contact (618) 948-2285.

November

- Basketball Capital Classic at Lawrenceville High School and Red Hill High School. Contact Chamber Office, (618) 943-3516.

Conclusion

For more information contact:
Lawrence County Chamber of Commerce
1112 Jefferson Street
Lawrenceville, IL 62439
(618) 943-3516 •
Fax (618) 943-4748

Tips

✔ Specialty stores, antique and craft shops.

✔ Fine dining at area restaurants — Steaks, fish, homemade desserts.

✔ Weekend racing—bombers, street stock, UMP modified, winged sprint.

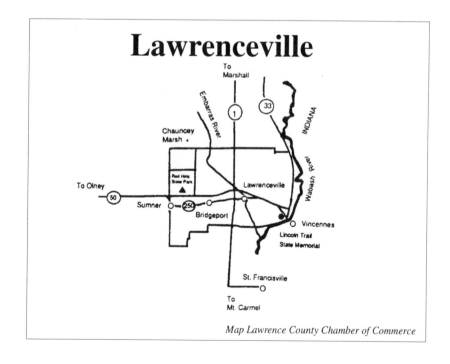

Lawrenceville

Map Lawrence County Chamber of Commerce

66 Welcome to Lawrence County, Illinois — Abraham Lincoln's entrance to Illinois. On the banks of the Wabash and Embarras Rivers, our county features Lawrenceville, Bridgeport, Sumner and St. Francisville, located at the Junctions of U.S. 50 and State Routes 1 & 33.

Lawrence County history includes the settlements of the Wabash Valley, or Oubache, a name that the French applied to the stream that separated Illinois from Indiana. The Wabash River was an early route the French used to reach the Mississippi from Canada. The French secured this route with the military post in Vincennes, Indiana. Early settlements radiated all around the fort opposite Vincennes in the fertile prairies of Lawrence County as early as 1762.

In 1763, by the Treaty of Paris, the whole territory came under British control. On February 18, 1779, George Rogers Clark crossed the river at St. Francisville and his American troops took the Vincennes fort on February 25, 1779. After the war of 1812, subsequent settlers rapidly moved in from Ohio, Kentucky, and Indiana to continue development of this new Northwest Territory.

A ferry was established where the Lincoln Memorial Bridge now crosses the Wabash. In March 1830, the Lincoln family crossed via ox-teamed wagons. The 21 year old Abe was with his father Thomas, step-mother Sarah Bush Lincoln and her two daughters and son-in-laws.

Lawrence County today remains a typical small community that offers warm hospitality, modern conveniences and simple country pleasures. Lawrence County respects its past and continues to believe in its future.

Visit Lawrence County, Illinois—Mid-American living at its finest. **99**

—Lawrence County Chamber of Commerce

Vandalia
Home of Illinois' Oldest Capital

Location
Located along 1-70, Exit 63 and U.S. Highway 51.

History
This was Illinois' capital from 1819 until 1839. In 1819 the State Legislature met in Kaskaskia and agreed to move the state's capital to the fertile valley of the Kaskaskia River. The town became a home for state politicians, who would later attain national attention. John Reynolds, Ninian Edwards, Stephen A. Douglas, and even Abraham Lincoln all cut their political teeth in the early capital site. Unfortunately for the inhabitants of Vandalia, in 1838, Honest Abe led a junta called the "Long Nine" that was successful in getting the state capital moved to Springfield the following year.

After the capital's activities left town, the town was left with serving as the county seat for Fayette County.

➺ Getting Started
Stop by the Tourist Information Center for information about Vandalia as well as free brochures about local, state and national sites. The Tourist Information Center is located at 1408 North Fifth Street, southwest of the intersection of I-70 and Route 51. Phone (618) 283-2728.

Attractions

Cumberland Road
The famous Cumberland Road, was the first highway built by the Federal Government, it opened up the interior of the country for development. The Madonna of the Trail statue marks the terminus of the journey. The road was started in 1811 at Cumberland, Maryland and completed in Vandalia, Illinois in 1838. The statue was donated by the Daughters of the American Revolution in 1928 in memory of the pioneer mothers who arrived in covered wagons.

Evans Library
This houses a large collection of items connected with Abraham Lincoln including books and photographs.

Fayette County Museum
(618) 283-4866
At the corner of Main and Ken-

nedy Streets you will find the century-old Presbyterian Church that houses the Fayette County Museum. Early American items date back to the time Vandalia was the state capitol. Listed on the National Register of Historic Places.

The Lincoln Life Mask
In the Old State Capitol you will find the life mask made for a statue of Lincoln in 1860 just after his election to the presidency.

Lincoln Trail Marker
You will find the marker in Rogier Park, south of Fillmore Street, along the trail used by Abraham Lincoln to travel between his home in Springfield and the capitol in Vandalia. Listed on the National Register of Historic Places.

State Cemetery
In 1823 the state of Illinois established the Old State Cemetery. Located in the cemetery are bronze markers giving biographical information on prominent citizens in the early history of the community.

The Little Brick House
(618) 283-0024
The Little Brick House is located at 621 St. Clair Street. The house has six restored rooms full of china, furniture, engravings and books belonging to early settlers when Lincoln attended the legislature (1834-39). It is listed on the National Register of Historic places. You will find old portraits and photographs of James Hall, the state's first literary figure and James Berry, who was the first talented artist of the state.
✪ Open by appointment

The Old State Capitol
The oldest existing building that served as the capitol of Illinois. The building was restored in the 1930s with rooms furnished as they were in its capitol period. Lincoln gave several speeches there, including his first protest against slavery. He also received his license to practice law there and the new city of Chicago received its city charter from the state capitol in Vandalia. It is open from 9:00am to 5:00pm daily, including Sunday. Buses are welcome. Groups of 25 must have reservations. It is handicapped accessible. For additional information write Site Manager, 315 W. Gallatin, Vandalia, IL 62471 or phone.
(618) 283-1161.
✪ Free Guided Tours

Annual Events
Vandalia is a hub of activity throughout the year with events

Old State Capitol

and activities. Write or call for listings and continual updates. (618) 283-2728.

April
- Lion's Club Community Sale in Ramsey's, held the first Saturday in April.

May
- Avenue of Flags and Memorial Day Service in Vandalia is held the last Sunday in May.

June
- Grande Levee — The celebration recalls the social life of Vandalia during its days as capital. A period celebration of arts and crafts, the event is held on the Old State Capitol grounds each year on the third weekend of June. It is kicked off each year with an old-fashioned ham and bean supper, ending on Father's Day. A must for the arts and crafts lover.
- Ramsey Daze in Ramsey — mid June.

July
- Fourth of July Parade and Cele-

bration in Herrick — Fourth of July.
- Team Penning Competition, mid July.
- Fayette County Fair in Brownstown, mid July.
- Prairie Days in St. Peter, 4th weekend in August.

September
- Labor Day Celebration in St. Elmo, first Monday in September.

October
- Lions' Halloween parade in Vandalia, Thursday before Oct. 30.

December
- Old State Capitol Candlelight Tours in Vandalia, second Sunday in December.

Recreation

Skydiving
The Archway Skydiving Center offers skydiving lessons and lift support for the more experienced skydivers from all over the midwest. Come join the divers or just be a spectator. The center is located at Vandalia's Municipal Airport. Call for more information (618) 283-4978.

Hunting
All types of hunting are available from upland game, waterfowl, to small and large game.
- Carlyle Lake — Water fowl, pheasant, deer and upland game hunting is a short drive from Vandalia. (618) 425-3533

- Keck's Marsh — Water fowl, pheasant, quail, dove, squirrel, rabbit and deer hunting is just outside of Vandalia. (618) 435-3740.
- Ramsey Lake State Park — Public hunting during the regular hunting seasons includes rabbit, pheasant, quail, squirrel and dove. (618) 423-2215.
- Vandalia Lake — The lake covers 660 acres and features quality fishing, boating, camping, picnicking and swimming. A city license is required and is available from the marina or City Hall. Camping facilities are available with hookups.

Shopping and Dining
A day of shopping in Vandalia can be a treat for the craft and antique lover. Vandalia offers everything from an old-fashioned soda fountain to steak house buffets.

Tips
✔ The Vandalia Airport is a full service airport for small aircraft. Two fully lighted runways, a maintenance facility, engine shop, 100 low lead fuel, jet A, and auto fuel available. The airport offers a courtesy car, free tie downs and hanger rental.

Conclusion

For more information contact
Vandalia Chamber of Commerce
P.O. Box 238
Vandalia, IL 62471
(618) 283-2728
or

Southwestern Illinois Tourism
and Convention Center
10950 Lincoln Trail
Fairview Heights, IL 62208
1-800-442-1488

---

66 Welcome to Vandalia, the second Capitol of Illinois and the Fayette County seat. We are friendly people helping to make your visit with us most pleasurable. We offer historical sites, skydiving, picnicking in seven parks, visits to our antique shops and various restaurants, boating and swimming at the Vandalia Lake. Hunting and fishing are available in season. 99

—*Vandalia Chamber of Commerce*

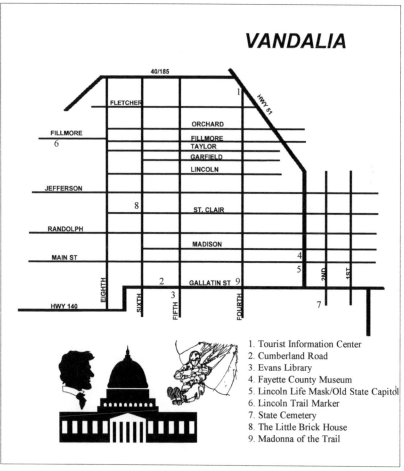

VANDALIA

40/185

FLETCHER

ORCHARD

FILLMORE
6

FILLMORE
TAYLOR
GARFIELD
LINCOLN

JEFFERSON

8

ST. CLAIR

RANDOLPH

MADISON

MAIN ST

4

5

2   GALLATIN ST 9

3

HWY 140

7

EIGHTH

SIXTH

FIFTH

FOURTH

2ND

1ST

HWY 51

1. Tourist Information Center
2. Cumberland Road
3. Evans Library
4. Fayette County Museum
5. Lincoln Life Mask/Old State Capitol
6. Lincoln Trail Marker
7. State Cemetery
8. The Little Brick House
9. Madonna of the Trail

Map from Paul Wentzel

Daytrip Illinois
Interstate 72

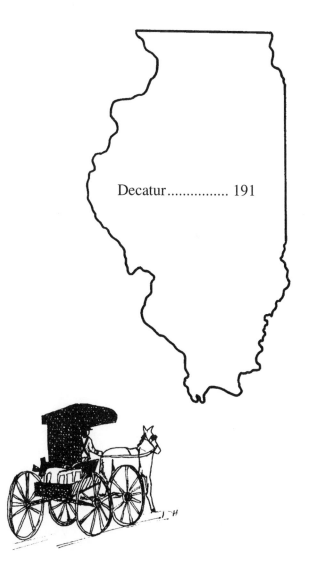

Decatur
Soybean Capital of the World

Location

Located along Interstate 72 in Macon County.

History

The seat of Macon County was founded in 1829. The first cabin was built by James Renshaw. In 1830 Abraham Lincoln, aged 21, settled about a mile west of town along the Sangamon River. It was here that young Abe split rails, plowed, and eventually studied the books that would propel him into a career in law and eventually politics.

Another famous Decatur resident was Richard J. Oglesby who arrived in 1836. Oglesby later became state senator, U.S. senator, governor, and a major general during the Civil War.

In 1854 the railroad assisted agriculture in sustaining the town's growth. By 1860 the town had reached a population of nearly 4,000 inhabitants.

Coal veins were unearthed in 1874. With resulting mining the population increased to more than 20,000 by 1900.

➡ Getting Started

Start your visit at the Decatur Area Convention and Visitors Bureau located at 202 E. North Street. The staff is ready to direct your path to make your visit a memorable occasion.

Attractions

Birks Museum
(217) 424-6337
1184 W. Main Street
The museum honoring the late Florence and Jenna Birks features a vast collection of more than 1,000 lamps, vases, and pieces of art glass. You will find turn-of-the century furniture made by Emil Galle and Gustav Stickley. Group tours available.
✪ Donations accepted

Gallery 510
(217) 422-1509
510 W. Decatur Street
The Gallery 510 Arts Guild Ltd. is a not-for-profit group of 25 dedicated local artists who have united to encourage, promote and

The James Millikin Homestead

enhance the visual arts. The gallery, located in a century-old landmark home in Decatur's historic district, features works by member and guest artists. One-person shows are held each month at this location. Open 1-4 p.m. Thursday through Sunday or by appointment. Art is also on exhibit monthly at the following locations: Tick building (corner of Water and North Streets); Decatur Airport, 910 S. Airport Road; Decatur Club, 158 W. Prairie Avenue; and Decatur Public Library, 130 N. Franklin, St. Free — 217 422-1509

Hieronymus Mueller Museum
(217) 425-7461 • Scovill Park
61 S. Country Club Rd.
Created and designed by former Smithsonian Institution staff, the fascinating legacy of Hieronymus Mueller and the Mueller family is told. Victorian, Edwardian, and prairie lifestyles come alive with the experiences of the first, second, and third generations. Open 1-4 pm, Friday-Sunday.
✪ Group rates available

Kirkland Galleries
In the galleries on the campus of Millikin University you will find

works from nationally known artists, area and student artists and photographic displays.

✪ Free admission

James Millikin Homestead
(217) 422-9003
125 N. Pine Street
This Victorian brick mansion was built in 1876 by banker James Millikin. The mansion has opulent wood and plaster work, elegant fireplaces, etched and stained glass.

✪ Donations accepted

Macon County Museum Complex
(217) 422-4919
5580 North Fork Road
See the prairie years and the Victorian Era come to life as you tour the museum. You will see the 1830 courthouse where Abraham Lincoln once practiced. Starting July, 2000 see "Lincoln In Macon County." Open year round.

✪ Donations are accepted.

Transfer House
Located in Central Park, the Transfer House is a trademark of downtown Decatur and is the hub of activity. Throughout the summer months outdoor events center around this historic landmark.

Walking Tours

In the 83 acres that make up the Historic District you will find

The Macon County Museum Complex

virtually every known type of architecture from pre-Civil War through bungalow, including Frank Lloyd Wright homes. Styles to be found are Italianate (1845-1880), Second Empire (1870-1890), Stick Style (1870-1890), Queen Ann (1880-1890), Shingle Style (1885-1903), Romanesque Revival (1875-1900) Georgian Revival (1890-1915).Neo-Classical (1890-1930) and the Art Deco (1920's-1930's).

Decatur boasts four wonderful walking tours. Below is information for Walking Tour Two and for a brochure of the other three walking tours call 1-800-252-3376 or (217) 423-7000.

For this tour, park your car on North College or West Prairie. Begin at the corner of North College and West Main—Walk east to Church Street. Walk one block north to West Prairie, head west to North College and turn north. Then turn east on W. William, walk two blocks to N. Church. You will pass First Methodist Church as you head north on Church to W. North Street. Two blocks west brings you to College Hill where you turn south. Approximate time of the walk is 50 minutes.

1 • *Dr. Will Barnes House, 500 W. Main Street—1891.* This Queen Anne mansion was built in 1871 by Lewis B. Casner. The house features a variety of dormers, a corner turret with a decorative cornice, a large stone column porch on the east and a porte cochere on the west.

2 • *Baldwin House, 452 W. Main—1879.* Italianate characteristics make this house one of great interest on the tour. Handhewn walnut logs from the two-room log cabin of William Hanks, Jr. have been used as ceiling beams in the kitchen.

3 • *W.H. Linn House, 300 West Main—1889.* This house is described as a castle because of its tower, massive porch and veranda.

4 • *First Presbyterian Church, 204 West Prairie—1890-2.* Romanesque style with a strong Byzantine influence.

5 • *Peter Loeb House, 300 West Prairie—1887.* Queen Anne style home with turrets and gables. Notice the variety of textures, window sizes, the stained and leaded glass.

6 • *Folrath House, 259 North College—1915.* Designed by architect England Dague.

7 • *Lyon House, 467 West William—1915.* This was originally built for lumber dealer George Lyon. Construction has a stucco covering over a wood exterior.

8 • *Henry Mueller House, 405 West William—1905.* Georgian Revivalist architecture was

Walking Tour Two

Map from Decatur Area Convention and Visitors Bureau

designed by W.O. McNabb. Notice that the second floor windows above the front entry create a Palladian effect.

9 • *Anderson House, 309 North Edward—1865.* The Italianate style is illustrated by long narrow windows, curved and straight window lintels and bracketed eaves. The masonry walls are 15 inches thick.

10 • *Ebenezer Missionary Baptist Church, 371 West William—1904.* Romanesque style. The corner stone was laid by the Masonic Fraternity on May 29, 1904.

11 • *Catto House, 364 West William—1880.* Italianate style.

12 • *V.H. Parke House, 307 West William Street—1866.* The Italianate style resembles the Millikin homestead a few blocks away.

13 • *Masonic Temple, 224 West William—1929.* An excellent example of Art Deco architecture.

14 • *First United Methodist Church, 201 West North—1906.* This English or modern Gothic church has a Byzantine dome. The building features blue stained-glass, hooded windows and twin flat-topped towers.

15 • Barnes House, 438 West North—1859. Colonial lines with a high-ceiling portico. There is a balcony featuring an ornamental iron railing.

16 • *Chamber-England House, 401 North College—1882.* The home was rebuilt in 1916.

17 • *Staley Mansion, 361 No. College—1881.* The home features French style leaded and stained glass windows.

Annual Events

Below is a sample of Decatur—Forsyth's popular festivals and events. The Decatur Area Convention & Visitors Bureau will customize a Festival Fun Tour for your special group. Call 1-800-331-4479 for dates, additional events and to arrange tours.

✦ **Festivals**

Mari-Mann Herb Fest. —Labor Day weekend — features herbal gourmet luncheons, herbal cooking, and craft demon-strations; herb garden tours.

Summer Start Festival and Boat Races. Memorial Day weekend on Lake Decatur. Hydroplane boat races, food, craft and commercial vendors, 5K run/walk, inline skate race, carnival and live entertainment on three stages.

World Championship Old Time Piano Players Contest. Memorial Day weekend. Some of the finest ragtime and old time music in the nation. Workshops and exhibits.

Gospel Music Festival. The best gospel groups from across the nation sing inspiring music for the entire family.

✦ **Summer Festivals**

Freedom Fest. Firecracker road run, food concessions, entertainment and fireworks.

Pride of the Prairie Midwest Country Western Dance Festivals. Workshops features the latest Country and Western dances.

Decatur Celebration. Free family festival featuring name entertainment, food booths galore, arts and crafts.

Yesteryear Fair. Sights, sounds and smells of yesteryear fill the air! Craft demonstrations, lots of food, book sale, antique show and sale.

Forsyth Fine Arts Fest. Juried art show and sale with professional musical groups playing throughout fest.

Big Band Festival. Big band musicians come from all across the country.

✦ **Fall Festivals**

Arts in the Park. Features over 70 artists.

Pumpkinfest. Family festival offers a giant craft show, food, carnival, pumpkin decorating contests.

✦ Winter Festivals

Greater Downstate Indoor Bluegrass Festival. Outstanding bluegrass, instrument dealer's trade show and more.

Decatur Symphony of Trees. Get in the holiday spirit with a visual feast of elaborately decorated Christmas Trees.

Christmas Walk on Merchant Street. Free horse-drawn carriage rides, performances and caroling, free refreshments.

Christmas Time at the Zoo. More than 80,000 lights and decorations and Santa Claus in his workshop ride the Artic Express

Annual Central Illinois Jazz Festival.

Satellite Attractions

❧ Forsyth

Located north of Decatur, on Interstate 72, the village of Forsyth a must for travelers. In June enjoy the Forsyth Park Celebration where you can enjoy sack races, games, contests for children, a softball game, races and many other activities. For more information call 217 428-6742.

Shopping and Dining

You will find shops of every description and the elegance of fine dining—airy restaurants, steak houses, ethnic dining, casual dining in a restaurant overlooking a beautiful lake.

Conclusion

For further information contact:
Decatur Area Convention and
Visitors Bureau
202 E. North Street
Decatur, IL 62523
217 423-7000 • 1-800-331-4479
FAX 217 423-7455
e-mail: decatur@midwest.net
Website: www.decaturcvb.com

Tips

✔ Decatur • Forsyth is the perfect hub for your "spoke" tours of Central Illinois sites. With the finest in hospitality, accommodations restaurants, and other facilities, our location makes it easy to move your group to and from wonderful sites just north, south, east, and west of the city.

66 Here in the heart of the Land of Lincoln, you'll find friendly people, outstanding services and year-round fun for the whole family.

Mari-Mann Herb Farm—continues to be one of the most popular attractions in Decatur. The Gingerbread House Gift Shop has one of the largest selections of herb products in the Midwest, and the Sugarplum Factory is home to a variety of herbal luncheons and high teas and herb programs.

Lincoln History—when the Lincolns moved from Kentucky, they spent their first year in Illinois, living in the western part of Decatur along the banks of the Sangamon River. Decatur has three excellent statues of Lincoln, one as a boy, one of Lincoln at 21 and Lincoln the lawyer.

Historic District—some 83 acres in size, the district is home to virtually every known type of architecture from pre-Civil War thru Bungalow, including Frank Lloyd Wright homes, Gothic and Italianate.

Family Activities—Scovill Park offers something for the whole family including Scovill Zoo and Oriental Gardens, Project Playground and the Children's Museum of Illinois.

Outdoor Activities—Rock Springs Center for Environmental Discovery is a popular attraction with hiking trails, cross country skiing, environmental programs and classes, and living history programs. Decatur is proud to have one of the largest park districts in the United States, including five public golf courses. Enjoy fishing and other water activities on Lake Decatur.

Museums—Birks Museum on the campus of Millikin University contains various collections of glass, crystal and china from such houses as Stueben, Wedgewood, Beleek, and Tiffany. The Macon County Museum Complex tells the history of Macon County and the surrounding area.

For more information on our area, please call the Decatur Area Convention and Visitors Bureau at 1-800 331 4479. We offer a full range of motorcoach services for the Tour Operator, including custom itineraries, free step-on guide and tour planning. Check out our Web at www.decaturcvb.com **99**

—Teri Freeze

Daytrip Illinois
Interstate 74

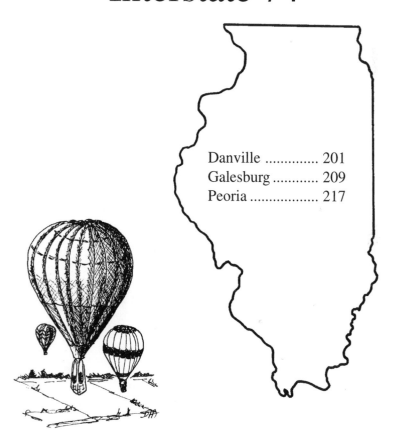

Danville
The Difference is Our People

Location

Danville in Vermilion County is located approximately 125 miles due south of Chicago on Illinois Route 1 and 85 miles west of Indianapolis on Interstate 74. It is within a 500 miles radius of nearly 200 cities with populations of 50,000 or more.

History

In 1765 Colonel George Croghan visited a Kickapoo Indian village and made the first written record of the Danville area. In 1801 Joseph Barron, an interpreter serving with General William H. Harrison, discovered salines in the region when the Kickapoo gave up some large tracts in 1819 to the U.S. Government, Barron returned to the area to survey the salt content for possible salting operations. Salt manufacturing began in earnest in 1824 when Major John W. Vance obtained a lease on the salines.

When Vermilion County was organized in 1826, the Salt Works settlement was chosen as its county seat. However, through the donations of land by Guy W. Smith and Dan Beckwith, the actual seat was laid out a few miles to the east of the salting operations. Beckwith's abilities as a surveyor destined the town's name to be named Danville.

In 1828 Gurdon S. Hubbard established a trading post in Danville. In 1831 Hubbard left the town for profiteering ventures in the then village of Chicago. In a letter to his brother-in-law Dr. William Fithian he wrote, "So far I have no regret for having moved to a smaller town."

Virginian Ward Hill Lamon came to Danville in 1847. The next year Lamon met with a lawyer by the name of Abraham Lincoln who had served the Eighth Judicial Circuit since 1841. The two began a law partnership that lasted five years.

➽ Getting Started

We invite you to stop by the Convention and Visitor Center located at 100 W. Main Street #146 to receive brochures, maps and information to help you get started visiting our area.

Attractions

Bunker Hill Historic Area
(Kennekuk Cove County Park)
(217) 442-1691

- *The Vermilion Chapel*
  The oldest frame structured church in the county was built in 1886. Open on Sunday during the summer season or by appointment.

- *Red Oak School*
  A one room schoolhouse built in 1914 and closed in 1956. Open on Sunday during summer or by appointment.

- *Newtown Store*
  The general store (1926-1979) has been authentically renovated. Open on Sunday during summer season or by appointment.

Department of Veteran Affairs Medical Center — Danville Area Community College
1900 E. Main
The former "Danville Home" was established by an Act of Congress in 1896. A driving tour of the grounds is permitted. A national cemetery is on adjoining grounds.

Illiana Genealogical and Historical Society
19 East North Street
Research Hours, Wednesday, Thursday, Friday, and Saturday 10am to 4pm. Tuesday evenings 5pm to 8pm. Call ahead for groups.

Springhill Cemetery
Situated between English and Voorhees Streets, two blocks east of Vermilion Street in Danville, the cemetery was established in 1864. Find the graves of Danville's founders and of Abraham Lincoln's friends and other historical figures such as General John C. Black and "Uncle Joe" Cannon.

Stony Creek Bridge
E. Main Street
Built in 1896, it has been placed on the National Register as one of the few stone arch bridges of its design remaining in the United States.

Lincoln Sites

Colonel Harmon Mansion
(217) 431-1332
522 E. Main

Built in the early 1850s and owned by Col. Oscar Harmon, attorney and friend of Lincoln. Lincoln visited the home and once ate Thanksgiving dinner there. The home now houses a restaurant open daily to the public.

Lamon House
(217) 442-2922
Lincoln Park, N. Logan Avenue
This 1840s Greek Revival Cottage was built by Joseph Lamon, cousin of Ward Hill Lamon, Lincoln's law partner and bodyguard. Open Sundays during the summer season or by appointment.

Lincoln Law Office Site
Commemorative plaque, 4 N. Vermilion

Vermilion County Museum
(217) 442-2922
116 N. Gilbert
Housed in a home built by William Fithian, Civil War surgeon and personal friend of Abraham Lincoln. The south balcony, from which Lincoln gave a speech in 1858, and the bedroom he used on his many visits remain as they were. Of special note, the Joseph G. Cannon's (Uncle Joe) room containing personal items of

Vermilion County Museum

Cannon who served in the U.S. House for 46 years and was Speaker from 1903 to 1911.

Satellite Attractions

✇ **Catlin**

The Catlin Museum
(217) 427-5766
210 N. Paris
Hours: Monday, Wednesday, Saturday, 9am-12pm and 1pm-4pm.

✇ **Georgetown**

Georgetown Historical House
(217) 662-8000
Corner of North Main and Hoffman
Sunday from 2pm to 4pm, June-August.
❍ Off season by appointment

✇ **Rossville**

Mann's Chapel
(217) 442-2922
Built in 1857, this is the oldest church in Vermilion County.
❍Tours available by appointment

Rossville Historical Society Museum
(217) 748-6045
108 W. Attica
Tuesday and Saturday 12-4pm

Tilton Historical Society
(217) 354-4832
201 W. 5th Street
Thurs., morning or by appointment

The Depot Museum
(217) 748-6615
Benton Avenue
The Depot Museum is open from Memorial Day through Labor Day. Saturday and Sunday 12pm to 4pm. Records are available for railroad buffs.

✇ **Salt Kettle**

Salt Kettle Rest Area off 1-74 East
Near the original salt mines site, this monument recognizes the first industry in the area, the Salt Salines.

Monuments

- **Civil War, Soldiers Circle** — Springhill Cemetery, Voorhees
- **Korean/Vietnam War Memorial** — SE corner Hazel and Williams
- **Revolutionary War Memorial** — Front of Federal Courthouse, Vermilion Street
- **Vermilion County Women's War Memorial** — Corner of Madison & Hazel
- **WWI Monument** — 201 W. 5th Street, Tilton
- **WWI Victory Memorial** —SW corner Main & Gilbert
- **WWII Monument** — W. Side Hazel Street

Historical Markers

Lincoln Markers —
8th Judicial Circuit

Intersection of U.S. Route 150 and Logan Avenue, Danville. On Il. Route 1 between Vermilion-Edgar County Line. 2 1/2 miles south of U.S. Route 150 on Vermilion-Champaign County Line, Kickapoo St. Park.

Lincoln's Last Speech in Illinois 1861 Plaque

Illinois-Indiana State Line, Northeast of Danville

Abraham Lincoln-Impromptu Speech 1858

Vermilion County Museum

Gurdan S. Hubbard Plaque

Inside Vermilion County Courthouse, Danville

Hubbard Trail Marker

306 S. Chicago, Rossville. It was erected in 1876 to mark the original trail.

Harrison Treaty Marker (1809)

East Ridge Farm, So. of C.H. 16

Indian Trail Marker (1834)

South of Sidell, Danville/Fort Clark Road

Annual Events

For a complete listing of events and further information call 1-800-383-4386.

Oldsmobile Balloon Classic Illinois

June

• Arts in the Park — Held in Lincoln Park the weekend following Father's Day. There is a regional collection of artists and performing art groups.

• Oldsmobile Balloon Classic Illinois — This is the largest nationally and internationally recognized balloon race in the state of Illinois with over 100 hot air balloons participating. Held the second weekend of June at the Vermilion County Airport.

• Turtle Races — Over 100 turtles compete in races throughout the day. Held at the Eastern Illinois Fairgrounds.

March

• N.J.C.A.A. Division II National Junior College Men's Basketball Championship — Danville Area Community College

Celebrity Way

A portion of highway runs through Danville recognizing the city's famous sons and daughters. Signs are marked at key intersections carrying the name and likeness of the celebrity as well as in what field that person gained recognition. Celebrities are honored by signs at these locations:

☆ *Uncle Joe Cannon,* former speaker of the House of Representatives, at Gilbert and Harrison Streets.

☆ Singer *Helen Morgan* at Gilbert and Seminary Streets.

☆ Humanitarian *Laura Lee* at Gilbert and Williams Streets.

☆ Entertainer *Bobby Short* at Gilbert and Fairchild Streets.

☆ Actor and Comedian *Jerry Van Dyke* at Vermilion and Fairchild Streets.

☆ Actor and Comedian *Dick Van Dyke* at Vermilion and Voorhees Street.

☆ Professional football player *Zeke Bratkowsk*i at Vermilion and Winter Avenue.

☆ Movie Star *Gene Hackman* at Vermilion and Lake Shore Drive.

☆ Actor and Dancer *Donald O'Connor* at Vermilion and Lake Shore Drive.

☆ Added in 1995 was Astronaut *Cmdr. Joe Tanner* at Vermilion and Shady Lane.

Shopping and Dining

Shopping is a true experience in Vermilion County. Treasures of the first settlers can be found in elegantly displayed antique and specialty shops. Many shops are located in beautifully restored homes while others can be found in the historic downtown business district. Shop for toys, jewelry, specialty gifts, clothing, primitives, or collectibles. For a brochure on specific shops and their hours call 1-800-383-4386.

There are many eating establishments from quick service to full service or seasonal specialty foods. No one will leave Danville hungry. Write or call for a list of restaurants in the area.

Conclusion

For further information contact:
Danville Area Convention and Visitors' Bureau
100 W. Main Street #146
Danville, Illinois 64832
(217) 442-2096 • 1-800-383-4386
FAX (217) 442-2137
www.danvillecvb.com

Tips

✔ Vermilion County offers a variety of parks and recreation areas which convey the majesty of the great Midwest. Every season ushers in something special for the great outdoors.

✔ Golf and tennis facilities are available and open to the public.

✔ The Art Council offers many cultural opportunities throughout the year. Just drop us a line or call and we will send you a list of scheduled events.

✔ Middle Fork National Scenic River has been designated a National Scenic River, the only one in Illinois. Canoe runs down the river are available from six hours to a full two and one-half days of adventure.

❝ Here in the heart of the Land of Lincoln, you'll find friendly people, outstanding services, and comfortable lodging. You'll find a unique community filled with fun and activities every day of the year . . . historic sites and attractions, sports, parks (over 11,000 acres), a scenic river, shopping, restaurants, antiques, arts, entertainment, museums, and more. Here you can enjoy fairs and festivals highlighted by Oldsmobile Balloon Classic Illinois, Arts in the Park, and an array of others.

Please contact the Danville Area Convention and Visitor's Bureau (800-383-4386) for information about the area. We hope you will enjoy a visit to Danville, where memories of the past and hopes for the future find harmony. ❞

—Jeanie Cooke

Travel Danville's "Celebrity Way"

Boiling Springs Road ⭐

Honoring the accomplishments of our native sons and daughters

Illinois Route 1 through the city of Danville

⭐ **Celebrity Way • Beginning/End**

	Shady Lane	Joe Tanner
	Liberty Lane	Donald O'Connor
	Lake Shore Drive	Gene Hackmann
	Winter Avenue (IL. Rt. 1)	Zeke Bratowski
	Voorhees Street (Vermilion Street)	Dick Van Dyke
Bobby Short	Fairchild Street (IL. Rt. 1)	Jerry VanDyke
Williams Street (IL. Rt. 1)	Laura Lee	
(Gilbert Street)	Helen Morgan / Seminary Street	
Harrison Street	Uncle Joe Cannon	
North Street ⭐		
Main Street		Martin Luther King
Martin Luther King Drive		Memorial Way

A project of the city of Danville

Galesburg
Get Away To . . .

Location
Located on Interstate 74 in Knox County.

History

George Washington Gale, a Presbyterian minister, conceived the idea of establishing a frontier town from the comfort of his Oneida, New York, parish. In 1835, after raising more than $20,000 for the effort from interested families, a committee was sent westward to locate a choice site. Good land was found in Illinois and from 1836-37 fifty families traveled a variety of routes to reach their newly acquired land parcels.

Galesburg became the home of Knox College which was chartered in 1837. Student labor for tuition greatly helped in the early building years of the town.

Strict moral codes and hard work ethics governed the community in those early growing years. A Galesburg family by the name of Ferris brought the town early fame. Olmstead Ferris experimented with popcorn and then introduced it to England where he popped corn before Queen Victoria and her court. Another Ferris invented the ferris wheel which was exhibited for the first time at the Columbian Exposition in Chicago in 1893.

In 1854 the railroad came to town and growth followed its arrival. The population in Galesburg in 1850 was about 880, but by 1856 the community had increased to 4,000. The city became a division point for the Burlington Railroad. This brought yet further construction and jobs.

During the period of the Civil War, Galesburg became an important station along the Underground Railroad.

➡ Getting Started

Drop by the Visitors Center to receive a visitors guide and calender of events. The center is located at 2163 East Main Street, Box 60, Galesburg, IL 61402-0060.

Attractions

When visiting Galesburg you have a feeling of nostalgia as so much of the city's heritage remains from days gone by. The architecture of the city has representations of Gothic Revival, Queen Anne, Neo-Classical, Georgian, Federal, Prairie, Italianate, and Romanaesque styles. An occasional hitching post reminds travelers of times past.

Browning Mansion
(309) 344-2839
325 North Kellogg Street
Built in 1858 as an Italianate-style square house, was later purchased by Mr. William Browning in 1886 after which he "Victorianized" it with the addition of bays, dormers and gingerbread. Today the Galesburg Historical Society owns the home, and it is open year-round except for major holidays.
✪ By appointment

Carl Sandburg State Historic Site
(309) 342-2361
331 East Third Street
On January 6, 1878, author and poet Carl Sandburg was born in the

Carl Sandburg State Historic Site

three-room cottage. Sandburg, born in this humble dwelling, in later life achieved international acclaim for his poetry and children's stories. He also wrote a six-volume biography of Abraham Lincoln. His ashes are buried behind the cottage in a small wooded park inscribed "Remembrance Rock." It is open year-round except major holidays. Hours: Daily, 9:00am-5:00pm.

Central Congregational Church
(309) 343-5145
Central Square
The Richardson Romanesque structure was built in 1898 of dark red sandstone transported from Michigan. The church is listed on the National Register of Historic Places. The building has beautiful rose windows and is located on the site of the Old First Church which was founded by the original settlers who arrived with George Washington Gale to start a religious community and college.
✪ Open year round

Galesburg Civic Art Center
(309) 342-7415
114 East Main Street
Ten exhibitions per year are held at the Art Center. The exhibits range from regional shows to annual national competitions called "Galex." Write or call for a listing of events that will take place.

Galesburg Railroad Museum
(309) 342-9400
Seminary and Mulberry Street
Tour a restored passenger train built by The Baldwin Locomotive Works in 1930. The fully-outfitted car and caboose were used by the Railway Mail Service and Railway Express Agency. An extensive collection of railroad memorabilia is housed in a 1923 Pullman parlor car as part of the museum. Open Memorial Day through Labor Day. Hours: Tuesday-Sunday, noon-5:00pm or by appointment.

Illinois Citizen Soldier Museum
(309) 342-1181
1001 Michigan Avenue
The museum houses artifacts from various wars from the War of 1812 through Desert Storm. It is located in the Robert Dunlap Room of the Admiral James Stockdale Building. Open year-round except on major holidays. Open Memorial Day and Veterans' Day. Monday-Friday, 9:00 am-2:00 pm; Sat. 9:00 am-4:00 pm.

Knox County Court House
(309) 343-3121
200 South Cherry Street
It took two years to build this sandstone building—1884-1886. The structure is reminiscent of the Romanesque period. It is open year round except for major holidays.

Orpheum Theatre

Hours: Monday-Friday, 8:30 am-4:30.

"Old Main" Knox College

The "Old Main" structure is the only remaining original site of the great Lincoln-Douglas debates held in 1858. You will find two large bronze plaques with the likeness of Abraham Lincoln and Stephen Douglas gracing the wall by which they stood. The building is registered as a National Landmark and is an example of American Gothic Revival architecture. Open September-May,

except major holidays. House: Monday-Friday, 8:00 am-4:30 pm, or by appointment.

Orpheum Theatre

(309) 342-2299
57 South Kellogg Street

The theater was built as a vaudeville house and hosted many early stars of stage and screen, including the late Jack Benny, George Burns and Houdini. Today it continues to reflect its former glory by bringing to its stage a diverse blend of top entertainment. The building shows a variety of architecture of the nineteenth century. Open year-round except major holidays. For admittance go to the Theatre Office at 60 S. Kellogg.

Annual Events

Visit us during one of our weekend events! Contact the Galesburg Area Convention and Visitors Bureau for dates and more information

February
• Chocolate Festival
March
• Rootabaga Jazz Festival
June
• Galesburg Railroad Days
• Seminary Street Taste
July
• Art-In-The-Park

August
• Knox County Fair
• Heritagefest
September
• Stearman Fly-In
• Taste of Galesburg
October
• Knox County Science Drive

Shopping and Dining

The downtown district is a bustling city center with a mix of historic and contemporary architecture which provides unique and exciting shopping. You will find over 130 retail stores with plenty of free parking. On the north edge of the city is the Sandburg Mall with over 50 merchants. At one time nearly abandoned, Seminary Street

Horse drawn antique carriage ride.

Photo by Robert Huddle

Historic Commercial District has been restored with specialty shops and marvelous restaurants. The catalyst that started the restoration was the Calico Cat. There you will find photos which chronicle the street's earlier days. It also provides visitor information.

The antique buff will find 10 different shops in which to browse and barter for goods. Antiques and collectibles from some of the Midwest's finest dealers are found in the Galesburg Antique Mall. The mall is located in a historically restored building on the corner of Main and Seminary.

You will find many dining opportunities. Write for a list of restaurants — fast food, family restaurants, and big chains.

Conclusion

For further information contact:
Galesburg Area CVB
2163 East Main Street
P.O. Box 60
Galesburg, Illinois 61402-0060
(309) 343-1194
www.galesburg.org\visitor

Tips

✔ Lake Storey Recreational Area offers year-round outdoor adventure (309) 345-3683

✔ Snakeden Hollow is a 2,470 acre State Fish and Wildlife Area. Great place for enjoying wildlife and seasonal fishing and hunting.

Get Away to Galesburg . . .

❝ You'll experience tradition and history when you visit Galesburg. The city surprises visitors with its accessibility and out-of-the-way charm, its historic buildings and modern day convenience, its strength of steel and its poet's sensitivity. Galesburg's got it all!

Galesburg is in the heart of Western Illinois, an area of the Prairie State rediscovered by modern day travelers. Conveniently located along Interstate 74, a major travel artery in the state, Galesburg is the perfect getaway.

Take the Victorian architecture, recreational facilities, cultural opportunities, great restaurants, and affordable lodging. Add a historic shopping district in the thriving downtown area, an antique mall in addition to several antique shops, and a modern mall. Mix with the Carl Sandburg State Historic Site, the Galesburg Railroad Museum, a Lincoln-Douglas debate site at Knox College's "Old Main," the restored Browning Mansion, and the Orpheum Theatre. Blend in lots of fun festivals and friendly people, the result is a great recipe for a stop while on a cross-country trek or for a weekend of wandering.

Using Galesburg as a hub city, you are within an hour's drive of riverboat excursions and riverboat gambling in both Peoria and and the Quad Cities. Monmouth (birthplace of Wyatt Earp and home of Western Stoneware, producer of Sleepy Eye pieces) is 15 miles west, Bishop Hill (a restored Swedish settlement from the mid-1800s) is 20 miles north, and Nauvoo, a Mormon settlement, is 90 miles southwest along the scenic National Great River road.

On behalf of the Galesburg Area Convention and Visitors Bureau, I cordially invite you to *Get Away to Galesburg . . .* a city rich in history, built on a tradition of pride, where you'll find lots to see and do. Come visit us. Galesburg loves company! ❞

—Mary Landon
Director
Galesburg Area CVB

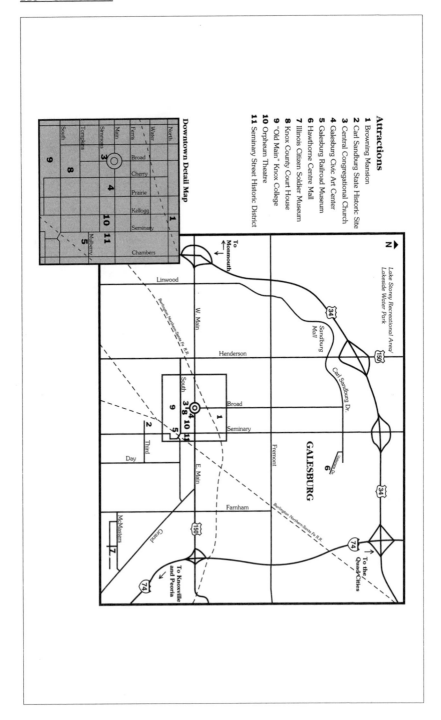

Attractions

1 Browning Mansion
2 Carl Sandburg State Historic Site
3 Central Congregational Church
4 Galesburg Civic Art Center
5 Galesburg Railroad Museum
6 Hawthorne Centre Mall
7 Illinois Citizen Soldier Museum
8 Knox County Court House
9 "Old Main" Knox College
10 Orpheum Theatre
11 Seminary Street Historic District

Downtown Detail Map

Peoria
Playing Better Than Ever

Location

Located on Interstate 74 in Peoria County.

History

The town named for an Indian tribe is the seat for Peoria County. Father Marquette and the explorer Joliet were the first non-Indians to venture in the area in 1673. In 1680, Robert Cavalier, Sieur de LaSalle, Henri de Tonti and Pere Louis Hennepin led a contingent of about 30 friars, artisans, priests, voyageurs, and Indian guides to the area. Just beyond Lake Peoria, they erected Fort Creve Coeur, "a heart breaking affair." Following LaSalle's exit, the fort was abandoned three months after its construction.

In 1691 the remnants of Fort St. Louis were moved to Lake Peoria where Lake Pimiteoui was established. Though the British gained control of the area in 1763, the treaties of the French and Indian War had little impact on the distant trading post. The village was visited by forces under the command of George Rogers Clark during the Revolutionary War.

French settlers sustained the village and by as early as 1764 it was referred to as Piorias with a nickname of AuPe which was short for Au Pioria or "to Peoria."

In 1812 the Illinois Militia, as part of the American forces, deported the French settlers whom they believed to be sympathetic to the Potawatami Indians, enemies of the American forces in the War of 1812. By 1813 Fort Clark was built and soon became the center for growth in the Peoria area.

By 1819 Americans ventured along the Illinois River to the former French settlement. They created what became Peoria County in 1825.

Peoria grew over the next ten years with an estimated population of 2,000. As travel and commerce on the Illinois River continued, Peoria grew even larger. By the late 1800s the infamous line "Will it play in Peoria?" began to spread through the country as traveling vaudeville acts, theatrical groups and musicians landed upon the river's shores. The years leading into the 1900s have given Peoria a memorable past which to this day gives modern Peoria a unique twist.

Getting Started

Before beginning your tour, stop by the Peoria Area Convention and Visitors Bureau located at 403 N.E. Jefferson Street. Information is available on dining, accommodations and attractions throughout the area. The Bureau will also send information to interested tourists. Please call their office at 1-800-747-0302 to have a packet sent to you.

Attractions

African American Museum Hall of Fame
(309) 673-2206
309 Dusable Street, Proctor Center

The museum is an educational institution depicting the life and culture of African Americas.

Illinois Historical Water Museum
(309) 671-3744
123 S.W. Washington
The museum is opened by appointment only. It features photographs and historical equipment once used in the purification of drinking water. The museum is located in a unique historically preserved building with turrets, gargoyles and winding staircases.

John C. Flanagan House
(309) 674-1921

Flanagan House

942 NE Glen Oak Avenue
This American Federalist style home was built in 1837 by John Flanagan. The home is the oldest standing residence in Peoria and is headquarters of the Peoria Historical Society. Tours are available Monday through Friday 10am to 3pm.

Lakeview Museum of Arts and Sciences/Planetarium
(309) 686-7000 or for planetarium (309) 686-NOVA
1125 W. Lake
The museum offers art and science exhibitions, a children's discovery center, and a planetarium featured in the *Guinness Book of World Records* as having the world's largest solar system model.

Pettengill-Morron House
(309) 674-4745
1212 W. Moss Avenue
This Mid-Victorian house, was built in 1868·by Moses Pettengill, a merchant from New Hampshire. On the National Register, the house actually portrays the life of the Morron family who were the last owners of the home. It offers the Butler's Pantry Gift Shop and candlelight tours at Christmas.

St. Francis Monastery
(309) 688-0094
3737 North Marybelle Avenue
This new monastery is known for its inspiring chapel and historic altar. The Marian Shrine has 1,500 relics of the saints on display. By appointment only, the hospitality center offers group lunch and dinner tours. Don't miss the spectacular Christmas display offered every holiday.

Wheels O'Time Museum
(309) 243-9020
Route 40
Located eight miles north of downtown Peoria on Illinois Route 40. Open by appointment only, the museum houses vintage and classic automobiles, gas engines, fire engines, airplanes, tractors, musical instruments, jukeboxes, toys, dolls, an animated miniature circus, and many hands-on displays.

Judge Jacob Gale House
Peoria Area Convention and Visitors Bureau
1-800-747-0302
403 N. E. Jefferson Street
Now home to the visitors bureau, the Judge Jacob Gale House was built in 1839 and still has the original Greek Revival style porch.

Peoria City Hall
(309) 674-8500
419 Fulton Street
This 1897 Flemish Renaissance style hall is on the National

Wildlife Prairie Park

Register of Historic Sites. The building has a classical style bell tower that was originally on Peoria's second city hall. Open weekdays.

Peoria Glen Oak Zoo and George Luthy Botanical Garden
(309) 686-3365
2218 N. Prospect Road
The zoo offers over 200 exotic and domestic animals as well as a petting zoo. The botanical gardens have four acres of herbs, perennial and award-winning roses. The conservatory houses an extensive collection of lush tropical rain forest plants, seasonal flower shows and a unique gift shop. Open year round.

Wildlife Prairie Park
(309) 676-0998
3826 N. Taylor Road
Wildlife Prairie Park
At this 2,000 acre zoological park, you can explore the pioneer farmstead complete with farm animals, a one-room schoolhouse, and a log cabin. Walk through intricate trails and view wolves, bison, black bear, cougar, and many more native Illinois animals in their

natural habitats. Located 10 miles west of Peoria on Interstate-74, exit on 82.

Satellite Attractions

❦ Brimfield

Jubilee College State Historic Site
(309) 243-9489
11817 Jubilee College Road
One of the first colleges built in Illinois, Jubilee College was founded by Philander Chase, the first Episcopal bishop of Illinois in 1840.

❦ Creve Coeur

Fort Creve Coeur
(309) 694-3193
508 Scenic Park Drive
A reproduction fort, trading house, Indian village and a small museum await visitors to this historic site. A picnic area with playground is available.

❦ Elmwood

Lorado Taft Museum
(309) 742-7791
302 N. Magnolia
The 1875 home was built by David Kemp and is now home to the Elmwood Historical Society. It houses a museum and a research library on the life and work of Lorado Taft, an Illinois sculptor.

❦ Lewiston

Dickson Mounds State Museum
(309) 547-3721
10956 N. Dickson Mounds Road
Explore 12,000 years of the Illinois River Valley's American Indian culture. Located in a rural setting, the museum includes artifacts, multi-media productions, interpretive exhibits and hands-on activities.

❦ Metamora

Illinois Mennonite Heritage Center
(309) 392-2518
Located on route 116 two miles west of Metamora, the center offers a museum, library and archives for immigrants from the 1820s to the present day. There is a restored barn, a grandfather house, native grasses, flowers and trees.

Metamora Courthouse
(309) 367-4470
113 E. Partridge
One of two remaining courthouses in the old Eighth Judicial Circuit, this courthouse is where Abraham Lincoln practiced law for twelve years. Built in 1845, the building was designed and built in the Classical Revival style using all native materials including locally kilned bricks.

✿ Pekin

Mineral Springs Park Pavilion
(309) 347-3178
Court Street
Built in 1904 by the Conklin-Reuling Company, the Mineral Springs Park Pavilion is one of the area's oldest park buildings. The park offers a lake for paddleboating and the annual Pekin Marigold Festival.

Dragonland Water Park
(309) 347-3178
Mineral Springs Park
This park offers two exciting water slides, a children's water play and sand area, sand volleyball, concessions and many family activities.

Tazewell County Courthouse
(309) 477-2201
414 Court Street
Dedicated in 1916, this courthouse was designed in the ever popular Classical Revival architectural style. A large interior court rises three floors to a spectacular glass highlight. Open weekdays.

Annual Events

The Peoria area offers a wide variety of annual events. For more information or a complete listing of events, call the Peoria Area Convention and Visitors Bureau at 1-800-747-0302. Annual festivals bring people from near and far to enjoy the picturesque countryside and the spectacular cityscape.

April
* Peoria Chiefs Class A Baseball Season — April through August. Pete Vonachen Stadium, Meinen Field.

May
* Metro Centre Farmers Market — Open May through October
* Race for the Cure — the largest all women's race of its kind, among the 56 national Susan G. Komen events. Metro Centre. Annually held the Saturday prior to Mothers' Day.

June
* Elmwood Strawberry Festival, Elmwood Town Square
* Old Fashioned Sunday, Glen Oak Park in Peoria
* Steamboat Days, Peoria Riverfront — annually held on Father's Day weekend
* Tremont Turkey Festival, Tremont
* The Return to Pimiteoui: An Intertribal Pow Wow, W.H. Sommer Park

July
* Independence Day Fire Works Spectacular, Glen Oak Park — Annually held on July 3
* Sky Concern, Peoria Riverfront Independence Day celebration — Annually held on July 4
* Heart of Illinois Fair, Exposition Gardens in Peoria

September
* Annual Pekin Marigold Festival, Mineral Springs Park in Pekin

- Annual Morton Pumpkin Festival, Downtown Morton
- Stark County Spoon River Drive, villages throughout Stark County

October

- Fulton County Spoon River Drive, located in 20 villages throughout Fulton County

November

- Nation's Oldest Santa Claus Parade, downtown Peoria
- East Peoria Festival of Lights and Parade, East Peoria

December

- Pettengill Morron House Candlelight Tours, Peoria
- St. Francis Monastery's Christmas Spectacular Indoor Display, Peoria

Shopping and Dining

The Peoria Area is a shopping haven with a variety of antique stores, shopping malls and plazas, specialty shops and art galleries. If it is food you crave, be sure to check out such unique dining experiences as seafood on the riverfront, home-brewed beer, mouth-watering barbecue, melt-in-your mouth steaks, and much more!

Conclusion

For further information on what the Peoria Area has to offer contact:
Peoria Area Convention and Visitors Bureau
403 N.E. Jefferson Street
Peoria, IL 61603
1-800-747-0302
www.peoria.org

Tips

✔ Don't miss Peoria's parks! They offer golfing, swimming, tennis, hiking, baseball, ice skating, and many more outdoor family activities!

✔ Peoria's rich vaudeville history still plays on today in the variety of art venues offered throughout the area. From dinner theater to opera and from jazz to blues, there is surely something to whet everyone's creative palette.

✔ Then there's the riverfront. Constantly undergoing transformations, visitors to the Peoria area won't want to miss the attractions and dining offered at this unique spot. Take a cruise and test your luck on the Par-A-Dice Riverboat Casino, or take an evening cruise aboard Peoria's own steamboat, The Spirit of Peoria. Plus a water taxi, with several drop-off points along the shores of East Peoria and downtown Peoria, to reach these hot spots in style!

❝ Scenic country sides, dazzling metropolitan lights and satisfied tastebuds await visitors on a daytrip to the Peoria area. With so many attractions to experience and see, try one of these suggested itineraries or create your own

For Antique Lovers Only

If it is something old you crave, spend a day browsing through antiques at the Illinois Antique Center or the Pleasant Hill Antique Mall. Located on Peoria's riverfront, the Illinois Antique Center offers two floors of booths and displays in a remodeled warehouse. While you're there, check out Willow Tree Books offering some of the finest used, antique and rare volumes, and taste a treat from Cafe Latte. The Pleasant Hill Antique Mall, one of the states largest malls located in East Peoria, offers a tearoom with home cooked meals and excellent homemade pies.

Fresh Air, Wildlife and Flowers

The great outdoors are a superb way to experience the scenic river valley Peoria calls home. The Forest Park Nature Center offers seven miles of hiking trails through a 500 acre wooded bluff that includes native prairie grasses and wildflowers. The 2,000 acre Wildlife Prairie Park, with such animals as buffalo, wolves, bears and bobcats, offers gift shops, playground areas, a petting zoo, and train rides.

A Stroll Through the Park

Family fun awaits visitors at Peoria's Glen Oak Park. Voted as one of the nations most beautiful parks, Glen Oak offers an outdoor amphitheater, a centennial playground, a zoo and botanical gardens. Located just a few blocks from Glen Oak Park is the Tower Park in Peoria Heights. Rising 175 feet via a glass elevator, this one-of-a-kind functional water tower offers the best panoramic view of the area.

Bring Out Your Inner Athlete

To catch a little diamond, rink or court side action, check out the Peoria Chiefs Class AA baseball team at Meinen Field, the Peoria Rivermen Hockey team at the Peoria Civic Center Arena or Bradley University Basketball. And if you want to get in on the athletic action yourself, visit Owen Center's indoor ice rink, East Side Centre's lagoon and water slide, or take a putt through the winding paths at Mt. Hawley Castle Miniature Golf. Whatever your sport, there's a venue to play it.

Lights, Microphone, and Entertainment

Whether it is a side splitting comedy or a roaring symphony you're looking for, such entertainment venues as the Jukebox Comedy Club, Peoria Symphony Orchestra, One World Coffee and Cargo Theatre, Zellmer's Dinner Theatre, Opera Illinois, or Peoria Ballet should satisfy visitor tastes. After all, Peoria's vaudeville days were the start of it all and one of several ways to "play in Peoria." **❞**

—GYC

The Peoria Area... Historical Sites and Major Attractions

- 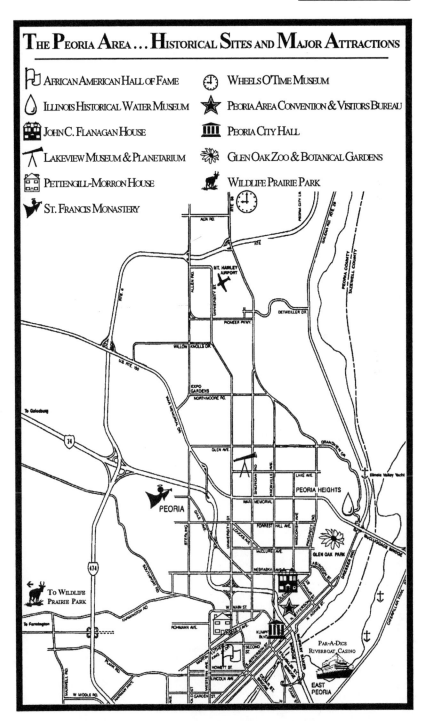 African American Hall of Fame
- Illinois Historical Water Museum
- John C. Flanagan House
- Lakeview Museum & Planetarium
- Pettengill-Morron House
- St. Francis Monastery

- Wheels O'Time Museum
- Peoria Area Convention & Visitors Bureau
- Peoria City Hall
- Glen Oak Zoo & Botanical Gardens
- Wildlife Prairie Park

Daytrip Illinois
Interstate 80

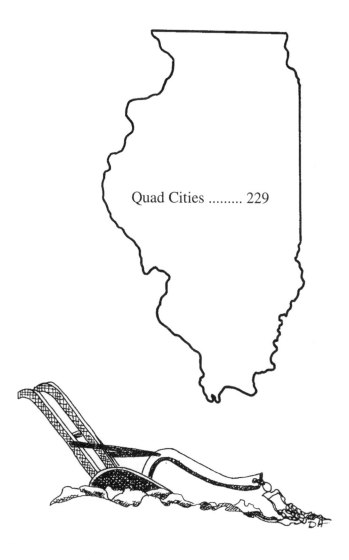

Quad Cities
Midwest Magic on the Mississippi River

Location

Served by Interstates 80, 88 and 74 and within a day's drive of several major metropolitan cities including Chicago, St. Louis, Des Moines and Minneapolis.

History

The connected towns of Rock Island, Moline, and East Moline in Illinois and Davenport and Bettendorf in Iowa are a conglomerate of history.

When Marquette arrived in the area in 1673, he found the Illinois, who were later supplanted by the Sauk and Foxe. In 1805 famous Colorado explorer Zebulon Pike also passed through the area.

Although Colonel George Davenport ventured to here in 1816 and constructed fortifications on what would later become Rock Island, settlers waited until 1828 to begin coming to this land by the Mississippi. This expansion was not welcomed by the inhabiting tribes. Atrocities on both sides caused the Black Hawk War. This unfortunate exchange resulted in the near extermination of the Sauk and Foxe, but secured the region for settlers to the region.

Rock Island County was organized in 1833. Its first county seat was Farhamsburg, and later Stephenson. The latter became Rock Island in 1841.

Rock Island was home for a short while to a doctor who owned the slave Dred Scott. Scott's petition for freedom went all the way to the Supreme Court, and its refusal of his freedom hastened the United States into the Civil War.

Steamboat traffic had a direct impact on local growth. In the 1840s and 1850s, as many as 1,900 boats docked in the Rock Island area. Logging also played a vital role in economic prosperity.

In 1843 the town of Moline was platted and five years later incorporated. The town became home to John Deere, who invented plows that could handle the gummy prairie soil. The Deere plant added to Moline's population, which by 1872 had reached 4,000.

Adjacent Rock Island became a center for the first railroads in the area in the fifties. In 1855 the first railroad bridge to cross the Mississippi was completed. The bridge became a hazard to river traffic and many boats commandeered by unwary pilots met their doom crashing into one of the bridge's piers.

These accidents prompted a lawsuit in 1856 against the Rock Island Railroad Company. The company was successfully defended by an up and coming lawyer by the name of Abraham Lincoln.

In 1862 Rock Island became the site of an arsenal. During the Civil War, the arsenal became a prision to more than 12,000 Confederate soldiers. Nearly 2,000 Confederate soldiers who died in captivity are buried at the Rock Island Arsenal.

Both lumbering and plow manufacturing contributed to the economic rise of Moline and Rock Island. These and other enterprises eventually led to the founding of East Moline, Illinois and of Davenport, Iowa.

➡ Getting Started

Enjoy the Quad Cities experience in Davenport/Bettendorf, Iowa and Rock Island/Moline/East Moline, Illinois.

Start your visit by stopping by the Convention and Visitors Bureau located at 2021 River Drive Moline, IL.
(309) 788-7800, 1-800-747-7800
www.visitquadcities.com
FAX (309) 788-7898.

The Quad Cities has four other welcome centers where you will find a full array of brochures, programs and information.

Mississippi Valley
Welcome Center
900 Eagle Ridge Road Exit 306
Interstate 80 at US
Highway 67
LeClaire, Iowa (319) 289-3009

Mississippi Rapids
Welcome Center
Interstate 80 Eastbound
Rapid City, Illinois
(309) 496-2145

Mississippi River
Visitors Center
West End of Arsenal Island
(309) 794-5338

Union Station Welcome Center
102 South Harrison Street
Davenport, Iowa
(309) 788-7800 Ext. 305

Attractions

MOLINE

Butterworth Center
(309) 765-7971
Visit the 1892 home of Mr. and

Mrs. William Butterworth. The house was built for Mrs. Butterworth, granddaughter of John Deere. ◎ Tours by appointment

Celebration Belle
(309) 764-1952 or 1-800-297-0034, Fax: (309) 764-1966.
Take a cruise on the 800-passenger paddlewheel riverboat. There are serveral excursions from which to choose.

Channel Cat Water Taxi
2501 River Drive
(Queen of Hearts dock)
Experience the magic of the Mississippi River from the Quad Cities' newest attraction —the Channel Cat Water Taxi. The Channel Cat is a 49 passenger ferry that connects Moline, Bettendorf and the village of East Davenport with regular hour-long loops across the Mississippi River. It also has room for 20 bicycles, which offers bikers the chance to extend biking trips between riverfront trails on both the Iowa and Illinois sides of the Mississippi River. For more information contact Metro Link at (309) 788-3360, fax: (309) 788-7515.

Deere & Company
Administrative Center
(309) 765-4235
World headquarters for the John

Deere-Wiman House

Deere company are located in Moline. The 20,000 square foot structure was designed by the late Eero Saarinen and houses historical John Deere products

✪ Free admission

John Deere Visitors Pavilion
15th Street and River Drive
(309) 765-8000
The pavilion features interactive displays on food and farming, climbable exhibits of agricultural equipment and a retail store.
(309) 765-1000, fax 765-1003
✪ Free admission

Deere-Wiman House
(309) 765-7971
817 11th Avenue
Charles Deere built this home in 1872. His descendants lived in the house until 1976.
✪Free Admission

Playcrafters Barn Theatre
(309) 762-0330
4950 35th Avenue
You can enjoy live theater in this refurbished dairy barn. Performances are in September, November, January, March, May and July. Call for exact dates.

Quad City Downs
(309) 792-0202
Intertrack racing via satellite from Chicago area tracks year round. Call for dates and post times.

Quad City Music Guild
(309) 762-3259
Summer theater in Prospect Park. Call for performance times and features.

ROCK ISLAND

Augustana College Art Gallery
(309) 794-7469
Centennial Hall 7th Avenue and 38th Street
Enjoy the changing exhibits in the gallery. You will also find a variety of interpretive programs. Closed in the summer months.
✪ Free admission

Black Hawk State Historic Site
(309) 788-9536
Blackhawk Road
The early Indian city of Saukenuk used to sprawl over the grounds that are now an Illinois State Park. Rock bluffs and wooded trails await the hearty explorer.

Chippiannock Cemetery
(309) 788-6622
2901 12th Street
Located on Manitou Ridge are 60 acres of unusual monuments and grave markers. Tour brochures are available in the office.

Circa '21 Dinner Playhouse
(309) 786-7733
Dinner shows and matinees are held in this beautiful 1920s

Black Hawk State Historic Park

vaudeville house. You will enjoy Broadway's finest musicals and comedies as well as children's theater productions.

Colonel George Davenport Home Arsenal Island

(309) 786-7336

George Davenport served with the Americans in the War of 1812 after which he established a log cabin trading post on the island in 1816.

Hauberg Indian Museum

(309) 788-0177

1510 46th Avenue

Artifacts from the Sauk and Fox tribes are on display featuring the geography and ecology of the upper Mississippi River.

✪ Free admission

Mississippi River Visitors Center—Lock and Dam 15

(309) 794-5338

The U.S. Army Corps of Engineers runs this display featuring the geography and ecology of the Upper Mississippi River.

✪ Free Admission

National Cemetery and Confederate Cemetery

Rodman Avenue

The final resting place for more than 1,900 Confederate prisoners who were incarcerated during the Civil War.

Rock Island Arsenal Museum

(309) 782-5021

Period weaponry along with educational displays are on display here.

The District

309 788-6311

This is a place worth exploring for fun, arts, entertainment and special events. You may call for a schedule of events. There are restaurants, night clubs, special musical events, festivals, games and great food.

Quad City Botanical Center
2525 4th Avenue
This conservatory with over 6,400 square feet features tropical trees and plants, a 14-foot waterfall and a bridge over reflecting pools. Flower shows and special events.
(309) 794-0991
fax: (309) 786-4982.

BETTENDORF, IOWA

Family Museum of Arts and Sciences
(319) 344-4106
2900-18th Street
This museum is filled with hands-on history and science exhibits for families.

DAVENPORT, IOWA

Adler Theatre
(319) 326-8555 Zip 52801
This art deco theater is tops in the country. You will find a variety of entertainment from musicals, rock concerts, pop concerts, symphonies, comedies to shows for the entire family.

Davenport Museum of Art
(319) 326-7804
1737 W. 12th Zip 52804
The museum houses over 3,000 works of art.

Quad City Symphony
(319) 322-0931

The lighted span of the Centennial Bridge link the Illinois and Iowa Quad Cities

P.O. Box 1144 Zip 52804
Write for place and schedule of
musical events.

**The Putnam Museum of
History and Natural Science**
(319) 324-1933
1717 W. 12th Street zip 52804
The museum features the
history and wildlife of the
Mississippi River valley and the
Quad Cities.

**VanderVeer Park
Botanical Park**
(319) 326-7818
215 West Central Park Zip 52803
The rose lover will find 1,800
roses that bloom from early June
to frost. Special floral displays
may be seen throughout the year
at the conservatory.
✪ Children Free

Wacky Waters
(319) 388-9910
Off Interstate 80 on North Fair-
mont
This is the largest water park in
the Quad City area.

Satellite Attractions

🍂 Aledo, IL 61231
Essley Noble Museum
1406 SE 2nd Avenue
309 582-2280
Almost 15,000 items dating from
1827 are on display, as well as a
one-room schoolhouse and an
agricultural shed.

🍂 Coal Valley, IL 61240

Niabi Zoological Park
309 799-5107
Box 13008 Niabi Zoo Road
Enjoy a family picnic, a train ride,
the education center and the more
than 400 animals from over 150
species.

🍂 Dixon, IL 61021
John Deere Historic Site
815 652-4551
Let a tour guide lead you through
John Deere's restored pioneer
home. You will see a blacksmith
at work in a reconstructed blacksmith shop. Tour the archeological
exhibit hall and the original site of
the blacksmith shop.

🍂 LeClaire, IA 52758

Buffalo Bill Museum
319 289-5580
200 N. River Drive
Take a historical look at the life
and times of Buffalo Bill Cody, a
native of LeClaire. Brochures
available for car tours.

🍂 Long Grove, IA
319 381-1114
Scott County Park
This recreated 1800s and early
1900s village is located on a three

acre site. Visit its 16 historic buildings.

🍃 **New Boston, IL 61272**

New Boston Museum
309 587-8440
302 Main
Visit this 1856 home with period items and Indian artifacts. Open Sundays 1-5 by appointment

🍃 **Princeton IA**

Buffalo Bill Cody Homestead
319 225-2981
Boyhood home of Buffalo Bill Cody. Explore the rich history of this outstanding government scout and Wild West showman.

Special Events

The Quad Cities hosts spectacular festivals, special events and sporting events every weekend all year long. Call 1-800 747-7800 for dates and additional updated events.

January
• Eagle Watch
• Bald Eagle Days
February
• Quad City Symphony Orchestra Concert—call for schedule
• QC Homebuilders Home Show
March
• "Symphony in Bloom" Lawn,

Garden and Flower Show
• WQAD-TV Kid's Count Expo
May
• Tour Season Opening of Col. Davenport House
• MIP Arts & Crafts Fair
• Quad Cities Jazz Festival
• Family Celebration at the Learning Campus
• Rhythm and Food Festival
June
• Rhubarb Festival, Aledo
• Quad City Air Show
July
• Mercer County Fair
• Rock Island County Fair Rodeo
• Old Fashioned 4th of July Celebration
• Amvets 4th of July Parade
• Firecracker Run
• Moline Riverfest
• Mississippi Valley Blues Fest
• John Deere Classic (PGA tourney)
• Bix Beiderbecke Memorial Jazz Festival
• Quad-City Times Bix 7 Mile Run
• Bix Street Festival
• Great Mississippi Valley Fair
August
• The Tug
• Ya Maka My Weekend/Boonoonoonoos!
• R.I. Argus Go Kart Gran Prix
September
• Rock Island Labor Day Parade
• Riverssance
• Quad Cities Marathon

October
- MIP Arts and Crafts Fair
- Laser Light Fright Night

November
- Festival of Trees
- Julmarknad

December
- Christmas Walk
- Messiah by G.F. Handel
- Christmas Victorian Walk

Shopping and Dining

Shop till you drop opportunities await visitors to antique stores, unusual gift shops, art galleries as well as stores for mall lovers. Fine dining awaits the traveler from fast-food to the finest cuisine.

Tips

✔ Quad City Airport offers convenient connections on four major airlines with 50 flights daily.

✔ 5,000 sleeping rooms range from intimate B & B's to luxury hotels and lodges.

✔ Three major convention facilities offer up to 100,000 square feet of meeting and exhibit space.

66 Whatever your reason for visiting, you'll have a magical time in one of the most affordable and exciting getaways you have ever experienced . . . the Quad Cities. Davenport/Bettenfort, Iowa and Rock Island/Moline/East Moline, Illinois.

The Quad Cities is a major metropolitan area of 400,000 located in Western Illinois and Eastern Iowa on the Mississippi River, just 160 miles west of Chicago, Illinois, and 175 miles east of Des Moines, Iowa.

The mighty Mississippi River has always been the Quad Cities number one draw, especially now with three riverboat casinos — Casino Rock Island, the President and Lady Luck. Non-gaming excursions are ever popular aboard the Celebration Cruises in Moline and River Cruises in LeClaire, Iowa. And the brand-new Channel Cat Water Taxi whisks you from one side of the Mississippi River to the other during spring, summer and fall.

Step back in time at the Buffalo Bill Cody Homestead, the Colonel Davenport House, or the Black Hawk State Historic Site. Or stop by the state-of-the-art visitors pavilion of Deere & Company to learn about Western Illinois' agricultural history. Or visit the Rock Island Arsenal and its museum to learn more about the role of the Quad Cities in the Civil War and in its U.S. military history.

There are more than a dozen museums offering 200 million year old fossils as well as a children's museum offering the most up-to-date fun. The brand new Family Museum of Arts and Sciences in Bettendorf is a brand new interactive museum where anyone can have fun and learn.

The Putnam Museum of History and Natural Science has undergone an expansion which doubles the space for learning and excitement.

Bald eagles migrate south to the Quad Cities each winter to the delight of birders and outdoor enthusiasts. From December through February, the birds fish in the open waters of the locks and dams and roost at night along the Mississippi's wooded bluffs.

Of course there is more to see and do in the Great Quad Cities. For more information, contact the Quad Cities Convention and Visitors Center Bureau, 102 South Harrison Street, Davenport, Iowa 52801 or 2021 River Drive, Moline, IL 61265-1472. **99**

—Joe Taylor
President/CEO, Quad Cities CVB

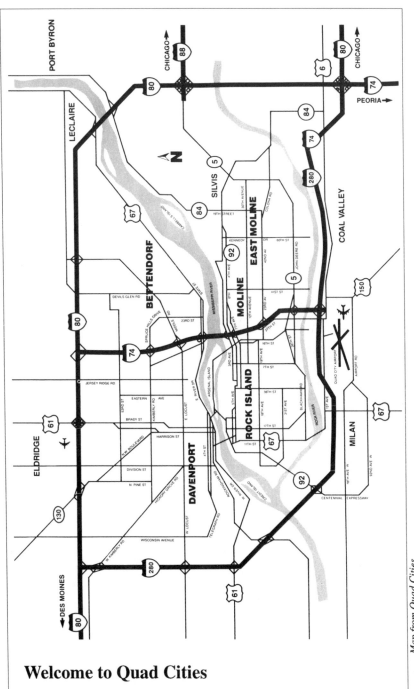

Welcome to Quad Cities

*Map from Quad Cities
Convention and Visitors Bureau*

Daytrip Illinois
Interstate 88

Aurora
City of Lights

Location
Located just 37 miles from downtown Chicago, Aurora's a town that celebrates its past with entertainment and attractions. Built on the banks of the Fox River, the area provides lots of outdoor recreation, family fun, shopping and entertainment for all ages.

History
Joseph McCarty, a New Yorker, came to the region in 1834 and found a large Potawatomi village. He constructed a sawmill on the Fox River. When the town was platted in 1836, more than a dozen pioneers had joined him.

In 1848 the introduction of the Chicago, Burlington and Quincy Railroad stimulated growth and assured the town's permanence. In 1857 Eastern Aurora and Western Aurora became a single entity. In 1881 Aurora became the first town in Illinois to light its streets with electricity. By 1890 the city had grown to more than 2,000 inhabitants.

➡ Getting Started
Begin your visit by stopping by the Aurora Area Convention and Tourism Council, 44 W. Downer Place, and let them help you plan your Aurora vacation. Call the AACTC at (800) 477-4369 or www.enjoyaurora.com for visitor guides, bike maps and a continual update on annual events.

Attractions

Aurora Art & History Center
(630) 906-0650 or 0654
20 E. Downer Place

Local history objects, photo exhibits, and museum gift store.

Aurora Regional Fire Museum
(630) 892-1572
New York and Broadway
The museum features photos from the great Chicago Fire of 1871. Other memorabilia, displays with uniforms, fire fighting equipment and motorized engines will be found there.

Blackberry Farm's Pioneer Village
(630) 892-1550

Paramount Arts Center

Barnes Rd. at W. Galena Blvd.
Children will enjoy the Discovery
Barn where they will find cuddly
lambs, pygmy goats, peep chicks
and a pen full of piglets. They can
enjoy rides on a carousel, a
miniature train or in a horse-drawn
carriage. Museums on the ground
portray a bygone era.

Grand Army of the Republic Memorial Hall
(630) 906-0654
23 E. Downer Place
The Memorial Hall houses Civil War
military memorabilia related to
Aurora.

Michael Jordan Golf Center
(630) 851-0023

Michael Jordan Drive
Superstar Michael Jordan has
chosen Aurora as the site for a golf
education center. The center has
covered and heated tees, a short
game practice area, putting greens
and an NBA-themed miniature
golf course for the kids. It's a great
place to pick up Michael Jordan
tee shirts and golf accessories.

Paramount Arts Centre
(630) 896-6666
23 E. Galena Boulevard
The 1930 era movie theater has
been restored to its original
splendor. The theater is listed in
the National Register of Historic
Places and has a seating capacity of
1,888. It hosts a variety of special

entertainment, from Broadway plays to a variety of local art exhibits.

Phillips Park
(630) 898-7228 General Information
(630) 851-8686 Aquatic Center
This is an old-fashioned city park with a newfangled water park. The 250 acre park has a small zoo, a colorful sunken garden, and an 18-hole golf course.

Schingoethe Center for Native American Cultures
(630) 844-5402
347 S. Gladstone Avenue
The center rotates displays of Native American artifacts.

SciTech
(630) 859-3434
18 W. Benton
SciTech has over 200 hands-on exhibits on weather, aquatic animals, light, electricity and sound, all housed in a historic post office. An outing packed with fun for the entire family.

Hollywood Casino Aurora
1-800-888-7777
Explore the excitement of Las Vegas-style dockside riverboat gaming, with blackjack, roulette, slots and more. Even if you're not a gambler, you'll enjoy a walk through the Hollywood Casino

Pavilion with its large collection of Hollywood movie memorabilia on display.

Walter Payton's Roundhouse Complex
(630) 264-BREW
205 North Broadway
Football superstar, Walter Payton, turned Aurora's historic railroad roundhouse into the Walter Payton Roundhouse Complex where you will find the area's largest microbrewery, an outdoor concert courtyard and restaurant. While there be sure to visit the **Walter Payton Museum**, where you will see Payton's Super Bowl Ring, a life size Wheaties Box and other mementos from his stellar career.

William Tanner House Historical Society
(630) 897-9029
Cedar and Oak Streets
Historic home with Victorian furnishings.

Satellite Attractions,

❦ **North Aurora**

Red Oak Nature Center
(630) 897-1808
2343 S. River Street
Nature center museum, hike and bike trails, a picnic area, cross-country skiing, canoeing. ❦

❧ Yorkville

Chapel on the Green
(630) 553-6777
105 W. Center Street
Here you will find an 1855 church building featuring an 1899 pipe organ and Heritage Hall.

Lyon Farm and Village
(630) 554-3064
Rte 71 Yorkville
Fifteen historical structures— write or call for schedule of special events.

❧ Oswego

The Little White School House
(630) 554-2999
Jackson at Polk Street
The restored Greek Revival building serves as a school house where you will find a collection of Oswego memorabilia.

Annual Events

We invite you to join us for one of the many exciting events held throughout the year in the Aurora area. For continual updates contact 1-800-477-4369.

May
• Native American Pow Wow — site for a contemporary celebration of Native American music, food, arts, dance and crafts.

• Bow Hunters National Tournament — 1,000 bow hunters gather from all over the U.S. to compete in this tournament.

June
• Mid-American Canoe Race — canoeists come from all over the United States to participate in a 22-mile race on the Fox River.
• Aurora Airport Air-Expo and Fly-In — takes place in Sugar Grove where you can view active duty military planes, WWII planes, ground battles and take an airplane ride.
• Civil War Days — takes place in Yorkville. A battlefield of the Civil War comes alive with Union troops and the appearance of President Lincoln. Artillery and infantry skirmish on the Crimmins Bridge.
• Blues on the Fox — Festival honors legendary musicians who performed at Aurora's Leland Hotel in 1937-38. Featuring a free blues stage in downtown Aurora and a "Blues Crawl" of area restaurants and pubs.
• Oswego Prairie Fest —"Festival of Brass".

July
• Independence Day fireworks and display over the Fox River.
• Sugar Grove Corn Boil at Sugar Grove. The best homegrown sweet corn in the state, car show, fire department tournament, children's zoo, commercial

Downtown Aurora Canoe Chute

booths, food and many more fun activities.

August

- Fox Valley RV and Outdoor Show — Large display of RVs, boats, trucks, lawn equipment, etc., for sale or viewing. Kane County Fairgrounds (630) 415-1263.
- Montgomery Fest — *Montgomery, IL.* The Montgomery Park comes alive with kiddie rides, games, a craft show, a parade, a corn boil, fireworks and much more.
- North Aurora Days — Fun for the whole family includes golfing, sand volleyball, community dancing, an evening concert, 5 and 10 K runs, and more.
- SoulFest — Homecooked soul food to celebrate heritage days. Live music, games for children and much more.
- Yorktown Riverfront Festival — *Yorkville, Ill.,* sponsors fun for the family with a carnival, food booths, entertainment, canoe racing, a fishing contest, etc.

September

- Yorkville Riverfront Festival. Annual festival showcases Yorkville's Riverfront Park located on Hydraulic Street. Carnival, hole in one golf on the river. Food and entertainment. Free Admission. For more information call (630) 553-4230.

November
- Christmas in the Country — *Sandwich*, IL. Christmas craft fair.

December
- Lehnertz Circle Christmas Display and drive-by fantasyland of Christmas lights.
- First Night Aurora — Enjoy the visual and performing arts while ringing in the New Year.

Shopping and Dining

There is an outstanding selection of shops and stores. You will find quaint boutiques, specialty shops, mega malls and major department stores to fit every person's need. The Aurora area is well known for its antique shops as well. There are many eating establishments from fast food to the finest dining.

Conclusion

For further information contact:
Aurora Area Convention and Tourism Council
44 W. Downer Place
Aurora, IL 60506
(630) 897-5581 • 1-800 477-4369
(630) 897-5589 FAX
Website: www.enjoyaurora.com

Tips

✔ There are a number of bike rental shops along the biking and hiking trails in northern Illinois. Most shops are open on weekends, so biking fun on the Midwest's best biking trails is easy to find.

✔ The Aurora Historical Society is a good place to start your visit to Aurora. There are displays of Victorian era Midwestern life, and mastodon bones found in Aurora.

✔ Aurora has the largest collection of public buildings designed by architect George Grant Elmslie. The Tourism Council has maps for self-guided walking tours of Aurora's historic district.

✔ The Hollywood Casino—Aurora is a good place to play, but it's also a great place for a family dinner. Surround yourself with Hollywood props in the Epic Buffet or enjoy the glamour of a gourmet meal at Cafe Harlow. The restaurants are open to the public.

Welcome to Aurora

66 The **Hollywood Casino-Aurora** offers the excitement of Las Vegas-style riverboat gaming, with blackjack, roulette, slots and more. Even if you're not a gambler, you'll enjoy a walk through the Hollywood Casino Pavilion, with its large collection of Hollywood movie memorabilia on display. Nearby, football superstar Walter Payton has turned Aurora's historic railroad roundhouse into the **Walter Payton Roundhouse Complex,** the area's largest microbrewery, outdoor concert courtyard and restaurant. While you're at the Roundhouse, be sure to visit the **Walter Payton Museum,** where you will see Payton's Super Bowl Ring, life size Wheaties Box, and other mementos from his stellar career. Another sports superstar, Michael Jordan, has chosen Aurora as the site of the **Michael Jordon Golf Center,** a golf education center with covered and heated tees, a short game practice area, putting greens and an NBA-themed miniature golf course for the kids. It's a great place to pick up MJ tee shirts and golf accessories.

For family fun, start at **Blackberry Farm's Pioneer Village**, a turn of the century village with costumed craftspeople who will help you re-live the farming days of yesteryear. There are several museum buildings on the site, and the kids will enjoy the miniature train rides and antique carousel. Another fun family place is SciTech, the interactive science and technology center. **SciTech** has over 200 hands-on exhibits on weather, aquatic animals, light, electricity and sound, all housed in a historic post office. **Phillips Park** is an old-fashioned city park with a new fangled water park. The 250 acre park has a small zoo, a colorful sunken garden, and an 18 hole golf course. For more outdoor fun, the Aurora area has the best **biking and hiking trails** in the Midwest. **99**

—Aurora Area Convention & Tourism Council

Blackhawk Waterways
A Moving Adventure
Through Northwest Illinois

Location

Blackhawk Waterways is made up of four picturesque counties—Carrol, Lee, Ogle and Whiteside. The counties can be reached by several highways and byways. The major access route is Interstate 88.

History

The Blackhawk Waterways Convention and Visitors Bureau was started in 1992 to increase the promotion of tourism in Northwest Illinois. We believe we have many fine places to promote for visitors and residents alike! We encourage people to visit our office and tour the fine community of Polo while on their trip.

Mississippi Scenic View

➡ Getting Started

Begin your visit by stopping by the Blackhawk Waterways Convention and Visitors Bureau located in the historic Burns House, on 201 N. Franklin Avenue in Polo. Stop in and we will assist in planning your day!

Historic Structures, Monuments, Museums and Statues

☙ Carroll County

Campbell Center, Mt. Carroll
(815) 244-1173
Seminary Street off Rt. 78
The 14 acre campus has been in continuous use since 1853. In 1980 it was listed on the National Register for Historic places

Carrol County Courthouse
(815) 244-9171, *Mt. Carroll*
Corner of Market and Main Streets
The 1858 courthouse is listed on the National Register of Historic Places. The county seat was located in Mt. Carroll in 1843. The northernmost and oldest section of the current courthouse was built at that time.
✪ Free admission

Lanark Museum
(815) 493-2423, *Lanark*
140 W. Lanark Avenue
A private museum features cobblers' benches, pottery, clothing, old-fashioned bedding and old cooking utensils.
✪ Free admission

Lanark's Paint the Town Project
(815) 493-2307, Ext. 12, *Lanark*
Lanark's Paint the Town Project painted the 1880s era downtown store fronts to display their unique architecture and hues.
✪ Free admission

Mt. Carroll National Register Historic District
(815) 244-9161
Visit over 30 different historic sites in Mt. Carroll's Historic District. Free brochureS available at the Visitor's Center or from local merchants.
✪ Free admission

Oakville Complex
(815) 244-3474
Between Rts 78 and 40 near Timberlake and the Oakville Golf Course, *Mt. Carroll*
This is a pioneer settlement that includes The Wietzel Cabin, Blacksmith Shop, McKean Granary, Peter Hay Cabin, Oakville School and Museum.
✪ By appointment only; leave message

Palisades Pre-Historic and Indian Artifacts
(815) 273-2741, *Savanna*
2 miles north of Savanna on Rt. 84
Artifacts and exhibits dating to

pre-historic times.

✪ Admission fee

The Soldiers and Sailors Monument and Annex
(815) 244-0221, *Mt. Carroll*
Mt. Carroll Courthouse lawn, Rt. 78
A monument was dedicated in 1891 in honor of the 1285 Carroll County men who lost their lives. Atop the monument is a cavalry man designed by the famous Lorado Taft. You will find this listed in *Ripley's Believe it or Not.*

✪ Free admission

✤ Lee County

Amboy Depot Museum
(815) 857-3814, *Amboy*
50 South East Avenue
This was the division headquarters for the Illinois Central Railroad. Today it houses local artifacts of Amboy and the surrounding area. Palmer Schoolhouse displays can be seen and outside is a steam locomotive.

✪ Free • Donations accepted

Amboy Pharmacy
(815) 857-2323 Fax 815-857-3466
202 E. Main Amboy
One of the oldest "Old Tyme Soda Fountains" left in Illinois. The store will bring back memories of the past with wooden shelves, floors and penny candy.

Franklin Creek Gristmill
(815) 456-2878, *Franklin Grove*
1872 Twist Road
Only truly water powered operational grist mill in Illinois.

Dixon Theatre
(815) 284-2715, *Dixon*
P.O. Box 682, S. Galena
The historic theater was built in 1920 and currently is being restored by the citizens of Dixon.

✪ Entertainment for all

HI Lincoln Building
(815) 456-3030, *Franklin Grove*
Classic 1860's stone building. Lincoln Highway National Headquarters.

Lincoln Statue
(815) 288-1840
Lincoln Statue Drive, *Dixon*
The statue depicts Abraham Lincoln at age 23 in his military uniform. He was a volunteer soldier, serving in the Blackhawk Indian War of 1832.

✪ Free Admission

Loveland Museum
(815) 284-2741, *Dixon*
513 W. Second Street
Featuring pictures and personal items of the town's founder, John Dixon, furnishings from a pioneer home, early farm tools, Native American artifacts, war items and more.

Donations accepted
✪ Free

Ronald Regan Boyhood Home and Visitor Center
(815) 438-28115 or
(815) 288-3404
816 S. Hennepin, *Dixon*
Visit the former President's boyhood home and visitors' center. The home was built in 1891 and has been restored. Guided tours available.
✪Admission

Sublette Armory
(815) 849-5432
203 W. Main, *Sublette*
Drive by and see one of the largest armories in the state of Illinois built in 1879. It housed the Co. F. 12th Infantry.
✪ Not open for tours

Sugar Grove Church and School
(815) 288-1890
Two and one half miles NW of Dixon on Palmyra Road to Sugar Grove Road, the school is over 100 years old, and served as a site for social gatherings in the community. It has been restored to its original condition.
✪ Free admission

☙ **Ogle County**

Aplington House
(815-946-2108
Corner of Locust & Franklin, *Polo*
An historic preservation museum focuses on the founding fathers, churches and one of the country's first six air stewardesses. Call for appointment
✪ Donations accepted

Battleground Memorial Park
(815) 645-2603, *Stillman Valley*
218 W. Main Street
Stillman's Run Memorial Park is the site of the oldest burial site in northern Illinois. Veterans of the Blackhawk War of 1832 are buried where they fought and died in the only war fought on Illinois soil.

Blackhawk Statue
(815) 732-6826, *Oregon*
Lowden Park, Lowden Road,
The statue stands 48 feet tall. It was designed by artist Lorado Taft and dedicated as a study of the character of the American Indian.
✪ Free admission

Burns House
(815) 946-2108
201 N. Franklin Avenue, *Polo*
Home to the Convention and Visitors Bureau, this is the first brick home to be built in Polo.

Civil War Cannons
(815) 732-3201
Corner of Rts. 64 and Illinois 2, at the Ogle County Courthouse
On the lawn of the county seat you will find two cannons. The one to the north is a Parrott-6 1/2" Naval rifle made in 1864 and weighing

Blackhawk Statue

special replica exhibit of the original blacksmith shop. Watch blacksmiths at work and learn about the first self-cleaning plow.
✪ Admission

Rochelle Railroad Park
(815) 562-8107
124 N. 9th St., *Rochelle*
See engines from 7 railroads and over 100 trains a day from an observation platform. Depot with gift shop.

Jarrett Prairie Center
(8151) 652-4551
7993 N. River Road, *Byron*
A hands-on natural history museum has living and preserved natural displays. You can climb through a real wolves den, watch industrious honeybees working in their see-through hive, dand view the heavens at Weiskopf Obersvatory.

9,722 pounds. The one to the south is a Columbiad built in 1846.
✪ Free

Flagg • Rochelle Public Library District
(815) 562-3431
619 4th Avenue, *Rochelle*
Founded by Andrew Carnegie in 1912, the interior has a wealth of oak woodwork and large windows. Placed on the National Register of Historic Places in 1973.

John Deere Historic Site
(815) 652-4551, *Grand Detour*
8393 S. Main, one block off Rt. 2.
In addition to the restored pioneer home of John Deere, there is a special replica exhibit of the original blacksmith shop. Watch blacksmiths at work and learn about the first self-cleaning plow.
✪ Admission

Lorado Taft Monuments
(815) 732-3201, *Oregon*
Famous sculptor Lorado Taft's

John Deere Historic Site

works are found throughout the area. In Lowden State Park you will find "The Muses," and in Mix Park you will find one of his beautiful sculpted fountains. They were erected in memory of Mr. & Mrs. Ruel Mared Peabody, pioneers in the area arriving in 1836.

Ogle County Courthouse
(815) 732-3201, *Oregon*
Corner of 4th & Washington,
This was built in 1892 and is on the National Register of Historic Places. Located on the grounds of the courthouse is a Soldier's Monument sculpted by Lorado Taft as a permanent record of the contribution of the men of Ogle County in the Civil War.

Ogle County Historical Society Museum
(815) 732-6876, *Oregon*
111 North Sixth Street
The museum houses memorabilia depicting Ogle County history.
✪ Free but donations accepted

Pride of Oregon
Hwy 2 North
Authentic paddlewheel boat. 102 feet of elegance and charm. Music, cocktails, dancing and fine dining. Located dockside of Riverside Restaurant. Call for complete schedule. 1-800-468-4222. Bus tours welcome.

❧ Whiteside County

Albany Indian Mounds State Historic Site
(309) 887-4335, *Albany*
Box 184
The mounds date back to 2000 B.C. As you walk the trails to the burial mounds, enjoy beautiful wildflowers along the path. Favorite activities of the site are cross country skiing and picnicking.

ASA Crook Home
(815) 537-5139
E. 3rd Street, *Prophetstown*
Whiteside county's first settler built the first frame house in the area in 1839. Open to the public.
✪ Donation accepted

Bears by Marge
(815) 659-2162, *Erie*
Main Street, Inside Village Variety Store
A toy museum is located in a loft! Dolls, toy trains and bears and more.

Dutch Windmill & Visitors Center on Great River Road
Authentic windmill built in the Netherlands and shipped to Fulton, Il by barge.

Carlton House Museum
(815) 772-4813 or (815) 772-3287
219 E. Main Street, *Morrison*
Twelve rooms of exhibits depict the history of Morrison. The museum is located in the oldest

Annual Autumn on Parade Festival

building in town.

✪ Free but donations accepted

Civil War Monument
(815) 537-5139
East 3rd Street, **Prophetstown**
Standing in memory of the Shiloh, Gettysburg, Kenisaw and Resaca battles stand the statues of a lone Civil War soldier.

Dillon Home Museum
(815) 622-6202
1005 E. 3rd Street, **Sterling**
Built in 1857 in the Italian Renaissance style, the home features the history of the Dillon family, Northwestern Steel and Wire and many fine antiques. Listed on the National Register of Historic Places.

✪ Admission

Heritage Canyon
(815) 589-2838
515 North 4th Street, **Fulton**
Located in an old 12 acre quarry on the Mississippi River is a restored, furnished mid-1800 settlement. Wander through wooded paths and hillsides that lead from one home site to another.

✪ Free but donations accepted

Little Red School House
(815) 625-0272
E. 11th Street, **Rock Falls**
Replica of an early 19th century American one room schoolhouse.

Morrison Historical Society
(815) 772-3287
Main Street, **Morrison**
Twelve rooms of exhibits depict the history of Morrison and the surrounding area history. This is the oldest building in town.

✪ Free but donations accepted

Ronald Reagan Birthplace
(815) 438-28115 or (815) 438-6395
11 S. Main Street, **Tampico**
Restored furnished apartment of our 40th president's birthplace. Photos, postcards, letters and souvenirs.

✪ Free admission. Call for guided tours. Open year round by appointment.

Old Settler's Cabin
(815) 284-3361
Lincoln Statue Drive, **Dixon**
A reconstructed log cabin built in 1894 as a tribute to the early settlers of Lee County. It was moved in 1969 to its present location and has been completely furnished.

Little Chocolatier

Blackhawk Chocolate Trail

This is a one of a kind experience as you roam through this beautiful countryside and country roads. Enjoy a day's trip on the **Blackhawk Chocolate Trail** where you will find some of the finest creators of this candy. Visit the general stores, bed and breakfasts, cafes, tea rooms, bakery, Log Cabin Lodge, gift shops and an old-fashioned soda fountain.

•• Carroll County

Fashions on Main
(815) 244-3111, *Mt. Carroll*
Dress and shoe store with 10 varieties of fudge, Fannie May Candy.

Opened Year round but closed on Holidays.

Sweet 'N' Counter
(815) 273-7340, *Savanna*
Open Year round. Old fashioned soda fountain and gift store. Holiday Amish made chocolates, chocolate phosphate sodas, chocolate sundaes, speciatlty chocolates such as soap and candles and chocolate covered peaches and coffee beans.

•• Ogle County

The Bakery at Conover Square
(815) 732-2545
201 N. Third, Oregon

Cookies, muffins, chocolate long johns, chocolate-filled long johns and brownies

The Cat & The Fiddle
(815) 562-4591, Rochelle
506 Sixth Avenue
Belgium Neuhaus Chocolate, chocolate mushrooms, truffles, gourmet chocolate covered nuts and blueberries, German chocolate, Swiss chocolate and liqueur chocolates.

The Cook's Collection
(815) 732-2926, Oregon
201 N. Third Street
Conover Square
Handmade fudge, Dutch chocolate coffee, dipped chocolates, sugar free chocolates and fudge, flavored cocoas and novelities.

Pinehill Fudge Collection and Historic B&B
(815) 732-2061, Oregon
400 Mix Street at Jackson
Free samples of exotic-flavored handmade fudge, Chocolate Gourmet Gift Gallery. Daily Chocolate Tea Parties. The "Originators of the Blackhawk Chocolate Trail.

White Pine Inn
(815) 946-3817, *Mt. Morris*
6712 W. Pines Road
Sweet Street Snicker's creme pie, chocolate sundaes, chocolate bark

peanut butter pie and chocolate specialities in the gift shop.

New York Bagel and Coffee Exchange
(815) 562-2435, *Rochelle*
340 May Mart Drive, Suite 115
Contemporary deli and gift shop with chocolate cheesecakes, chocolate chip bagels, pecan puddles, jumbo cashew puddles, chewy gooey chocolate pretzels, Swiss Mocha cake, Chocolate Cinnamon 14 layer cake, chocolate covered espresso beans, and much more.

↦ Whiteside County
Rock Falls and Sterling are located in Whiteside County and are part of the Blackhawk Waterways. See page 271 for more information about that area.

The Dutch Diner Family Restaurant
(815) 438-2096, *Tampico*
105 S. Main Street
Chocolate creme pie, peanut butter chocolate creme pie, Oreo, M&M, Snickers and Reese's flurries, hot fudge sundaes and hot fudge brownie.

Hillendale Bed & Breakfast
(815) 772-3454 or 1-800-349-7702, *Morris*
600 Lincolnway West (Rt. 30)
Apple chocolate pancakes, choco-

late cinnamon rolls, and/or chocolate fondue. Preparation time,30 minutes — everything is made fresh.

The Little Chocolatier, Inc.
(815) 626-2751 or 1-800-742-3240, *Sterling*
317 First Avenue
Hand-dipped chocolates, novelty candies, gourmet coffees and Espresso bar drinks.

Muffins 'N' More
(815) 624-7176 or
625-5116, *Rock Falls*
317 First Avenue
Chocolate chip muffins, chocolate pie, chocolate mousse and chocolate sundaes.

Fantasy Sweetes
(815) 622-3610
206 E. 3rd Street, *Sterling*
Reminiscent of Grandma's kitchen, smells of fresh baked cake, chocolate candies, brownies, chocolate deserts. Small cafe and whimsical gifts.

Youngstown Coffee House
(815) 626-3421 or 625-4130
201 E. 3rd Street, *Sterling*
Quad chocolate Raspberry muffins, Tiramisu, Carmel Fudge pecan torte, chocolate chocolate donuts, long johns, death by chocolate turtle cookies, mocha latte's and and cappuccinos, chocolate malts, the list goes on and on.

Annual Events

Many events are held throughout the year. Call or write for a complete listing of events and updates.

May
• Dutch Days Festival — *Fulton*. Wooden shoe dancing and wooden shoe making, authentic Dutch food, arts and crafts, parade, quilt show and much more. Held the first weekend in May. (815) 589-4545

July
• Let Freedom Ring Festival — *Mt. Morris*. Carnival, parade, car show, 10K run, queen crowning, food and fireworks. (815) 734-4114
• Dixon's Annual Petunia Festival — *Dixon*. Held in Page Park are a carnival, pancake breakfast, Taste of Sauk, craft show, kids day, children's events, car show, Beer Garden, Criterium, drum and bugle competition, parade, fireworks. (815) 2824-3361
• Fourth of July Celebration — *Prophetstown*. 3 on 3 basketball tournament at the high school, food, rides, games and fireworks at dusk. Prophetstown State Park. (815) 537-2301.
• Independence Day — *Mt. Carroll*. Parade starts at 5pm and ends at the athletic field. Food, music, entertainment and fireworks. (815) 244-9161.
• Freedom Festival — *Rochelle* at

Dutch Days Festival

Atwood Park. Parade, band concert, water wars, fireworks.
• *Byronfest* — A family festival including food, drink, entertainment, crafts, carnival, athletic events, car show, quilt show, children's fair and parade. (815) 234-5500.

August
• Carroll County Fair — *Milledgeville*. Farm animals, horse show, art, antiques, carnival rides, 4-H show, rodeo, tractor pull, demolition derby, country western show and food booths. (815) 493-2191.
• Whiteside County Fair — *Morrison*. Anniversary Harness racing, draft horse pull, tractor pull, demolition derby, carnival, country-western name entertainment, arts and crafts, hobbies, food booths, 6,000 exhibits and $90,000 in premiums. (815) 772-5189.

September
• Heritage Days — *Byron*. Family fun with quilts, crafts, antiques, art fair, children's games and movies, outdoor musical entertainment and lots of food. (815) 234-8535.

October
• Annual Autumn on Parade Festival — *Oregon*. Arts and crafts, castle tours, chase a pig, tug across Rock River, farmer's market, auto and tractor show, parade, 5K and fun walk/run, hayrides, quilt show, heritage craft demo's and much more. (815) 732-2100.

• Trail of Terror — A happening you will not want to miss from the last weekend in September through October 31. It is an experience of a lifetime. You will find fall festivals and events, haunted happenings, and pumpkin patches during the Halloween season. From Haunted happenings to scarecrow contests, antiques and crafts, festivals and pumpkin patches. There is plenty to do along Blackhawk Waterways' Trail of Terror. Write for more information or call 1-800-678-2108 to find out "Witch way do we go?"

Shopping and Dining

Anywhere you go you will find outstanding antique and craft shops, or you can shop one of the many country markets.

There are many fine restaurants throughout Blackhawk Waterways. Enjoy a mouth-watering lunch at one of the fine area restaurants. For those who enjoy staying at bed-and-breakfast, enjoy a leisure breakfast at one of the inns along the Rock River.

Tips

✔ Many of the family owned businesses on the chocolate trail celebrate the holidays, so please call ahead for holiday hours to avoid any disappointment.

✔ You will find every kind of outdoor recreation you can imagine. We are known as the "Great Outdoors." Our visitors guide has a map with the location of all river parks.

Conclusion

For further information contact:
Blackhawk Waterways Convention and Visitors Bureau
201 N. Franklin Avenue
Polo, Illinois 61064
1-800-678-2108 or
(815) 946-2108
email: bwcvb@essex1.com
Website:
www.promotion.com/bwcvb
visit the Trail's website at:
www.trail-of-terror.com

❝ Escape with us to the land of rest and relaxation. Blackhawk Waterways is a scenic four county area, including Carroll, Lee, Ogle, and Whiteside, in northwestern Illinois with something for everyone.

We'll put your head in a comfortable bed at any of our overnight guest establishments. Whether it is under the stars or under a roof, a good night's sleep is a good start to a great day. After your great night's rest, take a stroll through our green lush forests or state parks and observe all the natural wonders. Stop by a few of our gift, craft or specialty shops. You will be delighted at all the antiques, handcrafted items as well as imported and locally made merchandise.

Try our first-in-the-nation chocolate trail. Feast upon all types of chocolate and in the summertime don't forget to pack your cooler so you can take some treats home. While you're packing, pack a picnic lunch and then head to the river. You can take a pleasant drive, stop at any of the parks, go fishing, canoeing or catch a paddleboat cruise.

Next perfect your score at one of the many fairways, whether it is 18 holes or miniature golf. Enjoy captivating dinner theaters, where you can enjoy the shows and have a tasty meal. Visit our fun-filled haunted house, slide down a bed or see if this place is *really* haunted. You be the judge. Watch peaceful eagles soar, view wonderful lookout points and watch as a barge gently floats down the mighty Mississippi.

Finally, wind down and take a sentimental journey, visit historic sites, monuments, and statues that grace our scenic land. Enjoy artifacts of days gone by, watch as a blacksmith shapes steel, visit a steam locomotive, or see a cement figure 48' tall. Call for a FREE visitor guide 1-800-678-2108.

—Blackhawk Waterways
Convention and Visitors Bureau

Map from Blackhawk Waterways
Convention and Visitors Bureau

DeKalb
Discover DeKalb

Location

DeKalb is located approximately 60 miles west of Chicago off Interstate 88 (the East-West Tollway). Routes 38 and 64 also come straight into DeKalb from the neighboring suburbs.

History

The town and county were named for Baron Johann DeKalb, a major general in the Revolutionary War. Born of peasant stock in 1721, he acquired the noble title of Baron. He also showed military distinction in the German and French armies over a period of nearly 40 years. He fought with France in the American Revolutionary War and was killed in South Carolina in 1780.

DeKalb originally went under the name of Huntley Grove after Russell Huntley who arrived in 1837 from New York to purchase farmlands and sites on which to construct mills. In 1853 he helped secure the right-of-way for the upcoming Chicago and Northwestern Railroad. The population grew to 557. In the 1840s a name change took place and DeKalb became known as "Buena Vista" meaning "Beautiful View."

When the town was platted in 1853, it took the name of DeKalb after the county. Agriculture became an important part of the livelihood of the people due to the rich prairie soil and the advent of the railroad which allowed for easy shipment of crops as well as transportation of people into the area.

In 1874 Joseph E. Glidden patented an improved barbed wire that led to increase in the sale and use of the wire in the West. Working with Isaac Ellwood and Jacob Haish, the three men, produced barbed wire. The industry put DeKalb on the map, and, until 1938 the town was known as the "barb wire capital of the world." In 1938 the plants were closed and moved to Joliet and Waukegan.

A campaign was begun to get the Illinois Legislature to establish a Normal School for the training of teachers. The barbed wire "barons" were instrumental in the donation of land and funds to build a residential school for faculty and student housing. In 1895 Northern Illinois State Teachers College was founded in DeKalb. The first classes began in 1899 with 173 students and 16 faculty members. Today the school is a major educational institution, Northern Illinois University.

➡ Getting Started

Stop by the DeKalb Chamber of Commerce before you begin your visit to receive brochures, maps and helpful hints to start you on your tour of DeKalb. We are located on 122 North First Street, Suite E.

Attractions

Ellwood House Museum

(815) 756-4609

509 North First Street

The house is a grand Victorian mansion located in the heart of DeKalb. The home is graced with sparkling chandeliers, shiny gilt mirrors and gleaming woodwork. The home was built in 1879 by barbed wire baron Isaac Ellwood. When touring the mansion you will see what a complete household at the turn of the century was like. There is an English living room with a huge fireplace, the dining room is paneled with mahogany and there is a magnificent rotunda with a 3-story spiral staircase. There is a 1 1/2 hour guided tour which includes the 1891 playhouse and the Carriage House Museum where you will see exhibits on barbed wire history, antique farm equipment, carriages and sleighs. Stroll through the beautiful gardens and enjoy a peaceful walk under the majestic trees on the estate. The museum is listed on the National Register of Historic Places.

Egyptian Theatre

(815) 758-1215

135 North Second Street

A visit to the Egyptian Theatre will take you back to the age of movie palaces and ancient civilizations. The lobby cornices are decorated with lotus flowers and stars twinkle in azure skies above those seated in the auditorium. It is truly an internationally famous example of the Egyptian influence in theater architecture. You will see huge gold-colored statues of the seated pharaoh Ramses II which guard each side of the movie screen and stage in the restored 1929 theater. The theater was brought back to life in 1983 with the restoration of colorful wall murals featuring tableaus of Abu Simbal, the pyramids of Giza, the Sphinx, and a restful oasis. A visit to this theater will take you back to historic times when gentle breezes wafted off the Nile. The theater hosts 45-50 live stage events each year as well as 30-35 movies in a magnificent and beautiful setting.

❂ Closed January, July and August

Gurler House

(815) 756-4259

205 Pine Street

Built in 1857 for George Gurler who owned the dairy and creamery, this house is the best example of Greek Revival architecture in DeKalb. Gurler was a founder of the first American Farm Bureau and DeKalb Ag Research Corporation now De-Kalb Genetics. You are welcome to walk around the house and, in May through October, the beautiful perennial gardens are open to walkers. The home is on the National Register of Historic Places.

Joseph F. Glidden Homestead
921 W. Lincoln Highway
Local farmer Joseph F. Glidden built this historic house in 1861. The brick barn on the grounds commemorates the birthplace of barbed wire. The Joseph F. Glidden Homestead Association was formed in 1995 to preserve the house and barn for the operation of a barbed wire museum and research center.

Northern Illinois University
(815) 753-1000
Castle Drive and Lincoln Highway
Established in 1895, the school brings in thousands of visitors and students. You are welcome to come and stroll through the campus, relax in the Martin Luther King, Jr. Memorial Commons in the center of the campus, visit the

seven museums, attend the many plays and concerts offered, visit the art gallery, and cheer for the NIU Huskies at Chick Evans Field House and Huskie Stadium. Walking tours of the campus are held Monday through Friday at 1:30pm and 12:00pm on most Saturdays.

Stage Coach Theatre
(815) 758-1940
1516 Barber-Greene Road
This is one of the oldest community theaters in Illinois. In 1996 it celebrated its 50th season. The summer season runs from the middle of June to the middle of September. Call for schedule of productions or write Stage Coach Players, Box 511, DeKalb, IL 60115.

Annual Events

For more information on the events listed below and other events to be scheduled call (815) 756-6306.

July
• Art at Ellwood Art Fair and Sale — This is a juried show with all work for sale. More than 100 artists and craftspersons from Illinois and the Midwest exhibit on the spacious lawns of the Ellwood mansion. Food and refreshments on the grounds. (815) 756-4609.

- Drum Corps Midwest Championship — This is where the top drum and bugle corps in the Midwest compete for the championship of "Best in the Midwest". It is held at Huskie Stadium Drive and Annie Glidden Road. (815) 756-6306 or (414) 327-2857.
- DeKalb Air Show — This is an established airshow featuring unique airplanes. The show includes military and civilian aerobatic routines. It is held at the DeKalb Taylor Municipal Airport located on Peace Road & Pleasant Street (815) 746-6306.

August
- Ice Cream Social and Band Concert — The entire family can enjoy an old-fashioned ice cream social held on the spacious lawn of the Ellwood House Museum. There will be a band concert, games and activities for kids. There will be a large variety of homemade cakes and ice cream. Tours of the Ellwood Mansion by admission (815) 756-4609.
- DeKalb Corn Fest — Community corn festival with musical acts, food vendors, carnival, children's art fest, crafts, garage sales and antique auto show. Free corn served on Saturday. Held downtown, Route 38, between 1st and 4th Streets. (815) 748-CORN.

Shopping and Dining

There are plenty of antique shops and auctions in DeKalb as well as good places to find a meal.

Conclusion

For more information contact:
DeKalb Chamber of Commerce
122 N. First Street, Suite E
DeKalb, Illinois 60115
(815) 756-6306
FAX (815) 756-5164
Web Site: www.dekalb.org.

Egyptian Theatre

66 Just 60 miles west of Chicago, DeKalb has a relaxed pace and an easygoing lifestyle. The city is also home to a major university and a growing and diverse business community that springs from a strong manufacturing and agricultural heritage.

While DeKalb is located in the midst of some of the richest farmland in the world, manufacturing put the city on the map. The barbed wire industry was born here in the 1870's and barbed wire made in DeKalb helped to fence the West.

Northern Illinois University is the state's second largest with an enrollment of 22,000 students. The beautiful campus covers 500 acres with more than 50 buildings. Visitors are welcome to take a self-guided tour around the heart of the campus. Outstanding intercollegiate athletics, theater and musical performances are available to the public throughout the year.

The DeKalb Park District has 20 parks, 2 golf courses, picnic facilities, a municipal pool with water slide, and a band shell where the DeKalb Municipal Band performs free concerts every Tuesday evening during the summer.

DeKalb is a diverse community providing a variety of cultural and leisure activities for visitors and residents. 99

—DeKalb Chamber of Commerce

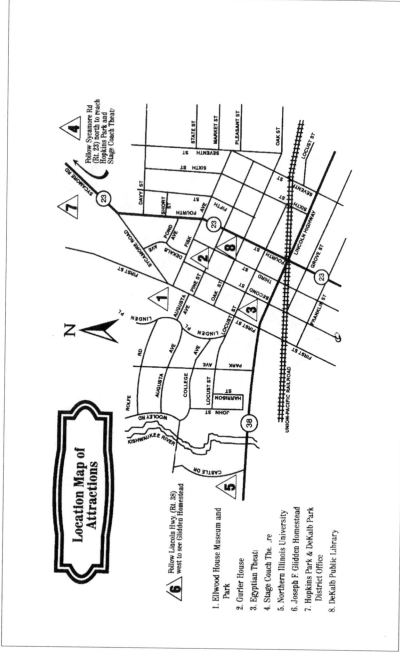

Location Map of Attractions

N

Follow Sycamore Rd (Rt. 23) north to reach Hopkins Park and Stage Coach Theatr

Follow Lincoln Hwy (Rt. 38) west to see Glidden Homestead

1. Ellwood House Museum and Park
2. Gurler House
3. Egyptian Theatr
4. Stage Coach The...re
5. Northern Illinois University
6. Joseph F. Glidden Homestead
7. Hopkins Park & DeKalb Park District Office
8. DeKalb Public Library

Map from
DeKalb Chamber of Commerce

Rock Falls
Proud of our Past, Confident of the Future

Location

Rock Falls part of the Blackhawk Waterways is located on Illinois Route 40 and US Route 30 along Interstate 88. We are 120 miles west of Chicago and 30 miles from the Mississippi River. Rockford is 60 miles northwest of us and the Quad Cities are 50 miles southwest.

History

The city lies on the south bank of the Rock River. Imagine life there in the beginning with boats, Indian trails guiding wagons, log cabins and meat from wildlife. In 1832 Blackhawk and his warriors followed paths that are now paved streets. In pursuit of Blackhawk nineteen hundred US troops camped in the area, among which whom Jefferson Davis, Zachary Taylor, Samuel Whiteside, and Abraham Lincoln as well as 23 others came from New Salem to lead a company of volunteers against Blackhawk.

In 1839 Edward Atkins, A.B. Wheeler, Isaac Merill and Daniel Brooks laid out the mile square town of Rapids City on the tract where Rock Falls now stands. A contract was let to build a canal which would facilitate navigation up the river, bringing the town prosperity for a time. When financial panic hit the country, the town became a ghost town. During the same winter a tribe of about 30 Winnebago Indians camped in the vicinity. They left in the spring of 1844, never to return again.

The river became the center of the township and interests were always centered around it. In 1867, A.P. Smith bought 65 acres of land on the south side of the river and hired a surveyor to lay out the town of Rock Falls. Citizens voted to incorporate their town into a city and on April 16, 1889, they became a city.

In 1890 Congress appropriated $500,000 to build the seventy-five mile long Hennepin Canal, from Hennepin to Milan, on the Mississippi. This section of the canal was dedicated in 1895. Because at times the water level in the canal was insufficient, a feeder canal was finally built from Rock Falls, but only after several years of dispute with other communities.

In 1898, construction was begun on the 29 mile feeder. A dam was built across Rock River to raise the water level for a proper flow into the canal through the feeder. 25,000 people attended the opening day celebration.

The only lock on the feeder at that time was the one at Rock River. For many years there was a large grain elevator at Mile Nine, where farmers took their grain to be shipped. Unfortunately, the usefulness of the canal was short lived because of better highways and large trucks. The canal fell into disuse, but today it is a recreational paradise.

➡ Getting Started

Stop by the Chamber of Commerce office where you will find brochures and maps to help you tour our area. We are located at 601 West Tenth Street. We will also help you with information about our sister city Sterling just across the route 40 bridge on the north side of the Rock River.

Attractions

Behren's Country Village and Muffins 'N More
(815) 625-5116
Prophetstown Road, off Route 30
The village is located on a beautiful family farm. It has a collection of Country Style Shops, you will find gift and craft items, quilting supplies and classes, a wooden ware, children's shop,

Path along the feeder at Rock Falls

Christmas Crib, flowers and plants and a village eatery.

⊙ Buses and groups welcome

Centennial Park

(815-625-0272
East 11th Street and Avenue D
Playground equipment, baseball diamonds, tennis courts, soccer fields, sheltered picnic areas, restrooms, a jogging and fitness course, paddle boats and canoes for use in ponds and lagoons.

Crystal Lake

1800 New High St. & Route 30
815-622-5974, *Rock Falls*
Open 7 days a week in season, June-August. Biggest Beach in Northwestern, Illinois. Volleyball, food, swimming and sun.

Hennepin Canal Parkway

The Hennepin Canal began in 1890 and is considered to have been an all-water version of Interstate 80. It opened a direct link between the Upper Mississippi Valley and the east coast. Considered at times to be the wrong size, first too large and then too small, commercial usage became disappointing. In 1951 the Corps of Engineers closed it to commercial navigation and today it is a recreational mecca.

The recreation area is 104.5 miles long and from 380 feet to one mile wide. The parkway, is shaped like a T, is located in Rock Island, Bureau, Henry Lasalle and Whiteside counties. It includes 3,000 acres of land and over 35,000 acres of water. The water for the canal is drawn from the Rock River, and the dam across the river between Sterling and Rock Falls forms a 2400 acre lake known as Lake Sinnissippi, the actual reservoir.

Originally the Hennepin Canal had 32 locks. Today four of the mainline locks have been restored to working condition. The canal crosses nine major streams or rivers in aqueducts, six of which are still in use. There is a Visitor Center Complex near Sheffield for information, displays, flush toilets, drinking water, playground equipment, picnic areas, boat launching ramps, marina and maintenance headquarters. Other recreational facilities include boating. fishing, hiking, bicycling, horse trails, snowmobiling, vehicles, migratory waterfowl hunting, and cross country skiing For more details about the park and other state parks contact:
Site Superintendent
Rural Route 2
Sheffield, Illinois 61361
(815) 454-2328

Jim Arduini Boat Launch

(815) 625-4500
East 2nd Street at Upper Dam

Little Red School House in Centennial Park

Boat ramps into the Sinnissippi Lake area of the Rock River, has a scenic river view, picnicking, parking for boat trailers. It is adjacent to the Hennepin Canal and the starting point of a path for walking, canoeing, jogging and bicycling.

Little Red School House
(815) 625-0272
E. 11th Street
The Centennial Village School #1 is a replica of an early 19th century American one room schoolhouse. Open Memorial Day thru Labor Day 12pm-5pm

Rainbow Falls Adventure Golf
1109 W. Route 30, *Rock Falls*
Right next to the Dairy Queen. Great Fun for the whole family.

Lower Dam Park and Bowman Family Memorial Park
(815) 625-0272
Lower Dam near 1st Ave.
Beautifully landscaped river walk, fantastic fishing and boat ramp. There is security lighting after dark.

Rock River Antique Center
(815) 625-2556
2105 East Rt. 30
Quality antiques are in this 14,000 square foot mall, all on one level.

They have a knowledgeable sales staff, large lighted showcases and booths, dealer discounts. They will buy single items or complete estates. The center is on seven acres with plenty of parking. Starting in April a monthly outdoor flea-market is held the last weekend of every month through October.

Selmi's Greenhouse and Farm Market

1206 Dixon Avenue, *Rock Falls*
(815) 626-3830, May-June
Wonderful greenhouse plants, strawberries late May and June. Super sweet corn in July and August. Large variety of fresh veggies all summer. Pumpkin world and harvest veggies September-October. New for kids is the educational agricultural center and exhibits.

Twin City Mall

209 W. 2nd Street
(815) 625-0991, *Rock Falls*
Antiques, collectibles, crafts, herbal creations, quilts, teddy bears, reproduction furniture, Coca Cola items, certified dealer of Georgetown dolls, baskets, dolls and accessories. Old and new everything inbetween.

Seward-Riverside Park

(815) 625-0272
East 2nd Street and Rock River
1.6 acres along the Rock River has abundant wildlife and playground equipment. This is the site of the Annual Rock Falls River Chase boat races.

Satellite Attractions

❧ Sterling

Dillon Home Museum

(815) 622-6202
1005 E. 3rd Street
Built in 1857 in the Italianate Renaissance style. The home features history of the Dillon family, early owners of North-western Steel and Wire. The home has many fine antiques and artifacts. Exhibits of local history and a Mini Railroad Museum are housed there. It is listed on the National Register of Historic Places.
❍ Admission

American Heritage Antique Center

202 1st Avenue, *Sterling*
(815) 622-3000
20,000 square feet of antiques and collectibles and much more. Offering a multitude of museum pieces to enjoy. Features the Youngstown Coffee House.

Annual Events

All Year (815) 625-6188
• Rock River Valley Skydivers — Jumping every Saturday and Sunday, weather permitting. Training begins in May.

June-October
- Rock Falls Farmers Market — From seven a.m. to noon every Saturday morning for the purchase of locally grown produce and baked goods.

June
- Soaring Contest — Region 7 SSA sponsored by Chicagoland Glider Council. (630) 907-0442
- Annual Fly-In/Drive In Breakfast— Open to the public to watch a variety of aircraft. Sponsored by the EEA Chapter 410. Door prizes will be awarded. (815) 625-6556.

July
- Sterling/Rock Falls Jaycees Fireworks — An all day 4th of July celebration with refreshmentments, entertainment, fireworks at dusk.
- Rock Falls River Chase — The American Power Boat Association sponsors a Six State Regional Championship Race. Two days of exciting hydro races, food booths and events. Lucky Duck Race for $1,000 1st prize. (815) 625-4500

August
- Central State Regional Girls Softball Tournament — Hosted by, Rock Falls Girls Little League. Winners of the respective Senior League (ages 13-15) and Big League (ages 16-18) will advance to the World Series. (815) 626-1049

- Fall Fest on the Rock — Lawrence Park Island located between Rock Falls and Sterling. Antiques, crafts, collectibles, food vendors, petting zoo, entertainment, quilt show and sale at the Rock Falls High School Gym. (815) 626-0991

September
- Mexican Fiesta Days, Rock Falls/Sterling — Folkloric dancing, open house and entertainment, parade, food stands on the street, fiesta dancing, queen contest and coronation. Ends with a soccer tournament. (815) 622-0536

October
- Pumpkin World at Selmi's Farm a time of the year when ghosts and goblins come out. Activities center around a children-petting farm, free outdoor displays, fresh apples, pumpkins, squash and apple cider! Bring your camera and video. (815) 626-3830
- Sterling/Rock Falls Jaycees Haunted House — (815) 626-7924

November
- Rock Falls Hometown Holidays — Friday, features live Reindeer, Love Light Tree Ceremony, Christmas Walk, living windows, wagon rides and refreshments. Saturday has a parade, horsedrawn wagon

rides and entertainment. Mr. and Mrs. Claus will be at the children's party in the armory. Craft shows are at the Rock Falls American Legion and Rock Falls VFW. Sunday, the Festival of Praise (815) 625-4500.

Shopping and Dining

Shopping in Rock Falls can be exciting with its many antique and craft shops. The new Rock River Antique Center offers a new arena for the avid collector.

Dining can be enjoyable in the Rock Falls and Sterling area. There are many fine eating places at reasonable prices from fast food, pizzas, carry out, Chinese, Italian, Mexican, ribs, and the all time favorite deli to the family restaurant. Stop by the Dairy Queen for a delicious ice cream.

Tips

✔ In visiting state parks groups of 25 or more persons are not permitted to any site unless permission from the site superintendent is obtained to use the facility.

✔ Due to freezing and thawing periods, access to park facilities might be by foot only. Call ahead for weather information.

Conclusion

For further information contact:
Rock Falls Chamber of Commerce
601 West Tenth Street
Rock Falls, Illinois 61071
(815) 625-4500
www.rockfallsil.com
email: rfchambr@cin.net

Welcome to Rock Falls!

66 You will find our people friendly and our businesses eager to serve you! We hope you will spend some time here and come back often.

Be sure to visit some of our points of interest. Whether you enjoy antiques or collectables, are looking for recreation, or just want to relax, you are sure to find it here. The Feeder portion of the Hennepin Canal is one of our most unusual assets. Construction of the canals was completed in 1907 and served as a commercial waterway until 1951. The canal is being preserved today as an important link to the history of Northern Illinois. Its future is tied to recreation and natural preservation.

Centennial Park is close to our major motels and provides a scenic setting for exercise or relaxation. Visit the Little Red School house, which is an authentic reproduction of the one room school houses, which were so abundant in the 1920s. The park has a 20-station jogging/fitness course. Tennis courts are available, as well as softball diamonds, soccer fields, picnic shelters, paddle boats and canoes on the lagoons and many types of playground equipment.

We hope you can enjoy a few meals in town. There is a variety available, from fast food and family restaurants to ethnic and fine dining. We've got it all!

Again, we hope you will visit the Rock Falls area and we welcome any questions or comments concerning our town and its people. **99**

—Linda Thurm
President, CEO

St. Charles
A Place of Charm & Treasure

Location
Located on Interstate 88 one hour west of Chicago.

History
This community located along the Fox River was first settled in 1834. It is the former home of the Pottawatomie Indian tribe. Once "just a buggy ride away from Chicago." St. Charles is older than the large sprawling metropolis of Chicago. The town square still exists as it did when it was first platted in 1837. The town square is full of tall oaks that still shade benches where folks gather to discuss the happenings of the day. Many of the homes are registered as national landmarks.

➡ Getting Started
Begin your visit by stopping by the St. Charles Convention and Visitors Bureau located at 311 N. Second Street. We will be happy to provide you with information to discover for yourself "A Place of Charm and Treasure."

Attractions

Arcada Theatre
Main Street and First Avenue
The theater is a "movie palace," built in 1926 in the Venetian/ Spanish style. The interior was designed to create the feeling of a Spanish grotto. With a terra cotta exterior with an orange clay-tiled roof, it is a delightful contrast to its Victorian neighbors.

Franklin Medical School
Northeast corner of 1st Avenue and Main Street
The first medical school in Illinois.

Garfield Farm Museum
(630) 584-8485
3N016 Garfield Road
On this 1840s living museum you will find buildings that depict farm life in the 1800s. On the 212 acre site there are historic breeds of chickens and vintage farm equipment. Many of the buildings have been restored or reconstructed.
✪ Open June-September

Hotel Baker
100 West Main Street
Built in 1928 the hotel has been

restored to its original grandeur. It has reopened as a hotel with 54 rooms and a restaurant. You will find on top of the doorway a stained glass window depicting a majestic peacock to welcome visitors. An outstanding feature of the hotel is the Rainbow Room dance floor where you will see beautiful colored glass floor panels lit from below the floor. When the hotel opened its doors in 1928, it was known as the "Honeymoon Hotel" since many newlyweds chose to go there.

Pheasant Run
(630) 584-6300
1-800-999-3319

You will find all the comforts of home at this resort. Pheasant Run is known as a complete resort offering a limitless variety of activities, entertainment and special amenities for guests of all ages and interests. It has the charm of a quaint country inn. With over 30 years of experience, it offers live dinner theaters, children's theater, comedy club, and an 18 hole golf course.

Pioneer Sholes School
(630) 377-6161
St. Charles Township
LeRoy Oakes Forest Preserve
Dean Street
This is a restored one room school

Paddlewheel Boat on the Fox River

where students and teachers can re-enact turn of the century classes.

✪ Donations accepted

St. Charles Heritage Center

(630) 584-6967

215 E. Main Street

The center houses a photographic history of St. Charles, 19th century furnishings and a permanent collection of Indian artifacts.

St. Charles Belle or the Fox River Queen

(630-584-2334

Take a ride on one of the old paddlewheel boats docked at Pottawatomie Park and enjoy a one-hour cruise up and down the Fox River. You will have a breathtaking view of the St. Charles skyline. The river is bordered by a forest preserve and has changed very little since the Pottawatomie Indians inhabited its banks.

1843 Durant-Peterson House

(630) 377-6424

LeRoy Oakes Forest Preserve

This 1843 brick mason's prairie farm house has been authentically restored. Special family events can be held there during the year by calling for reservations. Open June-October

✪ Donations accepted

1850 William Beith House

(630) 377-6424

8 Indiana

This is a restored 1850 Limestone Greek Revival home.

Fabyan Villa Museum
Japanese Tea Garden

Fabyan Forest Preserve 1511 S. Batavia Avenue, Rt. 31 Geneva,Il. Fabyan Villa call: (630) 232-4811. This is a 1907 Frank Lloyd Wright restoration.

Japanese Tea Garden call: (847) 741-9798

Annual Events

St. Charles offers many festivals and events throughout the year. Below is a sampling of main events. Almost every weekend these events take place at either the Kane County Fairgrounds, Pheasant Run Resort Mega Center, LeRoy Oakes Forest Preserve or citywide. St. Charles hosts events such as The Pheasant Run Antique Show, Old House New House Home Show, Antique Toy and Doll World Show, Willmann's Doll and Bear Fair, Antique Decoy Show, Country Folk Art Festival, Pheasant Run Art, Craft, and Homespun Market; Day in the Country, Chicagoland Rec Room Antique Slot Machine and Juke Box Show. For a more compre-hensive listing of scheduled events and times write or call the Visitors Bureau.

Kane County Flea Market

Monthly Event
• Kane County Flea Market is held at the Kane County Fairgrounds on Randall Road between routes 64 and 38. This is one of the largest antique and collectible flea markets in the Midwest or anywhere! The market has been in existence over 30 years and becomes bigger each year. (630) 377-2252.

June
• Pride of the Fox RiverFest — held downtown along the Fox River. The celebration of summer focuses on the river, craft and fine arts shows, live entertainment, children's activities, and much more fun for all ages. (630) 557-2575 or (630) 377-6161.

July
• Concerts in the Park — Every Thursday evening from July 4 through August you will find free musical performances in the gazebo in Lincoln Park at Main and Fourth Street. Concerts start at 7pm until dusk.

mid-July
• Kane County Fair (630) 377-6161

August
• Fox Rox Downtown Festival— The town rocks with exciting tent sales, craft shows, Bluesfest and family activities. (630) 513-5386 or (630) 377-6161.

October
• Scarecrow Festival — Lincoln Park is the location for this wonderful, whimsical handcrafted scarecrow exhibit. Come and stroll through the park, taking the opportunity to choose your favorite scarecrow; indulge in a variety of delicious food; enjoy live musical entertainment, face painting, pony rides, making your own scarecrow and browsing through the arts and craft show held at Pottawattomie Park. 1-800-777-4373 • (630) 377-6161

Bicycling along the Fox River Trail

December

• Downtown Holiday Open House — This is a weekend long festive holiday open house. You can sample the holiday cheer and hospitality with in-store treats, entertainment and demonstrations. (630) 513-5386 or (630) 377-6161 for date and time.

Shopping and Dining

Shopping opportunities in St. Charles are never-ending. Whatever you are looking for you will find. Explore the historic districts where stores are tucked in around antique buildings and homes. A major shopping mall provides diversity. Antique stores are scattered throughout the city where you can spend a full day searching for that special treasure. Galleries, artisans, and crafts are all part of the shopping arena.

Dining in St. Charles can be a unique experience. Enjoy dining in a cafe with a literary flair, an old filling station, by the river, an authentic Irish pub, an authentic speakeasy, or purchase a box lunch to eat in the park. You will find plenty of places that are fabulous from ethnic foods to the all-American.

Conclusion

St. Charles offers fun and entertainment for all ages. Call us for a free colorful Visitors Magazine which includes attractions, lodging, shopping, dining and a complete calendar of events.

St. Charles Convention
    & Visitors Bureau
311 N. Second Street
St. Charles, Illinois 60174
(630) 377-6161
1-800-777-4373
www.visitstcharles.com

Tips

✔ Dress for the weather and wear comfortable shoes when attending events and festivals.

✔ The Fox River Trail is a recreational delight where you can follow beautiful paths running alongside the Fox River by bicycle or by a leisurely walk. Call for a free bike map 1-800-777-4373.

✔ Motorcoach parking is available.

✔ Call for directions.

❝ Welcome to St. Charles, Illinois, a place of natural charm and treasures. Nestled along the Fox River, beautiful St. Charles is one hour west of Chicago. This picturesque community, rich in historic architecture, unique shopping and restaurants, is the perfect destination.

Discriminating shoppers delight in browsing throughout downtown St. Charles, visiting antique and specialty shops in **Old St. Charles, Century Corners, Fox Island Square**. For our modern day shoppers, don't miss **The Charlestowne Mall**, just two miles east of the Fox River on Main Street, with over 120 stores, food court and a distinctive double-decker carousel.

When in downtown St. Charles, you can enjoy architecture from days gone by, such as the **1928 Hotel Baker** on the Fox River once known as "the honeymoon hotel." **The Arcada Theater** is a romantic Revival style building that was built in 1926 for silent movies and is still used today for your movie enjoyment. The centerpiece of downtown St. Charles is the **Municipal Center.** This 1940 Art Moderne style building has a tower capped by a diamond-shaped form which glows at night.

Outdoor recreation at Pottawatomie Park includes daily summer cruises on the scenic Fox River aboard one of two **Paddlewheel Riverboats**, golf, mini golf, canoeing and miles of bike trails.

St. Charles offers many events and festivals to complement your visit.

If time permits, plan a weekend at **Pheasant Run Resort and Convention Center.** This full service resort offers 18 hole golf, dinner theater, children's theatre, Zanies comedy Club, spa, shops, night club, swimming, tennis, restaurants and a fabulous Sunday brunch. Other lodging options include Best Western, Days Inn, Super 8, Holiday Inn Express, Country Inn and Suites, Courtyard by Marriott, Hilton Garden Inn and the historic Hotel Baker located downtown by the Fox River. ❞

—*St. Charles Convention & Visitors Bureau*

Wheaton
A Quality of Life

Location

Located in the heart of DuPage County along Interstate 88 and North-South Interstate 355 just west of Chicago.

History

The development of Wheaton is credited to its founding members Warren Lyon Wheaton, Jesse Childs Wheaton, and Eratus Gary, natives of Pemfret, Connecticut, who settled here in the 1830s. The gentlemen crafted the community as it is today. There were earlier settlers in the area but recognition must be given to these men—two teachers, and a carpenter—for creating the community that included a railroad, a college and a government center.

The town was named for the brothers Warren Lyon Wheaton and Jesse Childs Wheaton, who along with Eratus Gary recognized the importance of rail transportation. Many landowners of the day asked high prices for small portions of land in the area, while these men offered a three-mile stretch of land to the Galena and Chicago Union Railroad to bring the line through Wheaton. The first trains arrived in 1849 and railroad officials hung the sign "Wheaton Depot."

By 1853, the brothers plotted and officially recorded ten blocks of their land surrounding the railroad. They offered free lots to anyone who would build on them, as they recognized that for a town to develop, homes and businesses had to be constructed.

Warren and Jesse then pledged to support financially the establishment of Wesleyan College in Wheaton, known today as Wheaton College. The opening of the school in 1853 laid the cornerstone for quality education in the newly formed community.

By 1859 there was a population of 700 and the community was incorporated into a village. By 1890 the village was incorporated as a city with a population of 1,622.

Wheaton became the county seat in 1867. Land was needed to build a courthouse before the county seat could be moved from Naperville. Again, Jesse and Warren donated land and labor for the first courthouse which was completed in 1868. It was time to move the courthouse but Naperville was not ready to relinquish its reign. The story of the

"Midnight Raid" recalls how the men from Wheaton rode their horses and drove their wagons down the dirt-paved Naperville-Wheaton Road to "steal" the county records. As luck would have it, before the Wheaton men could get out of town with the loaded wagons, several Naperville men awoke and took chase. In the escape some plat books fell off a wagon and were retrieved by a Naperville loyal. They were sent to Chicago for safe-keeping while Naperville residents tried to get the courthouse to reverse the referendum. The fight ended when the "Great Chicago Fire" destroyed the evidence in 1871 and Wheaton was secure as the county seat of DuPage.

Getting Started

To help you get started stop by the Greater Wheaton Chamber of Commerce at 108 E. Wesley or call (630) 668-6464. We will supply you with information about DuPage County, which contains many of the suburbs of Chicago, all are readily accessible from many directions. In the county you will find an assortment of daytrip ideas.

Attractions

Billy Graham Center Museum
(630) 752-5909
500 East College Avenue

Located on the grounds of Wheaton College, the museum gives a unique and visual history of Christian evangelism and its influence on society. You will find Billy Graham's traveling pulpit, sermon notes and video presentations along with computer printouts of favorite crusades. Tours can be arranged by calling in advance. The Billy Graham Center Museum is always open for tours.

Cantigny
(630) 668-5161
1 South 151 Winfield Road
Cantigny is the estate of Colonel Robert R. McCormick, former editor and publisher of the *Chicago Tribune*. The centerpiece of the 500 acre estate is the McCormick mansion built in 1896. On the estate you will find a premier public golf course, a clubhouse offering a spectacular view of Swan Lake, the foremost military museum in the nation known as the First Division Museum and ten acres of formal gardens.

Cosley Animal Farm
(630) 665-5534
Gary Avenue and Jewell Road
Cosley is home to more than 35 species of animals. On the farm you will find an old train station, an antique railroad caboose, a 128-year-old barn, and a display of

Cantigny Estate

horsedrawn vehicles. Also featured there is a beautiful duck pond, the Vern Kiebler Learning Center and a gift shop.

DuPage Children's Museum
(630) 260-9960
1777 S. Blanchard Road
This is the place where children and adults learn together through its many exhibits, programs, workshops and materials that stretch thinking skills, stimulate creativity and provide intellectual challenges in the sciences and arts.

DuPage County Forest Preserve
(630) 665-5310
Illinois Prairie Path
Wheaton boasts a variety of recreational opportunities in its forest preserves. On the south of Wheaton is the Danada Forest Preserve which houses an equestrian center where hay rides and sleigh rides can be enjoyed. It also is a favorite place for dinners, meetings and weddings. Adjacent to the Danada Forest Preserve is Herrick Lake which offers nature hikes, picnics and fishing fa-

cilities. You will find bike paths intertwined throughout the Forest Preserve connecting to the Illinois Prairie Path. The Prairie Path is an extensive trail system extending throughout northern Illinois—a must for the avid bikers, runners and hikers.

DuPage County Historical Museum

(630) 682-7343
102 E. Wesley Street

Located in downtown Wheaton, the museum attracts residents of all ages to its three-story complex of exhibits. The main floor features historical pictures, clothing and toys from the mid-1850s to the present. The basement houses a working model railroad reflecting rail travel throughout the county. Educational programs give children the opportunity to learn about history with a hands-on approach.

✪ Groups should call in advance

Lincoln Marsh Natural Area

Located at the intersection of Harrison Avenue and Pierce Avenue is a 130 acre park featuring wetlands, prairies, and oak savanna.

Rice Pool and Water Park

The pool and park feature two water slides, an innertube water slide, 200 feet of zero depth edge, a diving well, 25 meter lanes for lap swimming, a waterfall and a water play area, a sand play area, sand volleyball courts, grassy knolls and lounge chairs for sunbathing, concession stands, and a spectator viewing area.

Wheaton History Center

(630) 682-9472
606 N. Main

The history center preserves, records and studies and interprets the rich architecture and cultural heritage of Wheaton. Special group tours and programs can be scheduled any day by appointment. For more information call the above number.

✪ Free admissions; donations appreciated.

Satellite Attractions

🌿 Argonne

Argonne National Laboratory

(630) 252-5562
9700 South Cass Avenue

Site of the advanced Photon Source X-Ray Project. It is one of the countries premier facility for energy-related research and development. Tour by appointment this space age facility that is exploring the secrets of inner space.

✪ Free admission

❧ Batavia

Fermi National Laboratory (Fermi-Lab)
(630) 840-3351
Another opportunity to explore the mysteries of the atom and find answers to the fundamental questions on the nature of matter.
➊ Free admission

❧ Darien

National Shrine of St. Therese Carmelite Visitor Center
(603) 969-3311
8501 Bailey Road
The best collection of relics and memorabilia of St. Therese outside of France. Museum contains copies of photos and an original oil painting of the Carmelite saint. Also toys and a prayer book from her childhood, a photocopy of her original autobiography, *Story of a Soul* and other items of interest. Open daily (closed holidays).
➊ Free admission

❧ Elmhurst

Elmhurst Art Museum
(630) 834-0202
150 Cottage Hill
The museum's award-winning structure contains a dramatic glass entrance gallery, three museum galleries, an educational pavillion and the Ludwig Mies van der Rohe McCormick house. Contemporary art. Free Admission

Elmhurst Historical Museum
(630) 833-1457
120 E. Park Avenue
Prize-winning museum features exhibits on national tours as well as collections and exhibits about Elmhurst history. Local memorabilia are contained in the 1892 residence of Henry Glos, the first village president.
➊ Free admission

Lizzadro Museum of Lapidary Art
(630) 883-1616
220 Cottage Hill Avenue
A unique experience to see collections of carvings from jade, hard stone, and various precious metals.
➊ Free admission on Fridays

Theatre Historical Society of America
(630) 782-1800
152 York Road, Suite 200
Examine the history of various types of theaters.
➊ Free admission

❧ Glen Ellyn

Stacy's Tavern Museum
(630) 858-8696
557 Geneva Road
A restored 1846 stagecoach inn is the backdrop for much of Glen Ellyn's past. Experience the art, technology, and culture of northern Illinois residents.

❦ Hinsdale

Robert Crown Center for Health Education
(630) 325-1900
21 Salt Creek Lane
The center offers educational programs for over 175,000 students, teachers and parents each year on topics such as human reproduction, drug abuse, sex education, AIDS and general health.

❦ Lisle

Lisle Station Park
(630) 968-2747
918-920 Burlington Avenue
Located in the park you will find the Beaubien Tavern, Lisle Depot Museum and Netzley Yender House.

• *Beaubien Tavern*
918 Beaubien Tavern
Constructed in the 1830s this old Tavern served as a toll house for the Southwest Plank Road
✪ Free admission

• *Lisle Depot Museum*
(630) 968-2747
919 Burlington Avenue
This 1874 depot that served the Chicago, Burlington and Quincy Railroad today contains exhibits from Lisle's past.
✪ Free admission

Naper Settlement Museum

• *Netzley/Yender House*
920 Burlington Avenue
Make an appointment to tour this
1850s house once occupied by
Jacob Netzley, a local weaver.
✪ Free admission

The Morton Arboretum
(630) 719-2465
Route 53 and Interstate 88
An excellent place to find tranquility, this 1,700 acres contains
more than 3,000 kinds of trees,
shrubs, and vines from around
the world. Take advantage of the
12 miles of hiking trails or 11
miles of roadway to see them
all.
✪ Open daily year-round

❦ **Lombard**

*Enchanted Castle Restaurant and
Entertainment Complex*
(630) 953-7860
Roosevelt Road and Main Street
Nationally acclaimed as Chicago-
land's premier entertainment
complex! Featuring the Movie 'N
Motion ride; state of the art Q-Zar
Laser Tag Arena and the Black
Hole Virtual Speedway; Indoor
Miniature Golf; ImaGymnation
Station Playland; Bumper Cars;
and over 250 games. New Billiard
and Dart Room. Open Daily.

Lombard Historical Museum
23 West Maple Street
(630) 629-1885
The restored Victorian home

features rooms furnished with
artifacts that exemplify the
lifestyle of the emerging middle
class during the late 19th century
when Lombard was incorporated.
Open Wednesdays, Saturdays and
Sundays.

❦ **Naperville**

*Naper Settlement a 19th Century
Village*
(630) 420-6010
523 S. Webster Street
Venture back into the 19th century
as costumed tour guides interpret
this recreated village. Various
tours are offered to the homes,
shops and museum. This is
Chicagoland's only 19th-century
village that brings the Victorian
and pioneer past to life.

❦ **Oak Brook**

*Czechoslovak Heritage
Museum, Library and Archives*
(630) 472-9909 • 1-800-LIFECSA
122 W. 22nd Street
Highlights the history and culture
of the Czech Republic and
Slovakia, through authentic folk
costumes, lead crystal, china
ceramics, embroidery and historical displays. Open Monday-
Friday and every second Saturday.
✪ No admission fee, donations
welcome.

Graue Mill and Museum
(630) 655-2090
Spring and York Roads
The only operating water-powered grist mill in Illinois was originally built in 1852. A variety of crafts are exhibited along with artifacts from the period.

🌿 **Oakbrook Terrace**

Drury Lane Theatre
(630) 530-8300
100 Drury Lane
This is a 971 seat proscenium arch style live theatre featuring musicals, comedy, and Hollywood personalities. Dinner and/or theatre.

🌿 **Warrenville**

Warrenville Historical Society Museum
(630) 393-4215
33S530 Second Street
The museum is housed in a renovated 1858 Church.
✪ Free admission

🌿 **West Chicago**

Air Classic, Museum of Aviation
(630) 584-1888
3N020 Powis Road
Many vintage World War II planes on display.

West Chicago City Museum
(630) 231-3376

132 Main Street
Located in the National Register Landmark 1884 Turner Town Hall. Explore the roots of West Chicago's past.

🌿 **Westmont**

William L. Gregg House Museum
(630) 960-3392
117 South Linden Avenue
View memorabilia from the early 19th century in this Victorian home.
✪ Free admission

🌿 **Willowbrook**

Arabian Knights Farms
6526 Clarendon Hills Road
Petting zoo and horseback riding are offered here.

🌿 **Winfield**

Kline Creek Farm
(630) 876-5900
1N 600 County Farm Road
The 1890s come to life at this living history museum where farm workers dressed in period clothes explain the day's activities, or enjoy a special event such as the annual Ice Cream Social or the Harvesting Festival. Open Thursday through Monday, except major holidays.
✪ Free admission

Annual Events

Write or call for a schedule of events held throughout the year in downtown Wheaton the Greater Wheaton Chamber of Commerce 108 E. Wesley, Wheaton, IL 60187 (630) 668-6464 or our website: www.wheatonchamber.org

For a listing of satellite attraction events in DuPage County call or write:
DuPage Convention and
Visitors Bureau
915 Harger Road, Suite 240,
Oak Brook, IL 60523
1-800-232-0502 or our website:
www.dupagecvb.com

Shopping and Dining

The wealth of various cuisines offered in area dining establishments is taking a culinary trip around the world. You will find the best hamburgers in the world, wonderful steaks, and fresh seafood. We guarantee a different taste sensation every day!

Shopping in DuPage County is a world-class experience. Discover prestigious stores with international reputations. There is a variety of antique shops and boutiques as well.

66 Everyone from history buffs to shoppers is sure to find plenty of adventure in Wheaton and the DuPage County area. Warm, inviting inns and prestigious hotels keep visitors pampered and comfortable for the duration of their stay.

Wheaton, the Dupage County seat, rolls out the red carpet for visitors. Our thriving historic downtown remains a civic center for the community. Its tree lined streets and red brick buildings provide an inviting atmosphere for strollers. Two parks within walking distance of Main Street provide excellent settings for a picnic or an occasional outdoor concert, and a visit to the DuPage County Historical Museum is just around the corner. Throughout the year many special events are held in the downtown including such activities as horse drawn carriage rides, which add to the turn-of-the-century charm.

On the south side of Wheaton, award winning Town Square Shopping Center displays an intimate atmosphere with charming shops and places to capture a moment of peace and a cup of hot chocolate or coffee. Just south of the Square are the Rice Lake, Danada East and Danada West Shopping Centers. An exciting variety of restaurants, specialty shops, bookstores and discount stores are waiting for our guests to Wheaton. 99

—*Greater Wheaton Chamber of Commerce*

Daytrip Illinois
Interstate 90

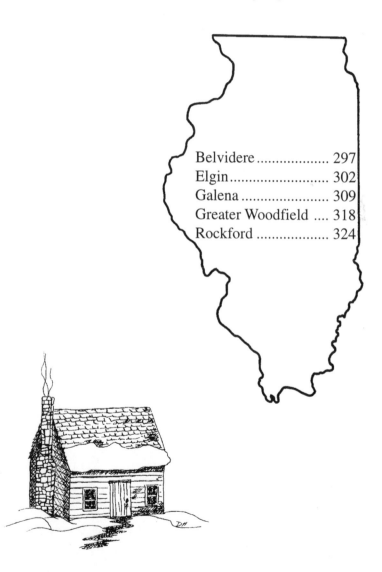

Belvidere
Beautiful to View

Location

Belvidere is located along Interstate 90 just east of Chicago and west of Rockford.

History

This principal stop along the Chicago-Galena stage route was founded in 1836. Following the Blackhawk War of 1832, Boone County, ancestral home of the Pottawatomi Indians, was settled by European-Americans in the summer of 1835. The natural interspersal of forest and prairie made the area such an enticing place to live that the first settlement was called Belvidere or "Beautiful to View."

Situated on the banks of the Kishwaukee River, the little village soon had a hotel, a blacksmith, several homes, some shops and a church. By 1845 a large grist and saw mill, the Baltic Mill, was erected and still stands today in the Belvidere Park.

The energetic pioneers who came from New England, Scotland, Norway, England, Sweden, Canada, Ireland and Germany then began to settle and farm the surrounding countryside.

With the advent of the railroad in 1852, the town and county began to prosper, In 1858 there were 2,500 inhabitants in Belvidere alone, along with three flour mills, four banks, forty stores, five hotels, two public schools and a couple of private academies.

➡ Getting Started

Begin your visit by stopping by the Belvidere Area Chamber of Commerce located at 419 South State Street. We have free brochures listings for specialty shops and lodging.

Attractions

Boone County Historical Museum
(815) 544-8391
311 Whitney Boulevard and
217 S. State Street
Exhibiting a variety of Boone County memorabilia, the museum features a Duxstad family log cabin, Civil War artifacts, a natural

history room, historic dolls, clothes, tools and transportation, from the 1906 Eldredge Runabout to Belvidere's first Chrysler production car in 1965. Open Tuesday and Thursday 8:30am-noon and 1-4pm, May through October. Also, 3rd Sunday of each month, 2-4pm. Call coordinator George Gibson (815) 544-8391.

Ida Public Library
(815) 544-3838
320 N. State Street
A 1987 addition to the original building is a beautiful blending of old and new which has tripled the volume size. It has also provided public meeting rooms and expanded the children's, audiovisual, youth and genealogy sections. Open Monday-Friday 9:30am-9pm. Saturday 9:30am-5pm.

Frank Lloyd Wright Petit Memorial Chapel
(815) 547-7642
1121 N. Main Street
The chapel, designed by Frank Lloyd Wright and erected in 1907, located in Belvidere Cemetery. Open daily 8am-sunset.
✪ Tours by appointment

The US Armed Forces Five Flags Living Memorial
(815) 547-6370
9700 Route 76
Dedicated to honoring all those who have honorably served, our country in war and peace, names of living and deceased veteran's appear on the memorial representing the U.S. from the civil war through current service.

Satellite Attractions

❧ Edwards Apple Orchard
(815) 765-2234
7061 Centerville Road
Poplar Grove, IL 61065
A Boone County tradition for family fall outings and fun is picking your own apples or visit the Apple Barn for apples, cider, donuts and many other tastes of fall. Attractions include a farm museum, coffee shop, farm animal zoo, children's maze and hayloft. Open September-Thanksgiving, daily 9am-7pm.

❧ Fiorello's Pumpkin Patch/Christmas
(815) 765-2587
3178 Illinois Route 173
1/2 mile east of Caledonia, IL
Mounds of bright orange pumpkins, golden cornstalks and colorful life-size paintings cheerfully greet visitors. The Harvest Barn offers cheeses, cider, preserves, candies, apples and Halloween novelties. There are painted pumpkins and gourds, weekend pony rides and face painting. Add to all this the

beautiful light displays, decorated Christmas trees and handpainted ornaments as Christmas approaches. Daily 9am-7pm, early September to late December.

Annual Events

The events and dates shown may be changed without notice. Please contact the Chamber of Commerce at (815) 544-4357 to verify.

✤ Spring

Annual Men's Canoe Race
1st Sunday in May
Held on Kishwaukee River, Gaden Prairie Bridge to State Street in Belvidere.

Annual Women's Canoe Race
3rd Sunday in May
Held on Kishwaukee River, Camp Epwroth to Main Street in Belvidere.

✤ Summer

Summer Concerts in the Park
June thru mid-July
Summer concerts are held at 7:00 pm every Sunday in Belvidere Park near the Baltic Mill, with a wide range of music for every taste. Presented by the Boone County Arts Council.
✪ Free

Blaine Folk Festival
2nd Sunday in June
11am-6pm Blaine, Illinois Methodist Church. Music, arts, crafts, homemade food. The festival is rain or shine.

Strawberry Festival
Mid-June
(815) 597-3011
Garden Prairie, 5 miles east of Belvidere on Rt. 20. Crafts, pony rides, music, food, games and hay rides. Good family entertainment.

Belvidere Women's Club Art Show
4th Sunday in June
Big Thunder Park
613 N. Main Street
Court House Square
All day over 100 artists will display, sell and compete in an outdoor setting. Children's corner, food, prizes, entertainment.

Wall to Wall Arts Festival
4th Weekend in June
Downtown Belvidere
The festival is in conjunction with the Woman's Club Art Show and the Boone County Arts Council's Concerts in the Park. Over 150 artists painted historic wall murals in 1997; thereafter, historic wall tours will be held. Future wall murals' are being anticipated. Food and entertainment are available.

Heritage Celebration and 4th of July Annual Parade

4pm Downtown Belvidere, 7pm Band Concert at Boone County Fairgrounds, 9:30pm Fireworks. All day activities at fairgrounds and Big Thunder Park.

✪ Free admission

Boone County Fair

August

Boone County Fairground Illinois Route 76 one mile north of Belvidere. 8am-midnight, Tuesday through Sunday. The second largest county fair in the state includes numerous displays, amusement rides, first rate entertainment by country music talents, and many foods for sale.

✦ Fall

Oktoberfest

2nd weekend in September Downtown Belvidere, 5pm to midnight Friday; 7am to midnight Saturday; 11am-5pm Sunday. German style bands, entertainment tent with beer garden, dancers, good food, carnival rides, parade, pancake breakfast and sports competitions.

Autumn Pioneer Festival

4th weekend in October
(815) 547-7935
7600 Appleton Road
Spencer Park, Belvidere

Crafts and life works of the mid-1800s. Boone County Conservation District.

✪ Free admission

✦ Winter

Hometown Christmas

1st weekend in December
Friday 6pm Lighting of the Community Christmas Tree, 6-9pm Victorian "Living" Window Displays, carolers, horse and buggy rides, tours of the Boone County Historical Museum, entertainment, festive foods and homemade holiday treats. Saturday,10am Parade with Santa. Sunday, Do-It-Yourself Messiah.

Shopping

Burd Antiques

(815) 764-2215
17293 Poplar Grove Road
2.5 miles north of Hwy 173. Open 9-6 Thursday thru Sunday, May to December. Antiques, collector items, country accessories and gifts. Visit the animal barn.

Exclusively Yours • Leiza George

(815) 544-0258
705 North State Street
This unique boutique is located in an historic Victorian neighborhood.

Flower Bin Specialty Shoppe

(815) 544-2800
424 S. State Street

Featuring balloons, gourmet gift baskets, and contemporary floral design and accessories.

Funderburg Antiques
(815) 547-8186
2111 Newburg Road
Warehouse with antique pine furniture and stained glass windows.

The Home Place Antiques
(815) 544-0577
615 S. State Street
Lamps and light fixtures, general line of quality antiques. Qualified appraiser. Over 20 years exper-

ience. Tuesday-Saturday 10am-5pm.

Ker-Ree Jewelry & Rock Shop
815 544-2722
2124 N. State Street
Black Hills Gold, crystals, gifts for all occasions. Unique rock shop.

Conclusion
For further information contact:
Belvidere Area
Chamber of Commerce
419 South State Street
Belvidere, IL 61008
815 544-4357 • Fax 815 547-7654
www.belvidere.net

Welcome to Belvidere . . .

❝ Today, Belvidere boasts a population of over 18,712 residents with another 18 thousand within the county, and has realized a productive meld of industry, agriculture and suburban living while retaining the small town amenities.

For those times when they are needed, urban offerings are just minutes away with Rockford being only twelve miles to the west while Chicago is a scant seventy-five minutes to the east.

Enjoy your visit, remember the special points of interest and special events and please come again. ❞

—Gloria Fay
Executive Director

Elgin
The City to Watch

Location

Located along Interstate 90 west of Chicago, take exit routes 31 or 25.

History

Following the Black Hawk War, James and Hezekiah Gifford came to the area in 1835. The enterprising James, along with the help of Samuel Kimball constructed a road to Belvidere that he hoped would attract stage traffic along the Chicago to Galena route. Within a year stages were stopping by twice a week.

In 1837, Kimball and James Gifford cooperated to dam up the nearby Fox River for the operation of a saw mill and grist mill.

Chicagoan B.W. Raymond came to the area in 1838 to the area with the hopes of founding a city. By 1847 the town of Elgin became a reality, and the following year Raymond was instrumental in coaxing the rails of the Chicago and Galena Railroad through the village. The city of Elgin was incorporated in 1854.

Milk, cheese and butter became the staple products of Elgin, especially by the development of condensing milk, a process refined by Gail Borden of Elgin. By 1875 condensed milk from Elgin was being sold in cities like New York. Watch manufacturing was another early industry of note in Elgin. Mimicking the same mass production techniques as Ford, Elgin watch manufacturers produced standardized goods at a rapid pace.

Beginning in 1872 the successful dairy trade made Elgin the seat of the Midwest Board of Trade for more than 40 years. By 1911 Elgin was producing more than 57 million pounds of butter.

➠ Getting Started

You'll find the Elgin Area Convention and Visitors Bureau at 77 Riverside Drive in historic downtown Elgin on the Fox River and find a Satellite Visitors Information Center at the Grand Victoria Riverboat Pavilion. Elgin, rich in history and ethnic diversity is experiencing a rebirth and revitalization. The Bureau represents thirteen communities scattered throughout Cook, Kane and McHenry Counties.

Attractions

Elgin Fire Barn #5 Museum

(847) 697-6242
533 St. Charles Street
Here you will see many old restored fire engines along with Elgin's first steam engine that dates back to 1869. The museum is listed on the National Register of Historic Places and is recognized for its Classical Revival style of architecture. Children will learn about fire safety and fire fighting.

Fox River Trolley Museum South Elgin

(847) 697-4676
Located on Illinois Route 31, three blocks south of State Street in South Elgin, IL. Ride a vintage 1896 trolley and view antique trolleys at this unique outdoor museum. An old time trolley will transport you along an authentic railway which has been in operation since Independence Day, 1896, a fun educational experience for the whole family. Open on Sundays from the second Sunday in May through the first Sunday in November.

Elgin Public Museum in Lords Park

(847) 741-6655
225 Grand Boulevard
The museum is the oldest building in Illinois built as a museum that still serves that purpose to see exhibits from dinosaurs to mound builders, you can visit prehistoric Illinois in this 1907 museum. Year round activities for children include the petting zoo in the park (seasonal).

Hemmens Cultural Center

(847) 931-5900
150 Dexter Court
The city of Elgin offers stellar entertainment in the 1,200 seat performing arts theater. You can count on Hemmens to host the best entertainment in the Midwest.

McHenry County Historical Society Museum

(815) 923-2267
6422 Main Street
The three buildings here dating back to 1847 include a museum in the 1870 Union School, the 1895

Fox River Trolley Museum, South Elgin

West Harmony one room school and a 1847 log cabin.

Old Main Museum
(847) 742-4248
360 Park Street
The area's historical museum was built in 1856. Displays include those of the Elgin Watch Company and the Elgin National Road Races. The museum is a National Historic Site.
✪ Call for hours

Valley View Model Railroad Museum
(815) 923-4135
17108 Highbridge

The sight and sounds of an HO miniature scale railroad work with animation and lots of track.

Visual and Performing Arts Center
Elgin Community College
(847) 622-0300 (Box Office)
The 700 seat main stage theater also hosts a 160 seat black box theater, an art gallery and a recital hall as well as arts classrooms. Call for a list of scheduled performances.

Haeger Potteries

Satellite Attractions

🌿 **Dundee**

Dundee Township Historical Society Museum
(847) 428-6996 (call for hours)
426 Highland
Learn about Alan Pinkerton, the famous local detective. Much of the museum is filled with Dundee's history dating back to the 1800s.

Haeger Potteries Factory Outlet
(847) 426-3033
West Dundee
Founded in 1871 on the beautiful banks of the scenic and historic Fox River the Haeger Potteries, today is under the direction of the fourth generation of the Haeger family. They are located on Van Buren Street, two blocks south of Route 72. Their pottery is accepted worldwide as the standard by which other pottery is judged. You will find an outstanding collection of ceramic accessories and original hand-turned pottery at factory prices.
✪ Free tours

Polar Dome Ice Arena
(708) 426-6751
Route 25 and 72
How about a daytrip on ice? Shows and public skating are on ice here.

Santa's Village and Racing Rapids/Family Theme Park
(847) 426-6751
Amusement rides and carnival games are adjacent to a water theme park.

🌿 **Huntley**

Huntley Factory Shops
(847) 669-9100
11800 Factory Shops Blvd. (exit 1-90 at Rt. 47)
Sixty five manufacturers are at

your beck and call. You will find fine quality merchandise at substantially lower prices. Special events and craft shows are regularly scheduled. Write or call for events listing.

❧ Marengo

Located west of Elgin along Interstate 90, this town was named for the famous Napoleonic battle in Italy. It was first settled in 1835 by Calvin Spencer from Ohio. He and his family operated a hotel in the village. Marengo is the home of Egbert Van Alstyne, who wrote the music for the song "In the Shade of the Old Apple Tree." Year round camping and recreation facilities are at Indian Oaks Park. In the winter you can come to the park and cut your own Christmas tree.

❧ Union

Illinois Railway Museum
(800) BIG-RAIL
7000 Olson Road
Take a nine mile ride on an antique steam locomotive and view other trains of yesteryear.
✪ Special events

Donley's Wild West Town
(815) 923-9000
Route 20 and South Union Road
Visit an old town that features gunslinger shoot-outs, pony rides and panning for gold.

The Depot/Information Center
(847) 426-2255
319 North Street, East Dundee
While obtaining information you will be taken back in time when you enter this vintage train depot. It has been renovated to accommodate the weary traveler along the Fox River Bike Trail.

Annual Events

May
• Valley Fox Trot — Nearly 10,000 participate in multi-distanced races. Pancake breakfast. (847) 931-6120

June
• Antique Music Sale and Show — Held annually in nearby Union.
• Scandinavian Children's Days — Vasa Park in South Elgin brings out the Viking in everyone.

July
• Illinois Railway Museum's Trolley Pageant in Union.
• Heritage Day — Festivities at the McHenry County Historical Museum.
• Algonquin Founders' Day Festival — Enjoy a golf tournament, parade, car show, fireworks and symphonic music.

August
• The Elgin Fine Arts Festival — A weekend of arts and music in the park.
(847) 695-7540

September
- Historic Elgin House Tour — (847) 741-2837
- Scandinavian Days — Vasa Park plays host to displays of Norse tools, costumes, food, and Viking fun for the whole family.

Shopping and Dining

Shopping can be a real adventure while you browse through the many shops in the area. You will find malls, antique stores, specialty shops, craft stores, and many more. There is something to fit every persons budget.

You will find dining at its best throughout the Fox River Valley. Write for a guide to restaurants.

Conclusion

For more information contact:
Elgin Area Convention and Visitors Bureau
77 Riverside Drive
Elgin, IL 60120
(847) 695-7540
Toll Free: 1-800-217-5362
FAX: (847) 695-7668

Visitor Information Center is located at the Grand Victoria Casino.

Tips

✔ Enjoy the golf courses in the Northern Fox River Valley. Call for a description and more information.
✔ The 36 mile Fox River Bike Trail offers biking enthusiasts trails winding through beautiful countryside and interesting cityscapes. Wild flowers, plants, birds, water fowl and small animals share the trail with nature lovers. Call or write for a map of the Fox River Bike Trail.
✔ Beautiful campgrounds are available. Write for a listing of campgrounds.

Venture Into the Northern Fox River Valley, IL

66 Our service area of thirteen municipalities offers visitors a great mix of events and attractions, with something great for everyone who visits.

Couples, singles and families, have many options to plan that perfect get-away.

The sophistication of great happenings such as music, the theater and specialty foods plus great outdoor activities, give couples a place to have fun and re-connect. Who could ask for more?

Singles will not be at a loss because the Fox River Valley is truly a friendly and comfortable place to visit. Knock yourself out shopping and attending craft shows and museums. Feel free to kick your shoes off and walk through the grass in any of our beautiful parks.

Families will tune into theme parks, hotel pools and the many fairs and festivals available year round.

For additional visitor information call 1-800-217-5360 and request our current visitors' guide. **99**

—Elgin Area Convention and Visitors Bureau

Galena
B&B Capital of the Midwest

Location

Arrive in Galena by driving through the area's scenic beauty on Highway 20. The drive can be one of the highlights of the trip.

History

Early lead mining assured the Galena area of eventual greatness. The Indians and later the French settlers mined the lead in what was then known as the Fever River Valley. LeSueur and Iberville led an expedition of 30 to explore the area in 1699. It was Le Sueur who discovered the Galena River in 1700. Galena means lead ore and "River of Mines" and the name stuck. By 1717 promoters were recruiting miners with "get rich quick" schemes. The remainder of the eighteenth century saw little growth in the area, but lead mining continued.

When steam trafficking became commonplace along the Mississippi River, lead mining in the Galena area began to boom. With the establishment of a post office, one of the first in northern Illinois, the town took root.

The rush to mine lead peaked in Galena about 1829. Throngs of miners brought elements of civilization which resulted in the addition of associated industries and more settlers. While other settlements were struggling with the construction of log cabins, Galena witnessed the erection of stone and brick mansions. By 1845 Galena was producing some 27,000 tons of lead, accounting for 83 percent of the U.S. supply.

Prosperity followed through the 1850s, but eventually the lead deposits began to dwindle. When the railroad bypassed Galena in 1855, the town lost its vital link to the outside markets. This prompted many miners to follow others out to the gold deposits in California.

The Civil War uncovered mixed loyalties within the town whose citizens came primarily from Virginia. However, Union sentiments prevailed and two companies were formed to support Lincoln's call for troops. Though he declined captaincy of one of the troops from Galena, Mexican American War veteran Ulysses S. Grant did agree to act as a drillmaster and went with the units to Springfield.

Getting Started

When you arrive in Galena stop by the Visitor Information Center located in the old train depot two blocks north of Highway 20 on the east bank of the Galena River. Hours are 9-5 Monday through Saturday and 10-4 on Sunday. Extended evening hours on weekends.

Visitor Information Center
101 Bouthillier Street
(815) 777-0203 or
800/747-9377
website: www.galena.org

Attractions

Galena boasts that 85% of the town is on the National Register of Historic Districts. In Galena you will find examples of 19th century architecture including Federal, Italianate, Greek Revival, Queen Anne, Gothic Revival, Second Empire, Romanesque Revival and Galena Vernacular. Zinc placques can be found on many of the buildings explaining their histories.

The Belvedere Mansion

(815) 777-0747
1008 Park Avenue
This 22 room mansion was built in 1857 for J. Russell Jones, steamboat magnate and ambassador to Belgium. Its architecture is Italianate style furnished with

Belvedere Mansion

formal Victorian pieces. You will find items from Liberace's estate as well as the famous green drapes from "Gone With the Wind."

City Brewery Mansion
(815) 777-0354
418 Spring Street
This limestone building was built in 1850 and operated as a brewery until 1881. You will see many displays about Galena's brewing history and learn about the different types of beer and how they were made.
✪ By appointment only

The DeSoto House Hotel
(815) 777-0090
230 S. Main Street
Known as the "best hotel west of New York City for its sumptuous accommodations and meticulous service," the hotel opened its doors in 1855 and underwent major renovations in 1980. It is listed in the National Register of Historic Places.

The Dowling House
(815) 777-1250
220 Diagonal Street
Built in 1826 of native limestone as a general store and residence, it is the oldest house in Galena. Vernacular architecture, it is furnished with primitive furniture and an extensive collection of Galena pottery.

Galena/Jo Daviess County History Museum
(815) 777-9129
211 S. Bench Street
This is the best place to start your visit to Galena. The museum is housed in this 1858 Italianate mansion with an hourly audio-visual show of Galena's progress of the town from its beginning to today. You will find permanent exhibits, one of which includes a Civil War Exhibit with Thomas Nast's original painting "Peace in Union."

Galena Post Office
(815) 777-0225
110 Green Street
Built from Nauvoo limestone in 1857-59 as a post office and customs house, the Renaissance Revival building is the second oldest continuously operating post office in the United States. If you mail a letter inside, it is post-marked "Galena."

Galena Public Library District and Historic Collection
(815) 777-0200
601 S. Bench Street
The library, built in 1907 in the Greek Revival style, was endowed by the Felt family. In the reading room is a mosaic fireplace in a wisteria pattern, in the style of Frank Lloyd Wright and the Prairie School architecture. You will find

Grant's Home

an extensive collection of historic documents.

Grant Hills Antique Auto Museum
(815) 777-2115
Highway 20 East
These antique, classic and special interest cars date from as early as 1912. There are also auto memorabilia, Ertl toys, Lionel trains, Galena pottery and many other collectibles.

The Old Market House State Historic Site
(815) 777-3310 or 815 777-2570
123 N. Commerce Street

The Old Market House served as a hub of community life during Galena's most prosperous era. The sesquicentennial of this Greek Revival building was celebrated in 1996. It was used as a multi-purpose building and continues that tradition today. Special events and exhibitions are held throughout the year. The Christmas season celebrates with "Santa's Workshop,"

Ulysses S. Grant Home State Historic Site
(815) 777-3310 or 815 777-0248
500 Bouthillier Street
Civil War hero General U.S. Grant

was presented this home upon his return to Galena in 1865. Now restored as it appeared during the post-Civil War period and the Grant Presidency, you will find many of the same furnishings used by Grant and his family. Grant's children gave the home to the city of Galena in 1905. Enjoy costumed interpreters telling about Galena's most famous citizen.

Vinegar Hill Historic Lead Mine and Museum

(815) 777-0855
8885 N. Three Pines Road
Enjoy a guided tour through the mine and the museum that features a wide variety of lead and ore samples and mining tools. Hard hats are provided.

Guided Tours

Enjoy a narrated guided tour on one of the trolleys. For group tours, bus tours or step-on guide service, call the toll free number. 1-800 747-9377.

Brill's Trolley Tours, Inc.

(815) 777-3121
102 N. Main Street
One-hour narrated tour.

Galena Trolley Tours Depot

(815) 777-1248
Fax 817 777-1283
Trolley Tours: This is a one-hour narrated tour. Executive Coach Tours: This is a two-hour narrated tour.

Satellite Attractions

✹ Apple River

Located on Stagecoach Trail this community owes its early growth to the Illinois Central Railroad which came through in 1854. A good time to visit this community is during the annual "Stagecoach Trail Festival" held each June.

✹ East Dubuque

Visit the Julien Dubuque Bridge which is the longest tied arch and cantileverted bridge ever built. The town offers visitors a variety of taverns and nightlife, restaurants and supper clubs as well as great parks, golf courses and marinas on the majestic Mississippi.

✹ Elizabeth

Enjoy a stroll down Main Street and the old-time feel of quaint shops, restaurants and galleries. Visit the Wedding Chapel in an 1875 country church. Another good time to visit is the last weekend in July when the annual Elizabeth Community Fair is held.

✹ Hanover

The Mallard Capital of the World and site of the Whistling Wings, the world's largest mallard duck hatchery. A popular attraction is the Mallard Duck Festival in September.

⚜ Scales Mound

The entire village of Scales Mound is a National Register Historic District and is listed in the National Register of Historic Places.

⚜ Stockton

This quiet country town is located among lush rolling pastures and is also distinguished by being the highest town in Illinois at 1000 feet above sea level.

Heritage League Museum, Stockton Township Public Library
815 947-2030
140 West Benton Street
Enjoy seeing memorabilia and artifacts from the early days in northwest Illinois such as farm implements, household items, vintage clothing and documents.

Scenic Drives

Continue your daytrip by driving through many of the winding scenic country roads of Jo Daviess County. Contact the Visitor Information Center in Galena for maps of the county. Some of the most scenic spots are these:
• Stagecoach Trail between Galena and Warren
• Blackjack Road between Galena and Hanover

• Derinda Road between Elizabeth and Mount Carroll
• Canyon Park Road between Stockton and Warren
• River Road and Blanding Road along the Mississippi
• The Great River Road, which runs along both sides of the Mississippi from the Minnesota headwaters to the Gulf of Mexico, begins in East Dubuque, passing through Galena and Hanover on the way south.

Annual Events

Calendars of Events are published twice a year. Before planning your trip please phone our toll-free number 1-800 747-9377 for confirmation of dates and events. The following is a brief run-down of long-standing annual events. Many more are added each year.

January/February
• Klondike Kapers
• An Evening with the Collectors
• Winterfest
• Illinois Special Olympics Winter Games
• Taste of Galena

March/April
• St. Patrick's Day Parade
• Boy Scouts of America Ulysses S. Grant Pilgrimage

May/June
• Stagecoach Trail Festival

• Galena Historic Home Tour
July/August
• Galena Arts Festival • Jo Daviess County Fair
• Willow Folk Festival • Chicago Bears Camp
• Menominee Country Fest • Galena Antique Car Show
September/October
• Ladies Getaway • Hanover Mallardfest • Ice Cream Socials
• East Dubuque Fun Day • Taste of Stockton
• Galena Country Fair • Warren Pumpkin Fest
• Galena Halloween Parade • Galena Historic Home Tour
• Elizabeth Autumn Craft Festival
• Stockton Scenic Trail Craft Fair
November/December
• Noveau Beaujolais Wine Celebration • Ski Swap
• Mistletoe Ball • Classic Holiday Concert • Country Christmas

Shopping and Dining

Shopkeepers pride themselves on personalized service. There is shopping galore and something for everyone. Galena is also known as the "choice antiquing town" by *Midwest Living* magazine. You will find many apparel shops, art galleries and studios, flower shops, book stores, Christmas shops and a wide assortment of craft shops.

Dining opportunities range from home-cooking to haute cuisine. You can breakfast with local farmers at the corner cafe or dine by candlelight on gourmet fare. "Come as you are"—we call it "casual elegance."

Tips

✔ You will find a few public parking lots downtown. They fill up fast as does much of the parking downtown. Watch for signs—restrictions are enforced.

✔ There is a free long term parking lot located across from the railroad tracks next to the Visitor Information Center. A weekend shuttle operates from May through October and is $1.00 for all day. Plenty of room and you may park as long as you wish.

✔ On special weekends parking is available on the edge of town with shuttle service provided to the festivals.

✔ Transportation—The nearest commercial airport is in Dubuque, IA. There is no train service, but the Greyhound Bus Line serves Galena via Highway 20.

❝ Galena, Illinois —With nearly 50 bed-and-breakfasts, Jo Daviess County is the B&B Capital of the Midwest and maybe even the nation.

Visitors call our 800 number and ask for the names of our B&Bs. When we say there are 50, there's a gasp on the other end of the line. But they are not quite so overwhelmed when we offer to send them a Visitor's Guide that describes each B&B in detail.

So . . . where's Jo Daviess County, and why does it have so many B&Bs?

Just three hours west of Chicago, Jo Daviess County is tucked away in the northwest corner of Illinois, where Iowa, Illinois and Wisconsin meet on the Mississippi River. The landscape is unlike the rest of the "Prairie State." offering rugged hills, rocky bluffs, wooded valleys and winding roads.

Galena, population 3,600, is the county's "crown jewel." The town was built by wealthy miners, merchants and steamboat captains, during the era following the nation's first major mineral rush in 1829, 20 years prior to the California Gold Rush.

Why so many B&Bs? Well, those early residents left a legacy of magnificent architectural treasures. Today's modern families of 3.2 people would rattle around in those mansions, and it's costly to restore and maintain a big historic home.

The B&Bs range from High Victorian to Fancy Farm, and the innkeepers are as diverse as the architecture — semi-retired couples, artists, teachers, single professionals and young ex-urbanite couples.

What else does Galena offer. The Ulysses S. Grant Home State Historic Sites,150 shops and galleries, great golf, interesting restaurants, hiking, biking and horseback riding; music and drama, Mississippi riverboat casinos and cruises, spectacular scenery and small-town ambience.

For a comprehensive Visitor's Guide just phone toll-free: 1 800 747-9377. ❞

Galena/Jo Daviess
County Convention and Visitors Bureau

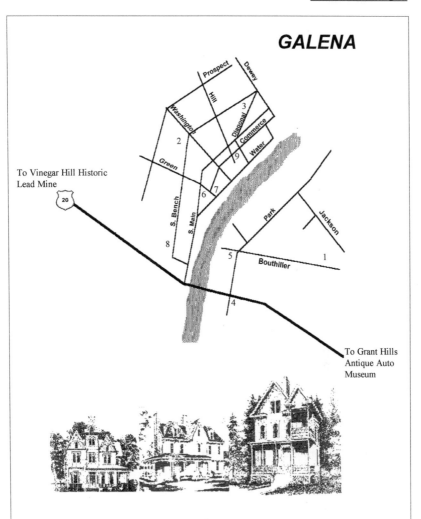

1. U.S. Grant Home
2. Galena/Jo Daviess County History Museum
3. Dowling House
4. Belvedere Museum
5. Convention Center and Visitors Bureau
6. DeSoto House Hotel
7. Galena Post Office
8. Galena Public Library and Historical Collection
9. Old Market House State Historical Site

Map by Paul Wentzel

Greater Woodfield
Chicago's Northwest Suburbs

Location
Located 35 minutes from downtown Chicago. The thirteen communities of Greater Woodfield are also a short drive away from the outdoor fun of Lake County and the Fox River Valley.

Greater Woodfield
Picture a region of lush cornfields and small bedroom communities, interspersed with hints of long ago farm villages and crisscrossed with country roads. Prior to 1970, this provincial territory, now known as Greater Woodfield, offered little resemblance to the metropolis of Chicago situated less than 23 miles to its southeast.

And then came Woodfield Shopping Center.

In 1971, the opening of the then world's largest enclosed mall, Woodfield Shopping Center, brought national attention to the region. Quick to follow were hotels, restaurants, and corporate centers, and soon, Greater Woodfield boasted a striking skyline of its very own.

This exciting edge city now has become a "hot spot" for meetings and conventions and more recently a tourist destination for folks who enjoy weekend getaways.

In addition to our famous mall, Greater Woodfield is home to Arlington International Racecourse, Medieval Times Dinner and Tournament, Rainforest Cafe, Dave and Busters, Lynfred Winery, JFK Health World Museum and more! Plus, the excitement and culture of Chicago are merely 35 minutes away.

More than 9,000 guest rooms in 42 properties from economy to first class resorts make finding the "right" home away from home easy. Each hotel features great weekend rates and special packages, and a FREE money-saving coupon book with values at hotels, restaurants, and attractions is distributed by the area's convention and visitors bureau.

Getting Started

For more information contact:
Greater Woodfield Convention &
Visitors Bureau
1375 East Woodfield Road, Suite
100
Schaumburg, IL 60173
1-800-847-4849
(847) 605-1010
(847) 605 0120 (fax)
www.chicagonorthwest.com

Attractions

❦ Addison

Dave & Buster's
(630) 543-5151
There is no place like Dave &
Buster's. The Million Dollar
Midway displays handcrafted
billard tables and a vast array of
games. It is a perfect playground
for grownups. Play a game of
shuffleboard, or enjoy virtual
reality and electronic simulators as
well as tried and true favorite games
of skill.

❦ Arlington

*Arlington International
Racecourse*
(847) 255-4300
This nationally known Thoroughbred racecourse is one of the most
beautiful in the world. Beautiful
flowers and lush lawns are a
magnificent backdrop for racing
enthusiasts. You can enjoy

watching from railside or enjoy one
of Arlington's elegant dining
rooms.

❦ Barrington

JFK Health World Museum
(847) 842-9100
This museum is a children's "hands-
on" health education and learning
center. It has more than 200
interactive exhibits, eye-catching
displays, oversized characters and
musical presentations to promote
good health and lifestyles. Open
Monday-Wednesday, noon to 5 pm;
Thursday-Friday, noon to 8pm;
Saturday-Sunday, 10am-5pm.
Admission charge.

❦ Elk Grove Village

Enesco's Back Door Store
The store offers many shopping
surprises at outlet prices —
Precious Moments, Easter and
Christmas ornaments, Cherished
Teddies, gifts for holidays,
birthdays, weddings, etc.

❦ Roselle

Lynfred Winery
(630) 529-9463
15 South Roselle Road
Producers of gourmet wines made
from Napa Valley grapes and fruits
from throughout the Midwest.
This is one of Greater Woodfield's
unique attractions. Call ahead for
tour availability and additional

information. Lynfred is open from 11 am to 7pm seven days a week.
❂ Free Tours

Rainforest Cafe
(847) 619-1900
Greater Woodfield boasts the first Rainforest Cafe in the area. One of the most intriguing experiences of a lifetime is when you are dining among parrots, fish, gallons of seawater and a real-life coral reef. You will be greeted by a nine-foot animated snake darting through fourteen foot banyan trees, as a nine-foot crocodile rests among 15 different live birds and periodi-cally wags its tail while rising out of a misty pond. The food is presented in a creative manner and served with tropical garnishes. After dining, shop for gifts from different parts of the world in the retail store located in the Rainforest. The curator of the Rainforest Cafe, who is a marine biologist, brings with him more than 20 years experience to the Woodfield Shopping Center where he educates people about the wonders and mysteries of the rainforest. Call for summer hours and additional information.
❂ Children two and under are free.

Rainforest Cafe

🍂 Long Grove

Historic Long Grove's shopping village has over 100 stores. Enjoy shopping in the unique country setting where you will find year-round Christmas items, Irish imports, Bohemian crystals, handmade crafts, distinctive clothing and antiques galore. While there take a carriage ride through the village. There are two outstanding events held in Long Grove — summer's Strawberry Fest and autumn's Apple Fest.

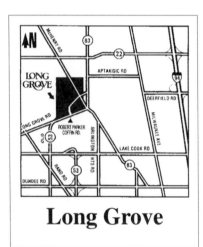

Long Grove

🍂 Schaumburg

Medieval Times Dinner & Tournament
(847) 843-3900
Located at the intersection of I-90 (the Northwest Tollway) and Roselle Road. You are invited by the Lord of the Castle to enjoy watching the state-of-the-art competition of jousting knights. You can enjoy a four course banquet served by your own serf or wench while watching spirited stallions perform intricate maneuvers. Fearless knights on horseback compete in games of skill and accuracy. A time to remember. Showtimes are 7:30 pm Wednesday and Thursday, 8:00 pm Friday and Saturday and 4:00 pm Sunday. Call for reservations.

🍂 Union

Donley's Wild West Town
(815) 923-9000
Fun for the whole family. Located at Route 20 and South Union Road. Take I-90 to US 20 and drive four and a half miles west to Union Road. Don't miss the excitement and charm of the Old West as it was when gunslingers and showdowns were a way of life. Visit the Blacksmith, Print Shop, Jail, Saloon, the Ole' Pawn Shop and the Town Telegraph Office. You can also tour The Museum where you will find collections of Editor and Victor phonographs, nostalgic music and memorabilia of yesteryear. Pan for gold at the Sweet Phyllis Gold Mine, saddle up for a pony ride, board the C.P. Hunting train, or watch a professional stunt team put on the wildest shootout you will ever see. Open Memorial Day to Labor Day.

Woodfield Shopping Center

Sunday through Thursday 10am to 6pm, Friday and Saturday 10am to 9pm April, May, September and October.

✪ Children under 3 are free

🍃 **West Dundee**

Haeger Pottery

(847) 426-3033

Founded in 1871 on the beautiful banks of the scenic and historic Fox River is the Haeger Pottery. Today it is under the direction of the fourth generation of the Haeger family. They are located on Van Buren Street, two blocks south of Route 72. Their pottery is accepted worldwide as the standard by which other pottery is judged. You will find an outstanding collection of ceramic accessories and original hand-turned pottery at factory prices.

Shopping and Dining

Woodfield Shopping Center

Located in Schaumburg Woodfield Shopping Center is Illinois' number one tourist attraction with 26 million visits this year. Located at Route 53 and Golf Road, the center features nearly 300 stores, including 40 restaurants and eateries.

Department stores include Nordstrom, Marshall Field's, J.C. Penney, Sears and Lord and Taylor. The Rainforest Cafe along with many restaurants and food specialty options please every palate and budget. Woodfield is the largest retail shopping center in the nation under one roof and provides more than 75,000 shoppers a day with choosing that perfect gift. For additional infomation or a brochure call (847) 330-1537 or 1-800-332-1537 outside Illlinois.

Museums in the Greater Woodfield Area

* **Arlington Heights Historical Museum**
  110 West Fremont
  Arlington Heights, IL 60004
  (847) 255-1225
* **George S. Clayton House Palatine Historical Society**
  224 East Palatine Road
  Palatine, IL 60067
  (847) 991-0333
* **Farmhouse Museum History Center**
  499 Biesterfield Road
  Elk Grove Village, IL 60007
  (847) 439-3994
* **Mt. Prospect Schoolhouse Museum**
  1100 South Linneman Road
  Mount Prospect, IL 60056
  (847) 956-6777
* **Roselle Historical Museum**
  102 South Prospect
  Roselle, IL 60172-2026
  (630) 351-5300
* **Schaumburg Historical Society**
  (1872 1-Room Schoolhouse)
  208 East Schaumburg Road

Schaumburg, IL 60194
(847) 843-0799
* **Spring Valley Nature Sanctuary**
  111 East Schaumburg Road
  Schaumburg, IL 60194
  (847) 985-2100

Tips

✔ For a calendar of annual events and a FREE coupon book, call or write the Convention and Visitors Bureau.

✔ For details on arranging conventions and meetings call 1-800-847-4849 or (847) 605-1010. The Greater Woodfield area is an ideal location.

✔ Greater Woodfield provides an unlimited source of group tour options for short stopovers, weekend getaways, shopping excursions, holiday events and access to Metropolitan Chicago.

✔ Brochures available free of charge for restaurant and attraction guides.

✔ Golf courses in the area welcome you.

Conclusion

For more information contact:
Greater Woodfield Convention and Visitors Bureau
1375 East Woodfield Road, Suite 100
Schaumburg, IL 60173
1-800-847-4849 • (847) 605-1010
(847) 605 0120 (fax)
website:
www.chicagonorthwest.com

Rockford
Forest City

Location

Rockford is located in north-central Illinois on Interstate 90 in Winnebago County. It is just 90 minutes from Chicago and Galena, 110 minutes from Milwaukee and 70 minutes from Madison. Rockford can also be reached by Interstate 39 or US Highway 20.

History

The seat of Winnebago County is bisected by the Rock River. Germanicus Kent and Thatcher Blake of Galena founded the town in 1834. Damming a tributary of the Rock River, Kent began a sawmill operation that provided homes to scores of New England settlers venturing into the area.

In 1835 Daniel Haight began his own settlement across the river, but in 1839 the two communities merged into a single entity named Rockford. Winnebago County was established in 1836 and in 1839, Rockford was chosen as its seat. Hopes for becoming a shipping port proved unsuccessful when it was determined that the Rock River was not navigable by steamboats. However, the arrival of the Chicago and Galena Railroad in the 1850s insured the town of success.

Industry soon followed. One of the early leaders of that effort was John H. Manny, he is credited with inventing a combination reaper and mower that rivaled the excellence of the efforts of the more famous Cyrus McCormick. Another successful Rockford industry was the manufacturing of hosiery. In 1870 John Nelson and W.W. Burson started this effort and by the 1930s their firm was producing more than 30 million pairs of hose a year.

In 1852 a large influx of Swedes brought a European culture to Rockford. Swedish craftsmen began a furniture business that added to the city's industrial base.

Discovery Center's Giant Bubble Maker

⇒ Getting Started

Stop by the Rockford Area Convention and Visitors Bureau located on 211 North Main Street. We will be happy to provide brochures and to help you plan your visit to our city. It is a fun city to visit.

Attractions

Anderson Japanese Gardens
(815) 877-2525
Spring Creek and Highcrest Roads
One of Rockford's world-class attractions, this formal five-acre Japanese garden has four waterfalls, ponds, paths and quiet areas for contemplation. Ponds are stocked with Japanese koai, Chinese grass carp and native fish and aquatic life. Wild mallards and wood ducks visit the pair of resident Australian black swans. An authentic Japanese tea house and guest house add charm, as do other traditional Japanese features such as lanterns, bridges, a stone pagoda, water basins, and gates. Seasonal workshops and demonstrations are held in the education center. Open May through October, 10am to 4pm Monday through Saturday, Noon to 4pm Sunday.
✪ Free for children four and under with paying adults.

Barons Glass Museum
(815) 624-2666

106 West Main Street
This museum houses one of the largest collection of eighteenth century Stiegel-type enameled glass in the world.
✪ Free admission

Burpee Museum of Natural History
(815) 965-3433
737 and 813 North Main Street
Two historic mansions house an assortment of nature displays from dinosaurs to rocks and minerals. A highlight of the museum is an exhibit entitled "Indians of the Rock River Valley" which covers Indian history back to prehistoric times.

Discovery Center
(815) 963-6769
711 North Main Street
From the stars to the hair on your head, you and your family can learn of the wonders of science through a host of displays and interactive exhibits.

Erlander Home Museum
(815) 963-5559
404 South Third Street
This 1871 brick home explains the history of early Swedish immigrants to the area.

Ethnic Heritage Museum
(815) 962-7402
404 South Third Street

Anderson Japanese Gardens — Viewing House on Pond

An 1850s home preserves the history of the six major ethnic groups that originally settled the Rockford area.

Graham Ginestra House
(815) 964-8333
1115 South Main Street
Rockford's first commissioned landmark is an 1857 home built in the Italianate style.

Magic Waters
1-800-373-1679
7820 North Cherry Vale Blvd.
Cool off and slide through a day of family fun at this 35 acre outdoor water theme park.

Midway Village and Museum Center
(815) 397-9112
6799 Guilford Road
Relive the past in this turn-of-the-century village complete with school house, blacksmith shop, hospital, police station and more.

Art

The Rockford area is well represented by a wide spectrum of daytrip opportunities.

Rockford Art Museum

(815) 968-2787

711 N. Main Street

The museum features regionally and nationally known artists throughout the year with dynamic and changing exhibits.

Rockford College Art Gallery

(815) 226-4034

5050 East State Street

Throughout the school year the gallery sponsors seven exhibits from contemporary to regional art plus artwork from college collections.

Entertainment

If you like to play at the "play," Rockford will more than meet your desires.

Coronado Theatre

(815) 963-4640

312 North Main Street

This 1927 theater, now used for concerts, has exquisite decor.

New American Theater

(815) 964-8023

118 North Main Street

From September through June you can enjoy the best in adult and family entertainment at this intimate arena theater.

Rockford College/Maddox Theatre

(815) 226-4100

5050 East State Street

Excellent theater and musical productions are presented during the school year.

Rockford Dance Company

(815) 963-3341

711 North Main Street

Come enjoy dance programs and guest performers from fall through spring. You will be entertained.

Rockford Entertainment League, Inc.

(815) 282-8111

1225 Clifford Avenue

From September to May this non-profit group sponsors Broadway road shows.

Rockford Symphony Orchestra

(815) 965-0049

711 North Main Street

From classic to contemporary, this is just the place to enjoy music, including opera.

Natural Attractions

Harlem Hills Nature Preserve

(815) 964-6666

Nimtz Road and Flora Drive

More than 98 acres of natural trails through woodlands and prairie can be explored at this nearby facility.

Klehm Arboretum and Botanical Gardens

(815) 964-8146

More than one mile of hard-surfaced paths crisscross this 155 acre former nursery site filled with a huge variety of trees and shrubs.

Recreation Path

(815) 987-8800
1401 North 2nd Street

Stroll along this 5.05 mile stretch of lighted and paved paths that will take you by many of Rockford's local landmarks.

Rock Cut State Park

(815) 885-3311
7318 Harlem Road

Pierce Lake and the surrounding terrain offer you a full spectrum of outdoor fun including sailing, fishing, hiking, biking and scenic picnicking.

Severson Dells Environmental Education Center

(815) 335-2915
8786 Montague Road

Miles of nature trails including guided discovery walks, environmental workshops, seasonal programs and a hands-on museum.

Sinnissippi Gardens Greenhouse and Lagoon

(815) 987-8858
1300 North Second Street

Enjoy these gardens along the scenic Rock River. The most beautiful you will ever see.

Special Tours

Forest City Queen

(815) 987-8893
324 North Madison Street

Cruise the Rock River and enjoy everything from informative narrations and entertainment to fine dining.

Lady of the Rock

(815) 877-7744
10 East Riverside Boulevard

This excursion cruise offers sightseeing from the river.

Trolley Car 36

(815) 987-8893
324 North Madison Street

Enjoy a 45 minute ride on an authentic reproduction trolley car past many of Rockford's natural attractions.

Sports

Rockford has many sporting activities that the whole family can enjoy.

Blackhawk Farms Raceway

(815) 389-3323
15538 Prairie Road

Sport car, motorcycle, and even go-cart racing fun from spring until fall.

Rockford Cubbies
(815) 964-5400
Catch the future major leaguers in this farm team for the Chicago Cubs.

Rockford Lightning
(815) 968-5222
300 Elm Street
Continental basketball fun is at affordable prices.

Rockford Speedway
(815) 633-1500
9500 Forest Hills Road
Come catch the thrill of NASCAR racing on this 1/4 mile asphalt track.

Annual Events

We invite you to call or write for a more comprehensive list of annual events to be held in Rockford.

January
• Illinois Snow Sculpting Competition — Teams from around the state compete in this national and international competition.

May
• Pec Thing — Semi-annual antique show with over 400 exhibits.

June
• Civil War Days — The Blue and

Civil War Days at Midway Village

Gray reenact the struggles of the Civil War at Midway Village

July
• 4th of July Festival — An all-day event starts with breakfast. Entertainment throughout the day provides, food, rides and the Ski Broncs Water Ski Show. The day ends with a fireworks display.

August
• Festa Italiana — This annual festival celebrates Rockford's Italian heritage.

September
• On the Waterfront — Enjoy Labor Day weekend, a 3-day festival filled with activities that the whole family can participate in and enjoy as Rockford celebrates this annual event down by the Rock River.

December
• Festival of Lights — Lighted displays and tableaux daily.
• Splendor & Majesty — An entertaining event for the whole family to enjoy has colorful costuming, sparkling choreography and special effects.
• First Night — The event is sponsored by the Rockford Area Arts Council in a special indoor and outdoor venue with window art, street performers, kids fest, teen dance, food, carriage rides, snow and ice sculpting, an indoor carnival, resolution luminaria and fireworks.

Shopping and Dining

Rockford boasts a whopping 400 restaurants with lots of brand-name eateries and an exciting collection of one-of-a kind ethnic and gourmet restaurants. The restaurants reflect the rich ethnic heritage of the city. Rockford is known as "Little Italy in Illinois" because of the thousands of Italian immigrants who settled here. You will find dozens of Italian restaurants. Thousands of people flock to the riverfront each year to partake of some of the world's finest food.

You will find five major shopping malls and a bustling "strip" of discount chains and off-price outlets, plus interesting specialty shops scattered all over town. Rockford is a test market for new chains such as Media Play and The Old Navy Store. The Cherryvale Mall offers childcare and supervised children's activities to make your shopping easier.

Conclusion

For further information contact:
Rockford Area Convention and Visitors Bureau
Memorial Hall
211 North Main Street
Rockford, Illinois 61101 USA
1-800-521-0849 (USA & Canada)
(815) 963-8111 Anywhere • v/tdd
1-800-691-7035 (FAX)
E-Mail: rkfdcvb.wwa.com

Tips

✔ You will find a full dozen golf courses in Rockford. It is said they have more golf holes per capita than any place in the world. Thus it is known as "Illinois' Holey City." Call or write for names and locations.

✔ Rockford boasts over 3,000 rooms at a couple dozen motels, hotels, resorts and several bed-and-breakfasts. Most of the major chains are present, and many of the properties have been built since 1990. The Best Western Clock Tower Resort and Conference Center is the largest with 252 rooms, four restaurants and more. You may obtain a list of motels, hotels and bed and breakfasts from the Visitors Bureau.

✔ We will help you plan your visit and have a good time. Write for a Fun Pack.

✔ Finally, look for festivals. That's where you will find the best of Rockford's arts, food, cultural diversity and recreation all rolled into one wonderful venue, whether it is *On the Waterfront* on Labor Day weekend, *First Night* on New Year's Eve or *Festa Ialiana* in August. These are just the tip of the iceberg.

✔ Rockford is often called the Forest City because of its beautiful tree-lined streets and thousands of acres of parkland and gardens. Public gardens are open regularly, and many private and public gardens participate in the annual Garden Glory Tour every summer. Call the Rockford Area Convention and Visitors Bureau staff and arrange for special tours by appointment. Call or drop them a line!

A TEAM THAT CAN'T BE BEAT!

66 As a relative newcomer to the Rockford area, I never tire of exploring this Big City. There is a delightful surprise around every corner, and I love sharing my discoveries with visitors. Did you know Rockford is Illinois' second-largest city?

Rockford has the culture, amenities and ethnic diversity of a Big City but the friendliness and safety of a small town. The prices won't blow you away, and it is easy to find your way around.

Look for first-class culture! The Rockford Art Museum is the state's largest outside of Chicago. There are the ballet, the symphony and several theatrical groups. Big names come to the MetroCentre, and there is always some kind of music or entertainment at our "architecturally significant" old theaters. Twice a week in the summer, you can enjoy a *free* band concert in Sinnissippi Park.

Look for great food! Swedish and Italian immigrants flocked here years ago, and you will find more than 50 Italian eateries and several Swedish restaurants, along with national chains and creative gourmet cuisine. The world is well-represented in our dining options, and ethnic groceries and farmer's markets dot the city and surrounding landscape.

Look for wonderful outdoor recreation! Thanks to the Rockford Park District and the Winnebago County Forest Preserve District, the Rockford area has the following areas: 7,000 acres of parks; Magic Waters, one of the Midwest's largest water parks; the championship Aldeen Golf Club, one of the eight public courses; SportsCore, a 105 acre complex of playing fields that attracts teams from all over the world; the Ski Broncs, who perform *free* water-skiing shows on the Rock River two nights a week all summer long; the Rockford Cubbies, a Chicago Cubs farm team that hit homers at Marinelli Field. 99

—*Kathleen Webster*
RACVB Public Relations Specialists

Daytrip Illinois
Interstate 94

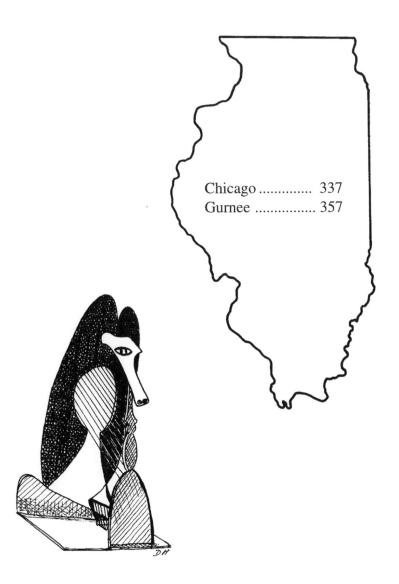

Chicago
"Windy City"

Location

Located on the western shores of Lake Michigan.

History

In September of 1673, Louis Joliet and Father Jacques Marquette led an expedition along the Mississippi to find a quick route to the Pacific. Traveling the various rivers to get to Lake Michigan, the party stopped for a day in what would eventually become the "Windy City." The land's significance was its portage proximity for travelers from the Chicago River to the massive lake. This opened up the Mississippi River Valley to the navigable northern lake system.

In 1696 Father Pinet established the Mission of the Guardian Angel to minister to the nearby Miami tribes. The stream running through the area was known to the Indians as the Checagou. This later evolved into the city's more familiar name.

The British seized control of the settlement in 1763 following the treaty ending the French and Indian War. Little remained of the French influence in the area. After the Revolutionary War the area became part of the newly formed United States, but British control would continue until Jay's Treaty in 1794.

Finally in 1803 Captain John Whistler, grandfather of the famous painter, took possession of the town and promptly constructed a fort near the river. He named the fort in honor of Henry Dearborn, then Secretary of the War in the Jefferson Cabinet.

Opposite the fort was a small settlement centered around a trading post begun by, Jean Baptiste Point Sable. In 1804, the Sable Trading Post was taken over by John Kinzie, a Scotch-Canadian trapper.

By 1812 the trading post spawned a village of some 40 inhabitants. When word reached the area that the British and their Indian allies were on the march, the decision was made to abandon the fort. On August 15, 1812, nearly 100 settlers and soldiers left the safety of the fort, led by Captain Nathan Heald. Two miles down the road the group was attacked by a band of Indians. In the ensuing fight, nearly half of the expedition was killed. The next day contingents of the local Potawatomi burned the fort to settle old grievances. One of the survivors was Kinzie, who four years later returned to rebuild his settlement. The decline of the fur trade thwarted further expansion into the region, but the Illinois-Michigan Canal project helped to found the town of Chicago, and in 1831 it became the seat of government for Cook County. The quiet settlement began in the year 1833 with only about 200 inhabitants, but by year's end, the settlement witnessed the passing of more than 20,000 travelers from back East enroute to the fertile farm land of the Midwest. Venturing along the Erie Canal to Buffalo, this army of settlers traveled by boat through the Lakes onto the harbor at Chicago. From there they could fan out into the river valleys to the south.

The wave of travelers brought merchants by the droves into the marshy settlement along Lake Michigan. Chicago became a city in 1837, and the following year witnessed the arrival of the steamboat that was used in a period of sustained growth. By the 1840's the reverse flow of goods through the city continued the upward trend of growth. By 1847, more than 450 stores graced the streets of Chicago which had 17,000 residents. Earlier New Englanders were later joined by waves of Irish, German, and Scandinavian immigrants.

As canal and rail routes began to connect Chicago with more and more distant fertile farmland, the city soon eclipsed the rival port of New Orleans as the point of choice for shipping. By 1848, Eastern cities as well as Europe could be supplied through the Great Lakes region to the north instead of the former southern route through the Gulf. In 1869, more ships arrived in Chicago Harbor than in the combined posts of New York, Philadelphia, Baltimore, Charleston, Mobile, and San Francisco.

Local merchants fought the introduction of the railroad for commerce trafficking. They preferred the added income from farmers driving their goods to the shipping ports. But their dissatisfaction went unheeded, and the burgeoning railroad increased the city's population to over 100,000 by the 1860's.

The invention of local George Pullman's sleeping car in 1864 spawned yet another industry for Chicago's growth and by 1870, the population rose to more than 300,000. The crowded living condition resulted in the construction of predominately closely packed, wooden houses. This error in judgment resulted in a fire on October 8, 1871, the Great Chicago Fire, reportedly started by Mrs. O'Leary's cow. It burned

17,450 buildings in 27 hours, claimed 300 lives, left 90,000 Chicagoans without homes and destroyed $200 million worth of property. An outpouring of humanitarian relief from as far away as Europe soon began the rebuilding project. Within three years, scarcely a sign of the fire remained.

With its inheritance as an industrial Mecca, it is not surprising that the modern labor movement found fertile ground for similar growth in the windy city. In 1877, rail and factory workers were led out on strike by Albert R. Parsons. This began a period of unrest that culminated in the 1886 Haymarket bombing. Parsons and three others were hanged for the incident.

In the midst of labor unrest the city continued its unparalleled growth. By 1890 the city was home to some one million inhabitants. The "gay nineties" saw expansion in the skyline of the city. In fact, an early Dictionary of American Slang defined "skyscraper" as, "a very tall building such as are now built in Chicago." The World's Columbian Exposition of 1893 was held in the capital of the industrial age. The celebration of America's 400th anniversary was an opportunity to show off the country's ingenuity to the rest of the world. Chicago was the fitting backdrop for this event that invited millions to witness the miracle of a new age.

Chicago had become the United State's leading ethnic center. More Scandinavians, Dutch, Polish, Lithuanians, Bohemians, Croatians, and Greeks resided in Chicago than in any other American city.

By 1930 the city's population had grown to over 3 million, and manufacturing produced some 4 billion in goods.

Getting Started

For more information about Chicago's many activities and attractions, call 1-800-2CON-NECT to request a free visitor information packet, or stop by any of the Chicago Office of Tourism's three visitor information centers located in the **Chicago Water Works** Visitor Center at 163 North Pearson Street at Michigan Avenue, in the Chicago Cultural Center at 77 E. Randolph Street, and in Illinois Market Place at Navy Pier, 700 E. Grand Avenue.

Attractions

The Art Institute of Chicago
(312) 443-3600 • TTY 443-3600
111 S. Michigan Avenue
Internationally renowned art institution, and comprehensive

*Photo credit — Chicago Photographic Co.
Chicago Department of Cultural Affairs.*

Preston Bradley Hall inside the Chicago Cultural Center

center for arts education and exhibition. Acclaimed Impressionist and Post-Impressionist collection. Galleries include Ancient Art, Japanese, Chinese and Korean, Modern Art (1900-1950) and the Thorne Miniature Rooms.

✪ Wheelchair Accessibile

Chicago Cultural Center
(312) 36-3278
TTY (312) 744-2947
78 E. Washington Street
Chicago's architectural showplace for the lively and visual arts celebrates its 100th anniversary in 1997. Join in the "Every Day's A Birthday" parties every afternoon in the Randolph Cafe. Free daily programs and exhibits cover a wide range of performing, visual and literary arts. Guided architectural tours of the landmark Chicago Cultural Center are offered every Tuesday, Wednesday and Saturday. A Chicago Office of Tourism visitor information center offers brochures, maps and calendars of events along with helpful representatives to assist visitors in planning their Chicago itinerary. The Shop at the Cultural Center sells products from Chicago area artists and attractions. The Corner Bakery Cafe is open seven days a week in the Randolph Street lobby. The Chicago Cultural Center also houses the Museum of Broadcast Communications.

DuSable Museum of African American History

(312) 947-0600

740 E. 56th Place

The oldest African American history museum in the United States, named for Jean Baptiste Pointe DuSable, a black fur trader and entrepreneur who was the first permanent settler in what became Chicago. It maintains an extensive permanent collection of artifacts, books, photographs, art objects and memorabilia, which total over 10,000 items. It presents the history and culture of Africans and Americans of African descent and holds a diverse array of public interpretive programs, including exhibitions, lectures, art education classes, workshops and African American history classes for young adults.

✪ Wheelchair Accessibility

Lincoln Park Zoo

(312) 742-2000

2200 N. Cannon Drive

One of the oldest zoos, started in 1868. This popular 35 acre zoo, with over 1,000 animals and 4 million annual visitors, is located in the heart of Lincoln Park. Free admission 365 days a year. The Great Ape House holds 24 of the world's finest gorillas. Children will enjoy the farm in the zoo and conservation station with hands-on activities for kids. A new glass-domed Regenstein Small Mammal and Reptile House opened in May of 1997.

✪ Wheelchair Accessibility

Lincoln Park Conservatory

(312) 742-7736

TTY-(312) 935-3718

2400 N. Stockton Drive

Modeled by architect Joseph Lyman Silsbee on London's Crystal Palace, the conservatory (1892) and its 18 propagating houses, cold frames and hotbeds now cover three acres. The three main galleries house extensive collections of palms, ferns, cacti and related flora. Many of the flowers in the gardens and landscapes of Chicago's parks are germinated in the conservatory's greenhouse.

✪ Wheelchair Accessibility

Mexican Fine Arts Center Museum

(312) 738-1503

1852 W. 19th Street

The largest institution of its kind in the US, this center is known for its annual *Day of the Dead* exhibitions in September. Two large galleries host activities ranging from fine arts exhibits to performances and community meetings. A $4 million expansion scheduled for completion in 1998 will triple the size of the museum.

✪ Wheelchair Accessibility

Museum Campus

The new museum campus has a friendly family park-like atmosphere that conveniently links the Chicago Park District to the *Shedd Aquarium, the Adler Planetarium*, and the *Field Museum on South Lake Shore Drive.* The design of the Museum Campus links Burnham and Grant parks with walkways and bicycle paths so visitors to the Adler Planetarium, Shedd Aquarium, and the Field Museum are able to walk between the three museums or enjoy a picnic in the park without crossing Lake Shore Drive. This relocates the north bound lanes of Lake Shore Drive to the west side of Soldier Field. Follow signs from Lake Shore Drive to the Museum Campus.

John G. Shedd Aquarium and Oceanarium

(312) 939-2438 •
TTY (312) 986-2302
1200 S. Lake Shore Drive
The world's largest indoor aquarium has more than 6,000 aquatic animals representing over 700 species from all over the world, including whales, sea otters, penguins, sharks and eels. The Oceanarium's Pacific Northwest Coastal Trail offers views of beluga whales, dolphins, sea otters and seals. Sea turtles, eels, and tropical fish are hand-fed by divers in the Caribbean coral reef. Free admission to the Aquarium on Thursdays.

✪ Wheelchair Accessibility

Photo—Willy Schmidt/City of Chicago

Adler Planetarium

Adler Planetarium and Astronomy Museum
(312) 922-STAR •
TTY (312) 922-0995
1300 S. Lake Shore Drive
The museum for astronomy and space exploration features sky shows, three floors of exhibits on astronomy, a domed Sky Theater, and a 77 foot "Stairway to the Stars" on a special effects escalator. See live telescope views of outer space from the Adler observatory following the 8pm Friday Sky Show. Special astronomer gallery talks are also scheduled. Major collection of artifacts on the history of astronomy includes sundials, astrolabs, and rare books from past centuries.
✪ Wheelchair Accessibility—Free Admission on Tuesdays

Field Museum of Natural History
(312) 922-9410 • TTY (312) 341-9299
Roosevelt Road at Lake Shore Drive (Follow signs to the Museum Campus)
Presents cultures and environments from around the world in a 6 acre natural history museum. Founded in 1893, to hold material assembled for the world's Columbian Exposition. Popular exhibits include "Inside Ancient Egypt," "DNA to Dinosaurs," and "Teeth, Tusks and Tar Pits."

✪ Free on Wednesdays
Wheelchair Accessibility

Museum of Contemporary Art
(312) 280-2660 •
TTY (312) 397-4006
220 E. Chicago Avenue
Located near the historic Water Tower, the MCA offers thought-provoking exhibitions of the finest art created since 1945 and a permanent collection featuring work by Calder, Kline, Magritte, Nauman, Paschke, and Warhol. A store, restaurant and sculpture garden also attract visitors. The first Friday of every month the museum hosts a "happy hour" party with entertainment and refreshments for members and guests.
✪ Wheelchair Accessibility

Museum of Science & Industry
(773) 684-1414 • TTY 684-3323
57th Street at Lake Shore Drive
Thousands of exhibits demonstrate scientific principles, technical advances and industrial applications. Designed specifically for visitor participation, exhibitions offer an interactive, hands-on learning environment. Also houses the Henry Crown Space Center and Omni-Max Theatre.
✪ Wheelchair Accessibility

Prairie Avenue Historic District

(312) 326-1480

1800 South Prairie Avenue

South of the Loop the Prairie Avenue Historic District is a living example of Chicago's past showcasing architecture ranging from untamed Prairie origins to the height of Victorian splendor. Chicago's architecture and history begin here. The landmark *Glessner House* (1887) and the *Widow Clarke House* (1836) have been joined by the newest museum in Chicago, the *National Vietnam Veterans Art Museum*.

National Vietnam Veterans Art Museum

(312) 326-0270

1801 S. Indiana Avenue

A new museum houses an international collection of Vietnam War art. "Vietnam: Reflexes and Reflections" is a permanent exhibition of paintings, drawings, and sculptures created by over 80 artists who have spent at least one tour of duty in Vietnam. An audiovisual presentation and artifacts of war are also on display.

✪ Wheelchair Accessibility

Navy Pier

(312) 595-7437

600 E. Grand Avenue

More than 50 acres of parks, promenades, gardens, shops, and entertainment attractions include the Skyline Stage's, lakefront performance venue, Crystal Gardens' six-story, glass enclosed botanical garden, historic Grand Ballroom with an 80-foot domed ceiling, the 15-story Ferris wheel in Navy Pier Park, and an old-fashioned musical carousel, an IMAX theater, Chicago Children's Museum, the Illinois Market Place retail store and visitor information center as well as shops and restaurants. Facilities are open year-round and feature special events and activities for the entire family. Sightseeing boat rides, bicycle rental and tours are also available.

✪ Wheelchair Accessibility

Chicago Public Library Harold Washington Library Center

(312) 747-4876

TTY (312) 747-4946

400 S. State Street

The world's largest public library has a collection of more than two million books. Visitors will enjoy the Winter Garden, the state-of-the-art auditorium, Beyond Words Cafe, and Second Hand Prose gift shop, daily programs and exhibits, and tours of the $1.4 million collection of art and sculptures.

✪ Wheelchair Accessibility

Chicago Children's Museum

(312) 527-1000

Navy Pier, 700 E. Grand Avenue

South walkway of Navy Pier with view of the Ferris Wheel

Photo: Willy Schmidt/City of Chicago

Fourteen hands-on, interactive exhibits offer education and enjoyment for children and adults. Special programs are offered throughout the year. Free family nights are on Thursdays. A second location recently opened at O'Hare International Airport. Called "Kids on the Fly."

✪ Wheelchair Accessibility

Chicago Board of Trade
(312) 435-3590
141 W. Jackson Blvd.
Located in an art deco landmark building, visitors can witness the trading activity at the world's busiest market place where investors from all over the world come to trade any of the over 60 agricultural and financial futures

and options contacts listed at the CBOT. A visitor center is located on the fifth floor, open weekdays.
○ Wheelchair Accessibility

Chicago Mercantile Exchange
(312) 930-8249
30 S. Wacker Drive
An international marketplace features the most diverse product line of futures and options available. Upper and lower trading floor Visitor Galleries allow viewers to see thousands of traders crowded shoulder to shoulder trading futures and options on currencies, interest rates, indexes and agricultural products.
○ Wheelchair Accessibility

The Hancock Observatory
(888) 875-VIEW
875 N. Michigan Avenue
View Chicago and surrounding states from the 94th floor of one of the world's tallest buildings. Open until midnight every day of the week. A new multi-media entertainment display opened in May, 1997.
○ Wheelchair Accessibility

Shopping

Magnificent Mile
A mile long stretch of Michigan Avenue reaching north from the Chicago River and wrapping around Oak Street. It is the most popular and renowned shopping district in Chicago, and includes vertical shopping malls, department stores, and some of the world's finest designer boutiques located on Oak Street between Michigan Avenue and Rush Street. Malls include Chicago Place, 900 N. Michigan Shops, Water Tower Place, and the Shops of One Magnificent Mile. Other shops include Banana Republic, Barney's, New York, FAO Schwartz, Giorgio Armani, Neiman Marcus, Sonia Rykiel, Tiffany & Co., Crate & Barrell, Nike Town, Sony Gallery, and Hammacher Schelemmer.

State Street
After a $24.5 million renovation of, That Great Street, State Street's, its shopping district has reclaimed the charm and glamour of the 1920's, including a cultural walk and a self-guided tour of more than 20 State Street buildings that possess cultural and historical significance. State Street shopping includes the flagship Marshall Field's Store, the Louis Sullivan designed Carson Pirie Scott department store, Toys R Us, discount retailers Filene's Basement and T.J. Maxx, plus the Gallery 37 store in the Renaissance Chicago Hotel.

New Maxwell Street Market
(312) 922-3100
Canal Street between Taylor Street

and Depot Place
The outdoor flea-market is open
year round, Sundays 7am-3pm.
Find antiques, collectibles, new
and used merchandise. Enjoy a
live blues band and over 30 food
vendors. Arrive early for the
largest selection.

Chicago Tours

Tour Black Chicago
(312) 332-2323
Guided cultural tours of Chicago's
African-American cultural, social and
artistic sites. By appointment only.

Eli's Cheesecake Factory Tours
(800) 999-8300
6701 W. Forest Preserve Drive
Guided tours of Chicago's famous
cheesecake manufacturing plant
includes samples, make your own
cheesecake, and the history of
family recipes and business. A
cafe-style restaurant is also open.
25 minute tours are offered on the
hour, Monday-Friday, 11am-3pm.

Loop Tour Train
(312) 744-2400
Seasonal tours (June-October) of
Chicago's downtown Loop
business district and historical
architecture are offered free-of-
charge with advance ticketing
through the Chicago Office of
Tourism Visitor Information
Center located at 77 E. Randolph

Street. Tours are offered four times
a day on Saturdays only.
✪ Wheelchair accessible

Chicago Neighborhood Tours
(312) 742-1190
Eight guided bus tours of Chicago's
diverse ethnic communities are
offered Saturday mornings at 10:00
am. Three and a half hour tours
offer an indepth look at the artistic
and cultural traditions of the people
who live and work in Chicago. In
addition to the weekly tours,
customized group tours including
lunch or dinner will be available by
pre-arrangement.

Audio Architecture Tour
(312) 744-2400
Self-guided walking tours of
Chicago's downtown Loop using
two 45 minute cassette tapes and
a walkman (a $50.00 returnable
deposit is required for use of the
walkmans).Tours cost $7.00 each.
Departure takes place from the
Shop at the Cultural Center, 77 E.
Randolph Street.

River and Lake Boat Cruises
Eight tour boat companies offer
sightseeing cruises of Lake
Michigan and/or the Chicago
River from April through October.
Call the Chicago Office of Tour-
ism at (312) 744-2400 for
information on the various com-

Photo: Peter J. Schulz/City of Chicago

Chicago skyline with Oceanarium and Sears Tower in far left.

panies. Most tours focus on architecture and two companies offer brunch, lunch, dinner and cocktail and moonlight (midnight) cruises. ✪Some are Wheelchair Accessible

State Street Culture Walk
(312) 782-9160

Self-guided walking tours of the historic architecture along Chicago's newly renovated State Street. Widened streets, '20s-style lampposts and subway entrances have returned "that great street" to its original splendor.
✪ Wheelchair Accessibility

Permanent & Open Run Events

- Vietnam: Reflexes and Reflections — National Vietnam Veterans Art Museum, Vietnam Veterans Arts Group (312) 326-0270.
- Best of Second City — Second City (312) 642-8189, Mondays.
- Dame Myra Hess Memorial Concerts — Chicago Cultural Center (312) 744-6630, Wednesdays.
- New Maxwell Street Market — Canal Street between Roosevelt Road and 15th Street (312) 922-3100, Sundays.
- The Oprah Winfrey Show — Harpo Studios. For tickets (312) 591-9222, weekdays.

Continuing Events

December

- A Christmas Carol — play, Goodman Theatre (312) 443-4940.
- ZooLights Festival — Lincoln Park Zoo (312) 742-2000.
- "That's Christmas Chicago's Merry Musical" — Shubert Theatre (312) 559-1290 x2067.
- Christmas Around the World/ Holidays of Light — Festivals of holiday traditions from around the World, Museum of Science and Industry (773) 947-3740.
- Skate on State — outdoor skating rink, State Street (312) 744-3370, November-March.

- Chicago Blackhawks Hockey regular season — United Center (312) 455-7000, through April.
- Chicago Bulls Basketball at the United Center, 1901 W. Madison Street, regular season, through April (312) 455-4000.

Annual Events

Listings are subject to change, to confirm dates and times please call or write to the Chicago Office of Tourism, 78 E. Washington Street, Chicago, IL 60602. To receive a free information packet call: 1-800-2CONNECT.

January

- Zooperbowl VIII — Lincoln Park Zoo (312) 742-2000.

February

- National African-American History Month at cultural institutions throughout Chicago. (312) 744-2400.
- Black Creativity — month long celebration of African-American creativity, Museum of Science and Industry (773) 684-1414.
- Chicago Auto Show — McCormick Place South, 22nd Street and Lake Shore Drive (312) 791-7000.

March

- Chicago Flower & Garden Show — Navy Pier (312) 321-0077.
- Spring Festival of Dance — various locations (312) 629-8696.

Wrigley Field — home of the Chicago Cubs.

Photo: Peter J. Schulz/City of Chicago

- St. Patrick's Day Parade — Dearborn Street from Wacker Drive to Van Buren Street (312) 942-9188.
- South Side Irish St. Patrick's Day Parade — Western Avenue from 103rd to 114th Street (773) 239-7755.

April
- Chicago Cubs Baseball Season — Wrigley Field (773) 404-CUBS.
- Chicago White Sox Baseball Season — Comiskey Park (773) 924-1000.
- Chicago Latino Film Festival — various theaters (312) 431-1330.

May
- Asian Pacific American Heritage Month — Asian American Heritage Council (703) 354-5036.
- National Tourism Month; Asian-American Heritage Month — Illinois Market Place, Navy Pier (312) 832-0010 x 2.
- Polish Constitution Day Parade — Dearborn St., between Wacker Drive and Van Buren Streets (773) 889-7125.
- Art Chicago — Navy Pier (312) 587-3300.
- Pier Walk (312) 595-PIER.

June

- 57th Street Art Fair — oldest juried art fair in the Midwest, 57th St. and Kimbark Avenue.
- Old Town Art Fair — oldest outdoor juried fine art fair, Lincoln Park West and N. Orleans Street (312) 337-1938.
- Chicago Blues Festival — Petrillo Music Shell, Grant Park (312) 744-3370.
- Chicago Gospel Festival — Petrillo Music Shell, Grant Park (312) 744-3370.
- Grant Park Music Festival — classical concerts, Petrillo Music Shell Grant Park (312) 742-7638.
- Loop Tour Train — Chicago Architecture Foundation guided tour of the Loop on Chicago Transit Authority (CTA) "L" trains. Free tickets at Chicago Office of Tourism Visitor Information Center in Chicago Cultural Center, 77 E. Randolph Street (312) 744-2400.
- Chicago Country Music Festival — Petrillo Music Shell, Grant Park (312) 744-3370.

July

- Gallery 37 — State Street between Washington and Randolph Streets (312) 744-8925.
- Independence Day Concert and Fireworks — Petrillo Music Shell, Grant Park (312) 774-3370.

- World's Largest Block Party — Old St. Pat's Church (312) 782-6171.
- Dearborn Garden Walk and Heritage Festival — street festival, 1300-1500 N. Dearborn Pkwy. (312) 751-0565.
- 5th Annual Chicago New Music Festival, July 25-26 at various locations (312) 341-9112.
- Newberry's 13th Annual Book Fair — Newberry Library (312) 255-3700.
- Venetian Night — Lake Shore Drive and Congress Parkway (312) 744-3370.

August

- Northalsted Market Days — 3200 to 3600 N. Halsted Street (773) 868-3010.
- Wicker Park Greening Festival —Damen Avenue and Schiller Street (773) 868-3010.
- Chicago Air & Water Show — North Avenue Beach (312) 744-3370.
- Chicago Jazz Festival — Petrillo Music Shell, Grant Park (312) 744-3370.
- Bud Billilken Parade and Picnic, 39th Street and King Drive to 55th Street and Washington Park. (312) 225-2400.

September

- Chicago Bears Football Season — Soldier Field (847) 295-6600.
- Opening of the Art Gallery Season — River North Gallery District (312) 649-0065.

- Chicago Blackhawks Hockey Season — United Center (312) 455-7060.
- Lyric Opera of Chicago — Civic Opera House (312) 332-2244.
- Chicago Symphony Orchestra — Orchestra Hall (312) 294-3000.

October

- Edgar Allan Poe Readings — Prairie Avenue House Museums (312) 326-1480.
- Chicago International Film Festival — various theatres (312) 644-3400.
- Chicago International Children's Film Festival — Facets Multimedia (773) 281-9075.
- Spooky Zoo Spectacular — Trick or Treating for children, Lincoln Park Zoo (312) 742-2000.

November

- Chicago Artists' Month Celebration (312) 670-2060
- Chicago Humanities Festival — (312) 422-5580.
- National American Indian Heritage Month — National Congress of American Indians.
- Newberry's Very Merry Bazaar, 60 W. Walton Place — Newberry Library (312) 255-3510.
- Magnificent Mile Lights Festival — Michigan Avenue from the Chicago River to Oak Street (312) 642-3570.
- Skate on State — State Street between Washington and Randolph Streets (312) 744-3370.
- Zoo Lights Festival — Lincoln Park Zoo (312) 742-2000.

December

- Holiday Candlelight Tours — Prairie Avenue House Museums (312) 326-1480
- Caroling to the Animals — Lincoln Park Zoo (312) 742-2000.
- First Night — Navy Pier (312) 595-PIER.

Chicago Festivals in Grant Park

For dates and information on festivals, contact the Mayor's Office of Special Events at (312) 744-3370.

June

- Chicago Blues Festivals
- Chicago Gospel Festival
- Chicago Country Music Festival
- Taste of Chicago, lasts into July

July

- Taste of Chicago
- Venetian Night

August

- Air and Water Show
- Chicago Jazz Festival

September

- Viva! Chicago Latin Music Festival
- World Music Festival and Celtic Fest Chicago
- World Music Festival 2000

Conclusion

For more information contact:
Chicago Office of Tourism
Chicago Cultural Center
78 East Washington Street
Chicago, Illinois 60602
(312) 744-2400

Tips

✔ To help you plan your trip ahead of time, call **1-800-2CONNECT.** You'll be mailed a visitor information packet which contains a quarterly calendar of events and official visitors guide containing maps, hotel, shopping and restaurant information.

✔ If you have access to the Internet, check out the city's "web site" at **http://www.ci.chi.il.us/ Tourism**. You can learn about everything from Chicago's world famous architecture to its multicultural neighborhoods and renowned museums. A calendar of Chicago events features an extensive listing of upcoming festivals, museum exhibitions, theatre productions and sporting events. Photographic images of Chicago's attractions appear throughout the text. Get visitor info off the state's web site — @http://enjoyillinois.com

✔ When you arrive in Chicago, take the blue line subway train from O'Hare Airport or the orange line elevated train from Midway Airport. Their fares are only $1.50

and you'll arrive in the city within 25-38 minutes. Just look for signs that lead you to "Trains to City" and you will be downtown in no time!

✔ Once you get off the train in the Loop, ask the train cashier for a map of Chicago's Pedway, the city's underground walkway system. By using these safe, well-lit tunnels you will avoid the weather and traffic above. The **Pedway** connects you to City Hall, Marshall Field's, the Chicago Cultural Center, and other Loop buildings.

✔ Walk through the Pedway to the Chicago Cultural Center where you will find one of the city's three **visitor information centers.** Pick up complimentary brochures, maps and schedules of events. Ask the friendly representatives to help plan your itinerary and answer questions.

✔ While you are in the **Chicago Cultural Center,** check out the daily schedule of free programs and exhibitions. You may encounter a free classical piano concert or an art exhibition. Walk up the winding staircases on either side of the building to see magnificent Tiffany stained-glass domes.

✔ Chicago is one of the only cities that lets you get a **skyline view from land.** Take a bus or taxi to Adler Planetarium, walk to the end of Navy Pier or sit on the rocks along Belmont Harbor and you will see a breathtaking view of the Chicago skyline from three very unique perspectives.

✔ If you want an aerial view of the city take the elevator to the 95th floor of the John Hancock Center and have a drink in the Signature Lounge. You'll most likely pay less for the drink than the admission to the Observatory and you will get a southern aerial view of the city that is engaging in both day and night.

✔ If you don't have the time to take in all of the sites, stop by the new **Illinois Market Place** at Navy Pier and preview Chicago and Illinois attractions in a retail setting. Video presentations and in-store displays combine with local artisan products, gifts and memorabilia to give you a "whirlwind" tour of several of the city and state's museums and cultural attractions—and let you take home a few souvenirs as well.

Welcome to Chicago!

" Chicago is a city of neighborhoods, and this guidebook can help you discover them. Chicago offers something for everyone— visit our museums, discover our architecture, explore our shops, dine in our restaurants, and enjoy our sightseeing tours.

Walking through the streets of Chicago is like walking through a museum of architecture. The first skyscraper was built in Chicago, and three of the world's tallest buildings are in Chicago. Sightseeing cruises offer visitors a unique vantage point for viewing waterfront architecture from Lake Michigan or the Chicago River, the only river in the world that flows backwards.

The world-renowned Art Institute of Chicago holds one of the largest and best collections of Impressionist paintings outside of the Louvre in Paris. Our new museum campus along our lakefront connects the Shedd Aquarium, the Adler Planetarium, and the Field Museum, must-sees for families. Further north along the lakefront, Navy Pier offers entertainment and activities for the entire family.

Downtown, the Chicago Cultural Center is the city's architectural showplace for the lively and visual arts, and offers free programs and events daily. North of the Loop, the Lincoln Park Zoo is free to the public every day.

Enjoy a guided tour of one of Chicago's unique ethnic communities on a Chicago Neighborhood Tour. Tour buses depart from the Chicago Cultural Center every Saturday morning at 10 am.

Visitors can receive additional information, including brochures and maps on Chicago's exciting events and attractions at one of our visitor information centers. They are located at Chicago Water Works, 163 E. Pearson Street at Michigan Avenue; the Chicago Cultural Center, 77 E. Randolph Street; or the Illinois Market Place at Navy Pier, 700 E. Grand Avenue. To order a visitor information packet, call 1-800-2CONNECT. Visitor information is also available on the Internet at http://www.ci.chi.il.us/Tourism.

Enjoy your visit to Chicago! **"**
—Dorothy Coyle, Director
Chicago Office of Tourism

DOWNTOWN CHICAGO

Gurnee
Chicago's Neighbor to the North

Location

Gurnee is located on Interstate 94 and Route 132 in Lake County.

History

What is now the village of Gurnee was first settled in the 1830s by pioneers who came on foot or horseback, in "prairie schooners," or by the Erie Canal and the Great Lakes.

A permanent bridge over the DesPlaines River near what is now Grand Avenue helped create an east-west road which connected McHenry County to the port of Little Fort (now Waukegan). The Milwaukee Road also ran through the area connecting Chicago and Milwaukee. From its earliest days, Gurnee was a hub of commerce.

In the 1830s the area was known as Wentworth after Long John Wentworth, a Chicago congressman. In the early 1870s the name was changed to O'Plain, a shortened form of Aux Plaines, the early spelling of the DesPlaines River.

When the Milwaukee Railroad went through in 1873, the town was renamed Gurnee Station. There is controversy whether it was named after either Louis Gurnee, a railroad surveyor, or Walter S. Gurnee, a Democratic leader and Chicago mayor. The name was eventually shortened to "Gurnee."

Gurnee became the first village established in Warren Township, but that came much later in 1928 when the village was incorporated.

Getting Started

For more information on Lake County contact:
Lake County Illinois Convention and Visitors Bureau
Riverside Plaza
401 N. Riverside Drive
Gurnee, IL 60031
(847) 662-2700

Attractions

Mother Rudd Home
(708) 263-9540
4690 Old Grand Avenue
The Mother Rudd Home is Warren Township's oldest building. It was formerly a stagecoach stop known as Marm Rudd's Tavern, and the

center of community activity. The building was renovated by the village of Gurnee and is now a museum housing local historical documents. The museum is open by appointment for those wishing to study the history of Gurnee and its people.

The Chicago-Milwaukee-St. Paul Railroad Station

In 1873 the first train stopped at the new Gurnee Station. The railroad station was named after one of its board members Walter S. Gurnee.

Gurnee Mills

It's bigger than Soldier Field attracts more visitors than Graceland, and offers more shopping values under one roof than any other mall in the four states surrounding Lake Michigan. Gurnee Mills Mall, the largest enclosed discount/outlet mall in the Midwest, opened its doors in 1991. Located midway between Milwaukee and Chicago, Gurnee Mills is the only major shopping center in the Midwest to combine manufacturers' outlets, department store outlets, specialty store

Gurnee Mill

outlets, super savings stores, off-price retailers and category dominant stores, offering shoppers endless options and excellent prices.

Visitors to Gurnee Mills enjoy an atmosphere that's both relaxing and exciting, traditional and contemporary. Built in 1991, Gurnee Mills' decor is suggestive of a traditional Midwestern Main Street. Two miles of storefronts, with natural light from the sky-lights, recall the simplicity of the American heartland while inlaid wood floors are reminiscent of old-fashioned wooden sidewalks. The decor is made exciting and contemporary through the creative use of neon lighting and colorful graphics and sign.

The center of the mall, Grange Hall, is designed in the Victorian style of an American variety store with custom-designed cabinetry for freestanding merchants, hardwood storefronts, poplar slatted ceiling and brass accents throughout. Small seating areas throughout the mall feature hip 50's style furniture and TV sets in retro color schemes, providing a whimsical contrast to Grange Hall's Victorian dignity.

For further information contact:
Gurnee Mills
6170 West Grand Avenue
Gurnee, Illinois 60031
(847) 263-7500
Fax (847) 263-2423
http://gurneemillsmall.com
mall@waa.com

Six Flags Great America
(847) 249-INFO

Six Flags Great America is located between Milwaukee and Chicago off I-94 at the Grand Avenue East exit.

The park is the Midwest's premier theme park featuring more than 30 rides plus spectacular shows and a variety of attractions. A general admission ticket is all you need for a fun-filled day of thrills, stunts, laughs and splashes. There are additional charges for food, drinks, merchandise and games of skill.

The park opens the last Sunday in April for weekends only. Daily operations begin about mid-May and last until September. The park opens at 10 a.m. daily; closing times vary.

A variety of themed areas highlights different aspects of Americana.

• **Carousel Plaza** welcomes each guest into the wonderful world of fantasy and excitement with a beautiful 10-story carousel.

• **Hometown Square** takes guests into rural America of the 1920s.

• **County Fair** recreates all the excitement and thrills of a real county fair as it would have been celebrated at the turn of the century.

- **Southwest Territory** transports guests back to a frontier western town, complete with a Spanish-style mission and gun-slinging desperados.
- **Yukon Territory** is an authentically landscaped area resembling the rugged days of the Klondike region during the Gold Rush era.
- **Yankee Harbor** transports guests to a fishing village on the eastern seaboard of the United States during the late 19th century.
- **Orleans Place** reproduces the aesthetic charm of New Orleans French Quarter circa 1850.

The greatest rides on earth range from the wildest roller coasters to soaking wet water rides to light-hearted family rides. Six Flags Great America has them all!

- **Viper** a single-track wooden roller coaster, features high-banked turns and drops, giving riders a thrill-a-second experience.
- **Batman The Ride,** the world's first suspended, outside looping thrill ride, it's the ultimate!
- **Shock Wave,** one of the world's tallest and fastest steel-looping roller coasters. Shock wave climbs 170 feet before taking its riders through seven loops at speeds up to 65+ mph.
- **American Eagle** is a favorite. This double-tracked racing wooden roller coaster gives its riders a beautiful eagle's eye view of the park before soaring down a 147-foot hill.
- **Iron Wolf** starts with a 90-foot drop, reaches speeds up to 55 mph and enters the first hair-raising loop. And you do all of this *Standing Up!*
- **Roaring Rapids**, we promise you'll get soaking wet on this white water rapids expedition.
- **Demon,** A spine-tingling roller coaster, drops its riders 82 feet and goes directly into two vertical loops, followed by a dazzling display of light and sound effects, and finishes with two corkscrew loops.

Introduced in 1997 you will find the:

- **Giant Drop** takes the ultimate plunge on a 227-foot tower that drops riders toward earth at a gut-wrenching 62 miles-per-hour! It is located at the site of the abandoned Loco Diablo Mine in the Southwest Territory.
- **Daredevil Dive** is a cross between bungee jumping and sky-diving, only for the daring. Flight times need to be scheduled early in the day. Additional fee required.

For more information contact:
Six Flags Great America
P.O. Box 1776
Gurnee, Illinois 60031
(847) 249-2144
FAX (847) 249-INFO

SIX FLAGS® GREAT AMERICA COASTER FACTS

BATMAN
THE RIDE
© 1994 DC Comics

- World's first suspended outside-looping roller coaster

- Opened 1992

- 2,700 feet of track

- Five inversions (two vertical loops and three "heartline spins")

- Each "heartline spin" provides 3 seconds of zero gravity

- Features suspended, chairlift type cars

- Maximum speed 50 m.p.h.

Batman® The Ride at Six Flags Great America

Satellite Attractions

Vernon Hills

Cuneo Museum and Gardens
75 acres of gardens, fountains, lawns and a 31-room Italian Villa furnished with priceless art. 18 rooms on exhibit.

Wadsworth

The Gold Pyramid House
Unique six-story, gold plated structure is a replica of a pyramid built over 6,000 years ago. The builder and his family live within the house. On site is a recreated King Tut Tomb.

Vernon Hills

Tempel Lipizzan Stallions
Rare white stallions perform in the tradition of Vienna's famed Spanish Riding School. Visit stallions in historic stables after each performance. Summer performances.

Highland Park

Ravinia Festival
Situated on Chicago's North Shore, the festival presents world-class entertainment featuring the Chicago Symphony Orchestra within in its 36-acre woodland setting. Summer performances under the stars.

Annual Events

August

- **Gurnee Days** — Organized by volunteers, the event is held from Thursday-Sunday. The event includes a bike rodeo, library show, pageant, teen dance, golf and volleyball tournaments, a 10K race and 2 mile fun run, a baby contest, bike and trike contests, Little Miss Gurnee Pageant, a community dance, a fire department open house, exhibits, food and games, a stage event, a volleyball tournament, a pancake breakfast, children's pony rides and parade. For more information (847) 623-7650.

Conclusion

For more information about places of interest and activities in Lake County, IL contact:
Lake County Convention & Visitors Bureau
401 N. Riverside Drive,
Suite 5
Gurnee, Illlinois 60031
(847) 662-2700
1-800-LAKE NOW
http://www.lakecounty.org

Lake County, Illinois
Chicago's Neighbor to the North ·

66 Lake County, Illinois, fondly referred to as the Great American County, is located between Chicago and Milwaukee on Interstate 94 with an eastern border rimmed by miles of blue Lake Michigans Shoreline and, to the west, an azure chain of sporting lakes sprinkled across the countryside. Within the confines of Lake County's 457 square miles one finds incomparable attractions, singular shopping, a host of culinary delights and a wide range of comfortable accommodations for individuals, families, groups and business travelers. Visitors are provided with the opportunity to experience an array of activities ranging from one of the midwest's largest shopping malls, to the midwest's premier theme park, performing Lipizzan stallions, an Italian villa, a replica of a pyramid, apple orchards, a county fair, a childrens' petting zoo, a hands-on energy museum, broadway musicals and symphony music, fishing, hiking and camping in two state parks. In addition Lake County boasts more than 29 public golf courses.

Top transporation amenities in Lake County range from easy access to Chicago's O'Hare International Airport and Milwaukee's General Mitchell International Airport to rail facilities such as the Milwaukee Road and the Chicago and Northwestern commuter trains. Our highways form a convenient system for reaching all the county.

Whether looking for a stop-over, a one-to-three day package or wishing to combine Lake County with a trip to the Chicagoland or the Great Lakes Region, one is guaranteed a most memorable experience.

Come see for yourself why Lake County, Illinois, is a mecca for all that's great in America.

Happy trails, 99

—Gail Svendsen
Lake County, Illinois Convention & Visitors Bureau

*Map from Lake County Illionis
Convention and Visitors Bureau*

Daytrip Illinois
Highway 20

Freeport
Refreshment for the Soul

Location

Located on Highway 20 just two hours northwest of Chicago and forty-five minutes west of Rockford, Stephenson County offers you a myriad of activities.

History

The town was founded by William "Tutty" Baker who came to the area in 1835. Building a trading post along the Pecatonica River, Tutty began a prosperous trade with the local Winnebago Indians. He offered travelers free ferry rides, meals, and lodging. Thus, the name "Freeport."

Getting Started

Stop by the —
Stephenson County Convention and Visitors Bureau
2047 AYP Road in Freeport.
1-800-369-2955 • 815 233-1357
FAX: 815 233-1358

Attractions

Fever River Railroad
815 232-6431
600 Fever River Place
This model railroad is something to see. It is a 103 by 24 foot HO scale model of a hypothetical railroad running from Duluth, MN to St. Louis, MO. It intersects with models of "real" railroads, each of which can be operated independently. Industries along the railroad right-of-way duplicate typical industries.

Freeport Arts Center
815 235-9755
121 N. Harlem Avenue
There are six permanent galleries featuring European, classical, Native American, Asian, ethnographics, and contemporary art. New exhibitions featuring regional artists and special topics rotate every eight weeks.

Lincoln-Douglas Debate Site
Douglas and State Streets
In 1858 two famous Americans debated the issues of states' rights and slavery. A statue, a boulder, and a plaque mark the spot where Abraham Lincoln and Stephen A. Douglas debated.

Lincoln The
Debater Statue
Taylor Park, E. Stephenson Street

Silver Creek Stephenson Railroad Steam Train

The statue, designed by Leonard Crunelle, was a gift to the city in 1929, presented to Freeport on the 71st anniversary of the Lincoln-Douglas debate.

Old River Historic District
Downtown Freeport
Several architecturally significant structures remain in original Freeport. You will find the oldest house in the area built in 1838 and the Wisconsin Road Bridge built of cast iron in 1885.

Silvercreek Museum
(815) 235-2198

2954 S. Walnut Road
Housed in the museum are 25 rooms of early Americana — 500 pieces of crockery, dolls, school-room and kitchen of times past, art exhibits, quilts, old-fashioned tools, agri-cultural equipment and numerous other historical artifacts.

Silver Creek and Stephenson Railroad Antique Steam Train
(815) 232-2306
Lamm and Walnut Roads
You may have a four mile ride on the train pulled by a 1912 Heisler steam locomotive. The antique red

caboose is reported to be the oldest in the state.

Soldiers Memorials
Stephenson County Courthouse
Galena and Stephenson Streets
Located on the southwest corner is an 1871 memorial inscribed with the names of soldiers from Stephenson County who lost their lives during the Civil War. On the southeast corner is a bronze statue honoring the soldiers of the Vietnam era.

Stephenson County Historical Society Museum
815 232-8419
1440 S. Carroll Avenue
This lovely Italianate home was built by Oscar and Malvina Taylor in 1857. It was the center of social activity in Freeport and is listed on the National Register of Historic Places. On the grounds are a one-room schoolhouse, a farm, an industrial museum, an arboretum and an authentic log cabin.

Tutty Baker Monument
Foot of Monterey Street
The monument located on Monterey Street was erected by the Daughters of the American Revolution in honor of William "Tutty" Baker, founder of Freeport.

Satellite Attractions

❧ Cedarville

Cedarville Historical Museum
Cherry Street
Located in an old stone jail house, the museum honors Nobel Prize winner Jane Addams who was born and raised in Cedarville. Miss Addams was famous for her humanitarian and social work.

German Valley Historical Museum
805 Church Street
The museum displays memorabilia relating to the early history of German Valley and its surrounding area.

❧ Kent

Blackhawk War Monument
Kent Road, south of Highway 20. Located at Kellogg's Grove, an early settlement established in 1827 on a mail route between Galena and Peoria, this monument is now on the National Register of Historic Places. The last battle in Illinois was fought here between the Blackhawk Indians and the militia in June, 1832. Abraham Lincoln helped bury five of the slain men. There is a picnic area, shelter, playground and a log cabin.

Stagecoach Trail
Follow an old stagecoach route established in 1830. The trail

Krape Park Waterfall

begins at the intersection of Highway 20 and Highway 73 and provides a beautiful view of one of the highest natural points in Illinois.

❦ Lena

Lena Area Historical Museum
427 W. Grove Street
Displays of area historical items are housed in the museum including quilts, farm tools, clothing, military exhibits and much more. Tour the first log schoolhouse of Lena, an old-time blacksmith shop, an Illinois Central Caboose, a barn, and the Lena Chapel.

❦ Winslow

Artesian Well at Paradise Cove
Edge of business district along Indiana Creek
Since 1927 thousands of gallons of pure water have flowed out of this natural artesian well located along Indian Creek. Watch flowing water continually turn a ten foot water wheel.

Annual Events

Over 100 special events from pancake breakfasts to major festivals occur throughout the year. Write or call for Stephenson County Calendar of Events brochure for complete listings and continual updates. 1-800-369-2955.

January
• *Le-Win Jaycees Winterfest* (Lena) —A weekend of winter fun for the whole family with sledding, cross-country skiing, sleigh rides, chili supper, pancake breakfast and more.

June
• *Stagecoach Trail Festival* (Lena) — A celebration of our Native American and pioneer heritage along the scenic Stagecoach Trail.

July
• *Steam Threshing and Antique Show* (Freeport) — Exhibits and demonstrations highlighting steam and horse power, plus a flea market, tractor and horse

pulls and antique steam train rides.

August

* *Tutty Baker Days Festival* (Freeport) — Celebration in honor of Freeport's founder with entertainment, arts and crafts, a carnival, sporting events, and more.

* *Stephenson County Fair* (Freeport) — Old-fashioned county fair with livestock judging, 4-H and commercial exhibits, a carnival, and major country western entertainment.

September

* *Lena Lions Fall Festival* (Lena) — Community celebration with games, carnival, entertainment, bike tour, and parade.

October

* *La-Win Jaycees Haunted Barn (Lena)* —Spooktacular fun in this top-rated barn of horror.

Shopping and Dining

You will find an assortment of gift shops, antique stores, craft shops, art glass, garden supplies, woolen supplies and much more.

Stephenson County offers a wide range of hotels, motels, bed and breakfasts, all reasonably priced.

Enjoy the best food selections you will ever find at moderate prices, flaky pie crusts, old fashioned malts, catfish, watermelon, home-made soups, cinnamon rolls, chili, variety of baked goods. Old fashioned cooking at its best.

Conclusion

For further information contact:
Stephenson County
Convention and Visitors Bureau
2047 North AYP Road
Freeport, IL 61032-8802
815-233-1357 • 1-800-369-2955
Fax: 815 233-1358
Website:
www.stephenson-county-il.org

❝ Stephenson County offers *"Refreshment for the Soul"* in the rolling hills of northwest Illinois. Its communities welcome the traveler to a gentler pace in this land of lush parks, unique attractions, abundant green fields, and hospitable people. Located just two hours northwest of Chicago, Stephenson County offers a myriad of activities — museums, recreation, historical sites, challenging golf courses, antique shops, and excellent lodging. The county includes the city of Freeport whose founder, William "Tutty" Baker, named it so because he offered travelers who rode his ferry across our Pecatonica River free lodging and food. Freeport was also the site of the second of the famous Illinois debates in 1858 between Abraham Lincoln and Stephen A. Douglas. The site is commemorated with a life-size statue of the two gentlemen in debate. Freeport's numerous parks include Krape Park with its old-fashioned carousel, duck pond, waterfall, picnic spots, and playground areas. Art and historical museums, an antique steam train, and excellent affordable lodging all await the traveler to Freeport.

The community of Lena is the beginning of the Stagecoach Trail, a scenic drive which follows a route established in the 1830s. The Trail offers antique stores with wonderful treasures, charming bed and breakfasts, cheese shops selling delicious locally produced specialties, hometown cafes and restaurants, and so much more. Lena also is the site of Lake Le-Aqua-Na State Park with a 40 acre lake for fishing and swimming, large tracts of wooded land, campgrounds, and hiking, cross-country skiing, and equestrian trails.

The village of Cedarville was home to the great humanitarian and Nobel Peace Prize winner, Jane Addams, who is remembered throughout the community including at the Cedarville Historical Museum and at her burial site in a lovely old hillside cemetery.

All of the many things to see and do are surrounded with the congeniality and warmth of the people of Stephenson County who want to share with you their very "special" world. ❞

—*Connie Sorn*
Executive Director

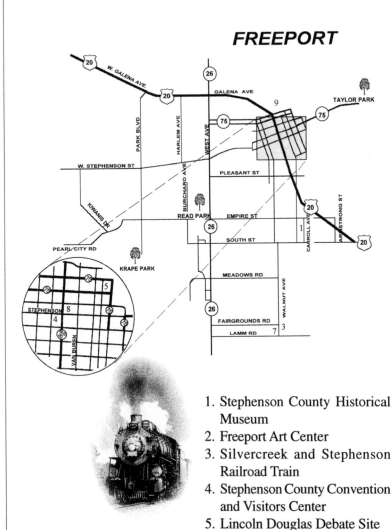

FREEPORT

1. Stephenson County Historical Museum
2. Freeport Art Center
3. Silvercreek and Stephenson Railroad Train
4. Stephenson County Convention and Visitors Center
5. Lincoln Douglas Debate Site
6. Lincoln the Debater Statue
7. Silvercreek Museum
8. Soldiers Memorial/County Court House
9. Tutty Baker Monument

Daytrip Illinois
Highway 36

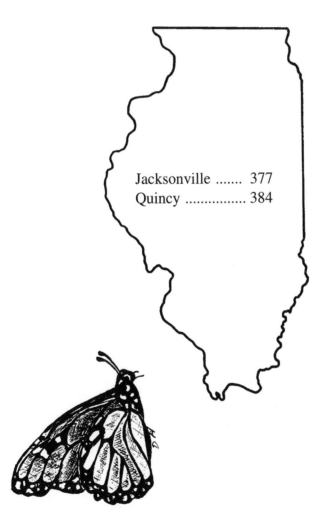

Jacksonville
Minutes Away

Location

Jacksonville is located on Highway 36 (Interstate 72), 230 miles from Chicago, 87 miles from St. Louis and 28 miles from Springfield.

History

Founded in 1825 and named for Andrew Jackson, the town contended unsuccessfully to become the site of the state capital and state university. But Jacksonville did manage to gain prominence as the seat of government for Morgan County. In 1835 a book entitled *Tour Through North America* stated that "Jacksonville contains about the same number of souls as Springfield, but is superior in buildings, arrangement, and situation."

Though first populated by southerners, Jacksonville later attracted many New Englanders who brought with them a strong abolitionist spirit. Consequently the town became an active station along the Underground Railroad.

Founded in 1829, Illinois College became a pillar of education in the community. The Reverend Edward Beecher became its first president. Its first graduating class in 1835 included future governor and U.S. senator, Richard Yates.

➡ Getting Started

Stop by the Jacksonville Area Visitors Center located at 155 West Morton Road. We offer handy information on historic sites, motels, restaurants, shopping, recreation sites and other local points of interest. We offer three walking tours. Call or write for a detailed brochure.

Attractions

Big Eli Wheel No. 17

Ferris wheels were first manufactured in Jacksonville in 1900. William E. Sullivan set up his first model on the public square. The business today is operated by the third generation. The company is the oldest firm in the country that makes ferris wheels as a stock item. The Big Eli Wheel No. 17 stands on the corner of Morton and

Main Streets in the community park.

1879 Bandstand

In 1878-79 two bandstands were erected, but only one stands today. The other bandstand was donated to the Smithsonian Institute in 1983. The remaining bandstand has been restored to its original state and is used for concerts and other activities on the Jacksonville Mental Health and Developmental Center grounds.

Governor Duncan Home

4 Duncan Place

The 17-room mansion served as the official governor's mansion during the term of Governor Joseph Duncan from 1834-1838. It is the only building left in Illinois that served in that capacity outside of Springfield. It is on the National Historic Register of Historic Places and it is fully restored. Many of the original Duncan family furnishings are still there. Adult donation $2.00.

✪ Children under 7 free

Heritage Cultural Center

125 North Webster
Illinois School for the Deaf

The Center displays Jacksonville history from 1800 through the mid 1900s. The center is open every Wednesday from 1:00-4:00 pm. Other tours by appointment.

Petting Zoo

(217) 245-4706

This is a children's paradise. A non-profit organization houses dogs and puppies, bunny rabbits, pygmy goats, miniature horses, llamas, kittens, hedgehogs, cockatoo, quaker parrot, various birds, dwarf hamsters and a pot belly pig for petting pleasure. Rides for children, face painting, and Bits O' Magic help make the petting zoo even more enjoyable. Contributions are accepted. Call for more information.

Historic Walking Tours —

A walking tour is a wonderful way to feel the nostalgia of days gone by, going down streets where history was made. Three walking tours are outlined in a detailed brochure available from the Visitors Bureau. Just call or write.

✦ *Walking Tour 1 — Begins in Central Park*

Approximately 8/10 of a mile, it takes about 30 minutes. Start at Central Park in the Downtown Plaza.

Central Park Plaza Monument

The sculpture grouping is a tribute to the men who fought in the Civil War and was dedicated in 1920.

Jacksonville Public Library

The library was completed in 1902

and opened its doors to the public on February 22, 1903.

David Strawn Art Gallery
331 West College

Built in 1880 for Phebe Gates Strawn, one of Jacksonville's wealthiest and most prominent families. The gallery houses rotating exhibits of locally and nationally known artists. The Miriam Cowgur Allen Collection of antique and collectible dolls is part of a permanent display. The second floor is in keeping with furnishings of the late 1800s.

Four Churches Corner
Four churches once stood at the intersection of West State Street and Church Street. Two of the original buildings remain, the Grace United Methodist built in 1910 and the Trinity Episcopal Church. The First Baptist church has been relocated and the Westminster Presbyterian Church was destroyed in 1967.

Morgan County Courthouse
300 West State Street

The courthouse built in 1869 is on the National History Register.

Farmers State Bank Building
200 West State Street

This is the first building in Jacksonville to be constructed of steel. It was built in 1912 and opened in 1913.

✦ *Walking Tour 2 — Begins in Duncan Park and is composed of two parts.*

Approximately 1.3 miles and takes about 50 minutes. The historic district begins in Duncan Park which is the site of the Governor Joseph Duncan's home. The tour covers architecturally and historically important buildings depicting much of Jacksonville's history.

Dr. Owen M. Long Home
The home was built in 1864 or 1865 and is of the Italianate style. Owner Dr. Long was an intimate friend of Abraham Lincoln, Ulysses S. Grant and Stephen Douglas. The home was later sold to James T. King, a hunting enthusiast and friend of Theodore Roosevelt.

The William S. Hook House
1042 West State Street

The solid brick home is covered with shingles and is an example of Shingle style architecture as well as an adaptation of Free style, rambling and Queen Anne style. William Spencer Hook became the owner in 1888. Upon his death it was inherited by his sister Fannie, who was known to dress in trousers and smoke cigars.

The Clay House
1019 West State Street

Built in 1834 on six acres of land the home of Porter Clay. The Clays had many famous visitors including Henry Clay and Daniel Webster.

The Bateman House
907 West State Street
The Gothic Revival home, built in 1851, was originally constructed of board-and-batten. It was home to Newton Bateman, the famous educator.

The Judge Henry B. McClure House
919 West College
The home was originally built in the 1850s a simple Greek Revival style. Later the home was enlarged into an Italianate structure.

The Octagon House
222 Park Street
The house was built in 1853-1888 from a design developed by Orson Squire Fowler, the nation's leading phrenologist.

The Fayerweather House
242 Park Street
The Gothic Revival style home was built in 1852 by Julian M. Sturtevant, a newcomer to Jacksonville, who married Elizabeth M. Fayerweather. Mr. Sturtevant later became a teacher at Illinois College in 1829 and in 1844 he was appointed president.

The Samuel Adams House
1120 West College Street

The home is a classic example of the Greek Revival style architecture. It was built by Dr. Samuel Adams in the 1840s.

Illinois College
1101 W. College
The land for Illinois College was bought in 1828. It is the oldest college west of the Alleghenies. The first degrees were granted in 1835 and Richard Yates, Civil War governor of the state, was one of the two graduates in the first class. The college became co-educational in 1903.

Illinois School for the Deaf
One of the oldest and largest schools for the deaf in the United States, the school was established in 1839. It opened in 1845 with two students. The Heritage Cultural Center is located on the 2nd floor of the main building

"Elm Grove"
Governor Duncan's Home
4 Duncan Place
The home was built in 1835 as the home of Governor Joseph Duncan. The capitol at the time was in Vandalia and there was no governor's mansion. Consequently, his home served as the official governor's mansion for the state.

The J.W. Lathrop House
817 West State Street

The Greek Revival style home was built in 1846 by John W. Lathrop. He was a prominent advocate of anti-slavery activity. Later in 1857 it became the home of John T. Alexander a pioneer cattle king.

The Augustus Ayers House
876 West State Street
August E. Ayers built the three-story red brick Italianate home in 1857.

The Moore House
856 West State Street
The Italianate home was built by Henry Owsley in 1853. It was sold to Joshua Moore in 1857 and remained in the Moore family for the next 117 years.

George M. Chambers House
829 W. State Street
This 1841 home is a blend of Greek Revival and Late Federal. In 1846 eight rooms were added, and since that time no architectural changes have been made.

The Rockwell House
724 West State Street
Ero Chandler, the first doctor in Jacksonville, built this house between 1828 and 1835. The woodwork and exterior siding are of black walnut. The beautiful leaded glass in the sidelights and transoms was brought to Jacksonville from New England.

The home was sold to Mr. Rockwell in 1838 and is still known as such.

✦ Walking Tour 3 — Begins at the Illinois School for the Visually Impaired.

356 & 360 East State Street
The homes on this street are considered to be a unit and have been in the Duncan family more than 100 years. The home at 356 E. State was built between 1856-1862. The home at 360 E. State was built between 1887-1890.

Our Saviour Church Rectory
462 East State Street
Started in 1895 the two-story, brick and stone house is of Queen Anne or Victorian design. The home has a hipped-roof with louvered cross gables. The wrap around porch has stone banisters with spindles protecting two entrances.

MacMurray College
447 E. College
The Illinois Conference Female Academy was founded in 1856 by a group of Methodist clergymen. It opened in the fall of 1847 one block west of the present Centenary Church. The college was originally known as Illinois Women's College. In 1931 it was renamed MacMurray College to honor

Senator James E. MacMurray, a major benefactor of the college.

339 East State Street
The home was originally built by Captain John Henry between 1848 and 1853. Today it is MacMurray College's presidential home.

Annual Events

Jacksonville is host to a variety of annual events each year. For further information write the Visitors Bureau.

March
• Farm Toy Show — Farm toys, construction toys, trucks and antique signs.
✪ Free admission

June
• Antique Auto Show — Class Automobiles from three states compete for 50 trophies.
✪ Free admission
• DTBA Flea Market
• General Grierson's Liberty Days
• Historic Home Tour — Lecture tour of four beautiful historic homes.

July
• July 4th Fair — Several days of fun for the family ending with an outstanding fireworks display.
• Fine Arts Fair — Artists from across the Midwest display, demonstrate and sell their works.
• Morgan County Fair

September
• IHSA Rodeo at Morgan County Fairgrounds

• Prairieland Heritage Museum Antique Steam Engine Show
• Cruise Nite Weekend

December
• Christmas Homes Tour and Tea

Shopping and Dining

You never have to leave Jacksonville to buy what you need — shopping is a pleasure. Downtown you will find historic "Central Park Plaza." Another shopping area is the Lincoln Square Shopping Center. A wealth of antiques shops are located in Jacksonville. If you enjoy antiquing, Jacksonville area is a must.

Dining at its best in Jacksonville. You will find family dining, fast food, fine dining, Mexican, Oriental and the all time favorite pizza restaurants.

Conclusion

For more information:
Visitors & Convention Center
155 West Morton Avenue
Jacksonville, IL 62650
1-800-593-5678 or
(217) 243-5678

Tips

✔ Many fine parks are located in Jacksonville with excellent recreational programs.

✔ Jacksonville has an airport to serve business and tourism. (217) 243-5824

✔ For the nature lover Lake Jacksonville and Goveia Beach await visitors with fishing, sailing, swimming, skiing, canoeing, hiking, picnicking and other outdoor recreation opportunities.

✔ The arts play an important role in the life of Jacksonville. Community theater groups are highly acclaimed. They offer a variety of productions throughout the year from drama to comedies, symphonies to choral groups. You will find outstanding performances. Write for schedule.

Greetings

❝ On behalf of the citizens of the Jacksonville area, I would like to welcome your interest in our community and offer best wishes for a pleasant visit.

The Jacksonville area offers a fine array of hospitality services and recreational opportunities. Our goal is to ensure that you have an enjoyable stay in our community.

The Jacksonville Area Visitors Guide offers handy information on historic sites, motels and restaurants, shopping, recreation sites and other local points of interest.

I trust your stay in Jacksonville will be an enjoyable one. Please call us or stop by the Visitors Bureau at 155 West Morton Road. ❞

Executive Director
Visitors and Convention Bureau

Quincy
Catch on to Quincy Illinois

Location

Quincy is located on the beautiful bluffs overlooking the Mississippi River 20 minutes off of Highway 36 (Interstate 72).

History

The seat for Adams County was named for the president of the United States, John Quincy Adams. The settlement began in 1822 when John Wood and Willard Keyes established claims in the vicinity. As other cabins appeared, the settlement became known as The Bluffs. Quincy's co-founder, John Wood, later served as Lieutenant Governor, and when Governor William H. Bissell died in office, Wood served out the remainder of the term as governor.

Because of a petition by Wood, the county of Adams was formed in 1825. When the commissioners were looking for a central place to select the county seat, Wood's partner, Willard Keys, led the group through "bogs, quicksand, and quagmires" to The Bluffs. At the end of the journey, Keys persuaded the commissioners to proclaim the settlement as the seat of government for the newly formed county.

Quincy rapidly became a thriving settlement along the upper Mississippi. In the 1830s it also became a focal point of local abolitionist activities. Reverend Asa B. Turner and Dr. David Nelson organized an abolitionist society that operated out of Turner's church named the Lord's Barn. The church was the scene of an early confrontation between abolitionist in Quincy and pro-slavery groups that originated in northern Missouri.

By the middle of the nineteenth century, Quincy had become the second largest city in Illinois. Livestock shipments from Quincy down the Mississippi to St. Louis promoted a period of early boom for Quincy. Added wealth created factories that began to produce plows, stoves, carriages and steam engines. By the 1840s more than 15 million dollars in goods were exported out of the western Illinois river town.

But post Civil War industrial growth throughout the rest of Illinois, coupled with the decline of steamboat traffic following the advent of the railroad hastened the decline in the Quincy economy. With railroads established elsewhere, Quincy had to settle for minimal community growth into the twentieth century.

➠ Getting Started

Stop by the Quincy Convention and Visitors Bureau located at 300 Civic Center Plaza, Suite 237 before beginning your tour of the city. We will provide brochures, maps and helpful hints to guide you through our three beautiful historic districts.

Attractions

All Wars Museum

(217) 222-8641
1707 North 12th Street
The museum is located on the grounds of the Illinois Veterans Home of Quincy. The home is one of the nation's largest and veteran homes. The museum contents displayed commemorate important moments in military history. Monday-Friday, 1pm-4pm. Saturday-Sunday, 1pm-4pm.

Calftown

(217) 223-5033
The South Side German Historic District encompasses most of Quincy's southwest quarter. In the late 1800s as much as 70% of the area was inhabited by German immigrants. Write or call for a walking tour pamphlet.

East End Historic District

(217) 228-4514
12th to 24th Streets, Maine to State
This district has been placed on the National Register of Historic Places as having the strongest architectural significance and integrity in Quincy. There is a grand collection of houses from every period and style since 1835.

Gardner Museum of Architecture and Design

(217) 224-6873
332 Maine Street
The Quincy Public Library is home to the Gardner Museum. You will find a variety of exhibits, programs and services. There are two temporary exhibits each year along with two permanent ones. The permanent exhibits are "A Kaleidoscope of American Architecture" which tells the history of Quincy's beautiful buildings and "Aspirations in Glass," a spectacular display of historic stained glass from churches in Quincy and the surrounding area. The museum is in the Richardson Romanesque style and is listed on the National Register of Historic Places.

Governor John Wood Mansion

(217) 222-1835
425 South 12th Street
The fourteen room mansion was started in 1835 and completed in 1838 by John Wood, founder of

Governor John Wood Mansion

Quincy and twelfth Governor of Illinois. The home was moved to a new site in 1864 where it remains today. It is recognized as one of the finest examples of Greek Revival architecture in the Midwest. The mansion houses the first piano in Quincy, Quincy-made stoves, a table used by Abraham Lincoln, a three-story Victorian doll house and an 1860 lithograph showing Quincy when it was Illinois' third largest city. Guided tours are available Saturday and Sunday afternoons, April-October. Weekday afternoon tours are given June, July, and August.

✪ Group tours are welcome.

Leyland London Tour Bus
(217) 231-2012
This is one of only two authentic double-decker buses in the United States. Groups of up to sixty-eight passengers can rent the bus to tour the historic and architectural areas of Quincy.

Quincy Art Center

Lincoln-Douglas Valentine Museum
(217) 224-3355 or (217) 224-5767
101 North 4th Street
Located in the restored Lincoln-Douglas building, the museum features a large collection of old and unusual valentines. The museum is a member of the National Valentine Collectors Association. Quincy's Paper Box Company, once the country's leading makers of valentine heart candy boxes, has graciously given the museum many beautiful valentine boxes which are on display.

Oakley-Lindsay Center
The center features a 30,000 square foot exhibition hall with 4,000 square feet of lobby. It has a multi-purpose theater that seats 500 people.

Quincy Art Center
(217) 223-5900
1515 Jersey Street
The center, located in the carriage house on the grounds of the former Lorenzo Bull mansion, is now home to the Women's City Club. This is a visual arts museum with annual and rotating exhibits. Its many activities include children's and adult's art classes and hands-on programs for students.
✪ Guided tours are by appointment only.

Quincy Museum
(217) 224-7669
1601 Maine Street
The beautiful Newcomb-Stillwell mansion is now home to the Quincy Museum. The Stillwell family donated the mansion to Quincy College in 1941, after which it was used as a dormitory. In 1980 the Quincy Museum acquired the property and restored the first floor to the style of the 1890s. An outstanding feature of the house is its window transom bars of solid stone and building materials of contrasting colors. All three floors house historic artifacts of the past. Children will delight in the discovery center where they have many hands-on-activities to enjoy. They can use the computers to learn through sight, smell and sound.
✪ Special classes are available for all age groups.

The Dr. Richard Eells House
(217) 222-1799
415 Jersey
The Ells house is an outstanding example of Quincy's mid-19th century architecture. It stands as the oldest two-story brick home in Quincy. The house was originally

Neucomb Stillwell Mansion and Quincy Museum

built in the the simple Greek Revival style and later altered into the Italianate style building you see today. Originally started in 1835, the house was a stopping point on the Underground Railroad where Dr. Ells helped several hundred slaves escape to freedom. Group tours welcome.

✪ Free admission

The South Eighth Street Bridge

The 1872 bridge spans Fern Hollow and Curtis Creek. Originally built of iron, wood and stone, the bridge eventually rotted and was in need of repairs. In 1889 the city council replaced the bridge by a completely stone structure. Today it serves as an outstanding example of architecture of the past. It is truly a landmark of the richness of Quincy's treasured past.

Villa Kathrine

(217) 224-3688
532 Gardner Expressway
This is a unique example of Mediterranean architecture with a beautiful view of the Mississippi River. The Islamic residence was built in 1900 and is listed on the National Register of Historic Places. The villa was built by George Metz, a native Quincian and world traveler. The top of the main tower is a replica of the famous mosque of Thais. Mr.

Metz lived in the villa alone with his 200 pound dog, a mastiff named Bingo. Today the villa is Quincy's Tourist Information Center. The grounds may be reserved for use by groups.

✪ Group tours available

Satellite Attractions

✤ Golden Illinois

Prairie Mill Windmill & Museum
(217) 696-4672
(217) 696-4819
The 1872 windmill is 92 feet high with sails eight feet wide and 71 feet long. The original three sets of millstones are still in place. The museum is filled with a collection of memorabilia of Golden and the surrounding area, plus a collection of windmill items.

✤ Old Emming's Bank Building Museum —
The Railroad Museum
(217) 455-3141 or (217) 696-4819
103-105 Quincy Street
The Bank Building has served in many capacities — offices for the steam mill, the Prairie Mill Windmill, a newspaper and a bank. It is filled with items from Golden's past businesses. The Railroad Museum houses a large display of railroad memorabilia, featuring dinnerware used on passenger trains, an authentic

ticket window, old books and toys of train displays and signal lanterns.

🍂 **Quinsippi Island**

The Mississippi Valley Historic Auto Club Museum
(217) 656-3791 or (217) 223-7909
Front and Cedar, Quinsippi Island
All American Park
Here you will find a large display of historic automobiles. The oldest vehicles on display are a 1917 Overland and a 1917 International Truck. The club was opened in 1968 with 35 contributing members

🍂 **Siloam Springs**

Fall Creek Scenic Overlook and Bridge
The bridge was constructed in the late 1850s for the expressed purpose of saving farmers the trouble of fording the creek during high water. It was open for public use until 1949. The one lane bridge, 14 feet wide and 110 feet long, majestically spans the Fall Creek Gorge. The 48 foot arch is the widest of any stone arch bridge built in Illinois to carry traffic. It was constructed of native natural stone more than 125 years ago and stands today as a monument to man's skill and ingenuity.

Siloam Springs State Park
One of Illinois largest parks covers

3,323 acres of beautiful woods, sparkling lakes and carefully maintained facilities. A great source of recreation and serene beauty just minutes away from Quincy.

Churches

Quincy has several historic churches that add to the visual and cultural landscape.
• St. John's Church of 1853
  7th & Hampshire Streets
• Salem Church of 1877
  9th and State Streets
• St. Francis Church of 1886
  17th Street and College Avenue

Annual Events

January
• Bluegrass Festival
May
• Dogwood Festival
• Gus Macker 3 on 3 Basketball
June
• Miller Gran Prix of Karting
• Pepsi Little People's Golf Championship
• D.A. Wiebring Pro-Am
• Quincy Warbird Convention
• Germanfest
• Quincy Gems Baseball
July
• Titan Firecracker Classic — Swim Meet
• Quincy Gems Baseball
August
• World Free Fall Convention

- Pepsi Jr. Masters Golf Tournament
- Masters Shooting Tournament
- Thunder on the Bay — Drag Boat Races
- Knights of Columbus Bar-B-Que
- Great River Golden Games
- Adams County Fair

September

- Arts/Quincy Riverfest
- Karting Klassic
- USPSA Shooting Tournament

October

- Quincy Conference
- Tin Dusters Fall Color Run

November

- Craft Shows

December

- Symphony of Trees (every two years)

Shopping and Dining

Discover what Quincy offers for the avid shopper. You will find "Shop 'til You Drop" opportunities here. We have art galleries, boutiques and crafts, as well as hunting, fishing and sporting goods stores. The Maine Center offers the shopper a variety of independent stores. We have a variety of antique stores both downtown and in country settings. We promise you won't go home empty handed.

Whether your appetite is large or small, you will find the perfect restaurant to fill the bill from tea rooms, family restaurants, fast food restaurants, specialty restaurants to fine dining. Write or call for a list of restaurants.

Conclusion

For more information contact:
Quincy Convention & Visitors Bureau
300 Civic Center Plaza,
Suite 237
Quincy, IL 62301-4161
1-800-97 VISIT
Website: www.quincy-cvb.org

66 Start with a beautiful location — on the bluffs overlooking the Mississippi River; add a wealth of authentically restored architecture; top it off with tree-lined streets that serve as a welcome mat for visitors from near and far; and it's not hard to see why dozens of regional, national and international events, and thousands of visitors, return to Quincy year after year.

Topping the list of Quincy's attractions is its treasure-trove of historic architecture. The city boasts three historic districts, including the East End Historic District with a grand collection of houses from every period and style since 1835. In fact, the corner of 16th and Main Streets has been called the most architecturally significant corner in the United States by *National Geographic* magazine.

In addition to the stately homes in the East End Historic District, Quincy's strong German heritage is evidenced in the hundreds of sturdy brick German cottages in the South Side German Historic District. And for a flair of the exotic, Quincy also has its own castle — Villa Kathrine — the only example of Moorish architecture on the Mississippi.

Quincy offers residents and guest alike a myriad of arts performances and activities one would only expect to find in a much larger city. Quincy is home to America's first community arts council, the Quincy Society of Fine Arts. The National Survey of Local Arts Agencies recognizes Quincy as the number one city in the United States for per capita arts support.

From the Muddy River Opera Company to the Quincy Symphony Orchestra; the Quincy Community Theatre to the Quincy Art Center, our fine arts community has something for everyone.

From the moment visitors enter Quincy, the warm, welcoming atmosphere of the community makes them feel at home.

Those looking for a peaceful getaway can find it around virtually any corner in one of the city's 26 parks. With more than 825 acres devoted to parks — from riverfront overlooks to a 27-hole golf course — it is easy to see why Quincy is a Tree City U.S.A.

The town offers much more than just scenic relaxation; Quincy also draws thousands of guests each year who are buzzing with the excitement of events such as the World Free Fall Convention, Miller Gran Prix of Karting, or the Pepsi Little People's Golf Tournament.

We welcome you to "Come and Catch on to Quincy.**99**

—Quincy Convention and Visitors Bureau

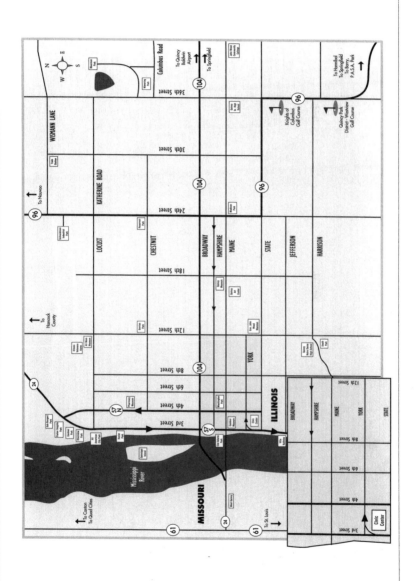

Daytrip Illinois
Highway 96

Nauvoo
Beautiful Place

Location

Located on Highway 96 along the scenic Mississippi River about 40 miles north of Quincy, Illinois, at the junction of Iowa, Missouri and Illinois.

History

The followers of Joseph Smith came to the area in 1839 after they were evicted from Missouri. What they found were a dozen old buildings in a place locally called Commerce. Smith renamed the village Nauvoo. The construction of a denominational temple began along with several other well built homes. By 1842 the population of the town had grown to nearly 15,000.

On June 27, 1884 Joseph and his brother Hyrum were being held at the Carthage Jail on charges of treason, when a mob stormed the facility, killing Joseph and Hyrum. Following Joseph's death, difficulties arose concerning church leadership. Several groups departed Nauvoo following various men. The largest group followed Brigham Young, President of the Quorum of Twelve, to the west and eventually to what is now Salt

Life as it was in the 1840s.

Lake City, Utah. Joseph Smith's family and his wife, Emma, remained in Nauvoo with many of the saints after the 1846 exodus.

Another schism struck Nauvoo in 1856 when Cabet was defeated for the ranking office of their commune. Cabet, angry at his fall from power, led a small band of followers to St. Louis. The remaining Icarians reorganized their commune, but by 1860 most had moved to Iowa and Nauvoo once again became a ghost town.

German settlers in the 1860s rebuilt the town yet again and their descendants have succeeded in preserving the old town.

➡ Getting Started

Begin your visit at the Nauvoo Chamber of Commerce Uptown Tourist Center located at 1295 Mulholland. A casette tape walking tour of Nauvoo is available. For more information call (217) 453-6648.

Attractions

French Icarian Museum
(217) 453-2437
2205 Parley Street
The museum tells the story of Icaria and has artifacts of the Icarian period in Nauvoo from 1849 to 1860. The museum's mission is promoting the preservation of French heritage in America.

Baxter Village
11 blocks east of Nauvoo State Park
You will find special shops offering a variety of Old Nauvoo cheeses, wines, sweet breads, pies, hand-blow glass, pottery, flowers and other gifts.

Nauvoo Restoration, Inc.
(217) 453-2237
A short movie is offered at the center telling the story of the Mormons in Nauvoo and a tour of the Monument to Women Statue Garden. Twenty restored homes and shops of the 1840s are shown with demonstrations.

Nauvoo State Park and Historical Museum
Park (217) 453-2512
Museum (217) 453-2767
The park offers fishing, camping, trails, wildlife areas and picnic areas. It is operated by the Illinois Department of Conservation. The museum, operated by the Nauvoo Historical Society, is located in the park on Highway 96 South. It is in an 1840s home where historical documents and artifacts can be seen from Native American, Mormon, Icarian and German periods of Nauvoo's history. It operates from May to October.

Gunsmith Shop in Old Nauvoo

Restored Sites of Old Nauvoo

Here you will find 25 historic homes, businesses and demonstration sites from the early 1840s. There is no charge and all sites are open daily.

- **Visitor Center and Lands and Records** — View an award winning film telling of the people who lived in Nauvoo from 1839-1846.
- **Monument to Women Garden** — There are thirteen life-size statues depicting women's roles in the home and society.
- **Sarah Granger Kimball Home** — One of the oldest existing structures in Nauvoo.

- **Nauvoo Temple Site** — The most imposing building in the Midwest of the 1840s.
- **Wilford Woodruff Home** — Home of the 5th president of the Latter Day Saints Church.
- **Carriage Ride** — Free carriage ride around restored Nauvoo.
- **Cultural Hall** — A quilt display and a short dramatic skit about the city.
- **Scovil Bakery** — Sample a gingerbread cookie baked in an 1840s oven.
- **Lyon Drug and Variety Store** — Restored store that carried medicines, hardware, shoes books and produce.
- **Heber C. Kimball** — A home built by early LDS leader fur-

nished with antiques and family pieces.

- **Stoddard Home and Tin Shop** — A shop stocked with equipment used by a tinsmith in the 1840s.
- **Post Office and Mercantile** — An 1840s post office and Merryweather's Mercantile Store.
- **John Taylor Home** — Home of the 3rd president of the LDS Church who served as editor of *The Times and Season* in 1845.
- **Printing Office** — Houses an 1840s printing press where *The Times and Season* and *Nauvoo Neighbor* were printed.
- **Browning Home and Gunshop** — Display of Browning guns.
- **Brigham Young Home** — The home reflects the skill and craftsmanship of Brigham Young as a builder and carpenter.
- **Blacksmith Shop** — Receive a horseshoe and "prairie diamond" ring at the Webb Wagon and Blacksmith Shop.
- **Seventies Hall** — The restored Missionary Training Center is a beautiful small chapel that was used as a place of worship and lectures in the 1840s.
- **Exodus of Greatness Monument** — Point of departure of the Latter Day Saints as they crossed the Mississippi River on the westward migration to the Great Basin.

Pottery Demonstration in Old Nauvoo

Photo by Ray Longhurst

- **Rizer Boot and Shoemaker** — Some of the original boot and shoemaking equipment owned by the Rizer family is on display.
- **Pendleton Log Home and School** — The backroom of the authentically restored log home was used as a school in the 1840s.
- **Brickyard** — Brick-making demonstrations.
- **Lucy Mack Smith Home** — Mother of the prophet Joseph Smith lived in this house in 1846.
- **Coolidge Home** — See demonstrations of early frontier crafts such as candle making, barrel making and pottery.

- **Pioneer Burial Grounds** — The principal burial ground in the 1840s is located on a beautiful and peaceful wooded four-acre site.

Restored Sites of the Smith Family.

- **Joseph Smith Historic Center** (217) 453-2246, 149 Water Street. You will see a multi-media presentation on Nauvoo history. Also, a guided walking tour past the Nauvoo House, and the Gravesites, and through the Joseph Smith Homestead and Mansion House is available.
- **Joseph Smith Homestead** — The land where the Homestead

stands is part of a 135 acre tract of land purchased by Joseph Smith. He purchased the land in 1839. Located on the land is an 1803 log cabin that was added onto in 1840 and again in 1858. Next to the summer kitchen you can see live demonstrations of life as it was in the 1840s.

- **Nauvoo House** — The Nauvoo House started in 1841 and never completed was intended to house new arrivals to Nauvoo. Today the hotel serves as a hostelry.
- **Joseph Smith Brick Stable** — It and other stables could hold up to 60 horses.
- **Nauvoo Mansion** —The man-

Blacksmith and Farrier

sion, built in 1843, was home to the Joseph Smith family for many years after his passing.

- **Joseph Smith Red Brick Store** — The store was built in 1841 as a general store, with Joseph as the proprietor. In 1890 the store was torn down, the bricks were taken uptown to complete a meat market. The present operating Red Brick Store is a reconstruction—1980. Pictures and paintings provide guidance to the reconstruction.

Annual Events

Many special events are held each year. For updates and changes contact the Nauvoo Chamber of Commerce Tourism Center or call (217) 453-6648 before planning your trip.

Monthly Event
- Tuesdays, January through March—Brigham Young University Faculty Lectures are held at the Nauvoo Restoration, Inc.

March
- "Soldiers of Humanity"—Exhibits open at the French Icarian Museum
- Bunny Trail — Sponsored by Nauvoo Chamber of Commerce

Memorial Day-Labor Day
- Historical Musicals nightly Monday-Saturday

June
- French Heritage Festival — French Icarian Museum
- Home Winmaker's Contest — Baxter's Vineyards

July
- Independence Day and Bastille Day Celebrations

August
- Nauvoo Grape Festival — The only place in America where you can see a spectacular event take place exactly as it was done at the festival in Roquefort, France.
- City of Joseph Outdoor Musical Program Hill east of LDS Visitors Center.

October
- Persimmon Festival — French Icarian Museum

November
- "How to Fair" — Nauvoo Restoration, Inc.

December
- Christmas in Old Nauvoo — All month
- Nauvoo Holiday Walk

Shopping and Dining

Baxter Village at 2010 East Parley Street is a shopper's delight. It has unique specialty shops with homemade goodies, glassware and stoneware, handcrafted items and much more.

You will find fine dining in Nauvoo from restaurants with AAA rating to short order meals. Call or write for a list of restaurants.

Conclusion

For information on lodging and camping write or call:

Nauvoo Chamber of Commerce
Tourism Center, P.O. Box 41
Nauvoo, Illinois 62354
(217) 453-6648
Website: www.visitnauvoo.org

Tips

✔ Free admission to visitors at Nauvoo.

✔ All sites are open daily.

✔ Guided tours are available.

❝Welcome to historic Nauvoo. You will find us located on a horseshoe bend of the the Mississippi River. More than 30 buildings have been restored and open to the public daily free of charge.

Besides the history of Joseph Smith the area is known for its wine-making. When the early immigrants first settled there they brought with them the knowledge of grape growing and wine making from the old country. It later became the largest grape-growing community in the Midwest. Prohibition came dooming the industry. Many of the wine cellars still exist today but they are privately owned and are not opened to tourists. In 1857 the grape industry revived when Cecil J. Baxter got a license to manufacture wine. About the same time Mr. Baxter started his business, a new industry was born when it was discovered that the cool moist wine cellars were ideal for curing and aging cheese. A new business was born and became known as Nauvoo's Blue Cheese Industry.

Today an outstanding event of the community is the celebration of "The Wedding of the Wine and Cheese". The festivities take place every year on Saturday and Sunday before Labor Day. Thousands of people flock here to celebrate the annual Grape Festival with a parade, a custom auto show, a grape stomp, an antique show, and a pageant called "From Quashquema to Nauvoo."

Come enjoy one of the most unique Daytrips you will ever experience.❞

—Nauvoo Chamber of Commerce

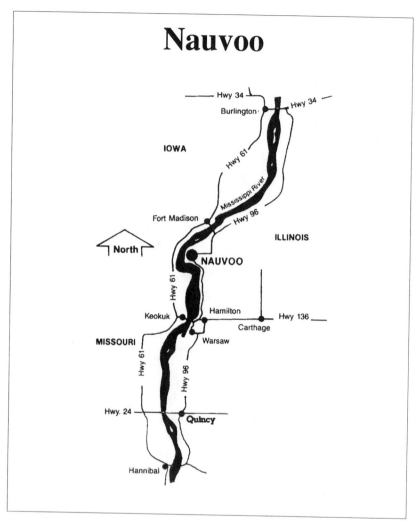

Nauvoo

Hwy 34
Burlington
Hwy 34

IOWA

Hwy 61

Mississippi River

Fort Madison
Hwy 96

North

NAUVOO

ILLINOIS

Hwy 61

Keokuk
Hamilton
Hwy 136

Carthage

MISSOURI
Warsaw

Hwy 61

Hwy 96

Hwy. 24
Quincy

Hannibal

Map from Nauvoo Chamber of Commerce

Welcome to the
State Parks of Illinois

The Department of Natural Resources manages over 260 state parks, fish and wildlife areas, conservation and natural areas. These sites represent the beauty and diversity of the Illinois landscape, from rolling grasslands and woodlands to craggy ravines and beautiful waterways.

Illinois' topography is unique. Many of the state parks are located on rivers and lakes. Outdoor recreational opportunities abound, including hiking, biking, camping, fishing, hunting, boating, canoeing and horseback riding. The DNR takes seriously its responsibility to maintain and preserve wildlife habitat, wetlands, rivers and streams.

Many of our state parks feature interpretive programs to help visitors gain a better understanding of Illinois' natural features, natural heritage and wildlife.

The Illinois State Park Lodges and cabins are available throughout the state for overnight or weekend getaways and family vacations. They include the lakefront Illinois Beach Resort on Lake Michigan; the Starved Rock Lodge on the Illinois River; The White Pines Inn cabins in northwest Illinois; the Inn at Eagle Creek on Lake Shelbyville; the new Carlyle Lakefront Cottages at Eldon Hazlet State Park on Carlyle Lake, the Rend Lake Resort on Rend Lake; Cave-in-Rock cabins on the Ohio River; the Giant City Lodge in the Shawnee Forest in Giant City State Park; and, the Pere Marquette Lodge near the confluence of the Illinois and Mississippi Rivers.

The Department of Natural Resources invites you to contact us for more information regarding the breathtaking beauty and outstanding recreational opportunities available at the state parks of Illinois. Please call 217/782-7454; TTY 217/782-9175, Ameritech Relay 800/526-0844, or visit our website at http://dnr.state.il.us.

—Brent Manning
Director

The maps on the following pages are reprinted with permission from *Illinois State Parks Magazine* © 1999 American Park Network.

Illinois State Parks Regional Map

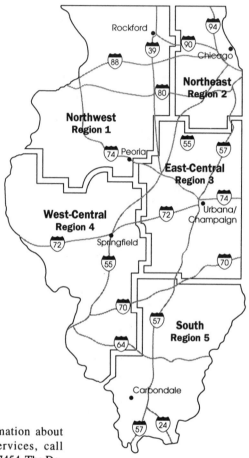

For information about special services, call (217) 782-7454. The Department can also receive calls from a TDD — telephone device for the deaf. If you have a TDD and have any questions, please call (217) 782-9175.

Northwest
Region I

For more information about sites in northwest Illinois, contact the Region 1 Office, Department of Natural Resources, 2612 Locust St. Sterling, IL 61081; (815) 625-2968.

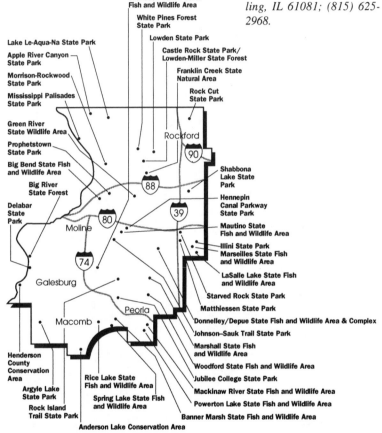

Snakeden Hollow State Fish and Wildlife Area

White Pines Forest State Park

Lowden State Park

Castle Rock State Park/ Lowden-Miller State Forest

Franklin Creek State Natural Area

Rock Cut State Park

Lake Le-Aqua-Na State Park

Apple River Canyon State Park

Morrison-Rockwood State Park

Mississippi Palisades State Park

Green River State Wildlife Area

Prophetstown State Park

Big Bend State Fish and Wildlife Area

Big River State Forest

Delabar State Park

Rockford

Moline

Shabbona Lake State Park

Hennepin Canal Parkway State Park

Mautino State Fish and Wildlife Area

Illini State Park

Marseilles State Fish and Wildlife Area

LaSalle Lake State Fish and Wildlife Area

Galesburg

Starved Rock State Park

Matthiessen State Park

Peoria

Macomb

Donnelley/Depue State Fish and Wildlife Area & Complex

Johnson–Sauk Trail State Park

Marshall State Fish and Wildlife Area

Woodford State Fish and Wildlife Area

Jubilee College State Park

Mackinaw River State Fish and Wildlife Area

Powerton Lake State Fish and Wildlife Area

Banner Marsh State Fish and Wildlife Area

Henderson County Conservation Area

Argyle Lake State Park

Rock Island Trail State Park

Rice Lake State Fish and Wildlife Area

Spring Lake State Fish and Wildlife Area

Anderson Lake Conservation Area

Northeast
Region 2

For more information about sites in northeast Illinois, contact the Region 2 Office, Department of Natural Resources, 110 James Road, Spring Grove, IL 60081; (815) 675-2385.

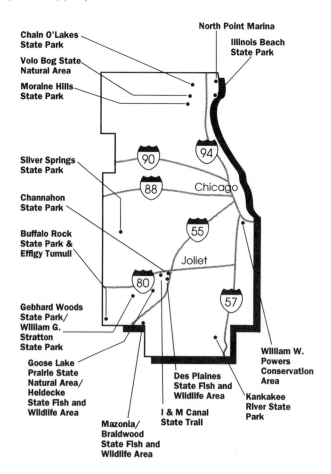

Chain O'Lakes State Park

Volo Bog State Natural Area

Moraine Hills State Park

North Point Marina

Illinois Beach State Park

Silver Springs State Park

Channahon State Park

Buffalo Rock State Park & Effigy Tumuli

Gebhard Woods State Park/ William G. Stratton State Park

Goose Lake Prairie State Natural Area/ Heidecke State Fish and Wildlife Area

Mazonia/ Braidwood State Fish and Wildlife Area

I & M Canal State Trail

Des Plaines State Fish and Wildlife Area

William W. Powers Conservation Area

Kankakee River State Park

Chicago

Joliet

East-Central
Region 3

For more information about sites in east-central Illinois, contact the Region 3 Office, Department of Natural Resources, 2005 Round Barn Road, Champaign, IL 61821; (217) 333-5773.

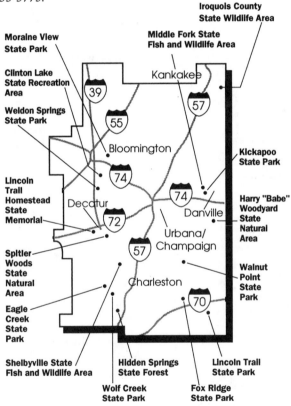

West-Central
Region 4

For more information about sites in west-central Illinois, contact the Region 4 Office, Department of Natural Resources, 4521 Alton Commerce Parkway, Alton, IL 62002; (618) 462-1181.

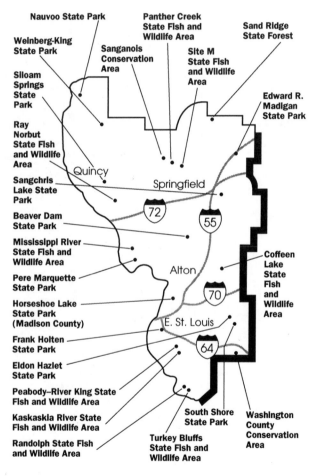

Nauvoo State Park

Panther Creek State Fish and Wildlife Area

Sand Ridge State Forest

Weinberg-King State Park

Sanganois Conservation Area

Site M State Fish and Wildlife Area

Siloam Springs State Park

Edward R. Madigan State Park

Ray Norbut State Fish and Wildlife Area

Quincy

Springfield

Sangchris Lake State Park

Beaver Dam State Park

72

55

Mississippi River State Fish and Wildlife Area

Coffeen Lake State Fish and Wildlife Area

Pere Marquette State Park

Alton

70

Horseshoe Lake State Park (Madison County)

E. St. Louis

Frank Holten State Park

64

Eldon Hazlet State Park

Peabody–River King State Fish and Wildlife Area

Kaskaskia River State Fish and Wildlife Area

South Shore State Park

Washington County Conservation Area

Randolph State Fish and Wildlife Area

Turkey Bluffs State Fish and Wildlife Area

South
Region 5

For more information about sites in southern Illinois, contact the Region 5 Office, Department of Natural Resources, 11731 State Highway 37, Benton, IL 62812; (618) 435-8138.

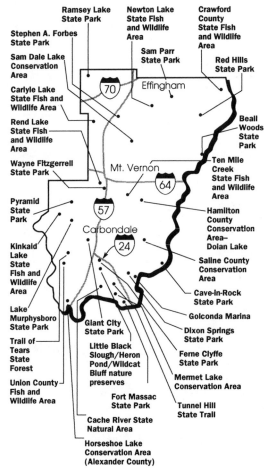

Ramsey Lake State Park
Newton Lake State Fish and Wildlife Area
Crawford County State Fish and Wildlife Area
Stephen A. Forbes State Park
Sam Parr State Park
Red Hills State Park
Sam Dale Lake Conservation Area
Carlyle Lake State Fish and Wildlife Area
Effingham
Rend Lake State Fish and Wildlife Area
Beall Woods State Park
Wayne Fitzgerrell State Park
Mt. Vernon
Ten Mile Creek State Fish and Wildlife Area
Pyramid State Park
Hamilton County Conservation Area– Dolan Lake
Kinkaid Lake State Fish and Wildlife Area
Carbondale
Saline County Conservation Area
Lake Murphysboro State Park
Cave-In-Rock State Park
Golconda Marina
Trail of Tears State Forest
Giant City State Park
Dixon Springs State Park
Little Black Slough/Heron Pond/Wildcat Bluff nature preserves
Ferne Clyffe State Park
Union County Fish and Wildlife Area
Mermet Lake Conservation Area
Fort Massac State Park
Tunnel Hill State Trail
Cache River State Natural Area
Horseshoe Lake Conservation Area (Alexander County)

Index

Travel Log Memories

Location:

Date:

Place Visited:

Those Present:

Best Memories: